Victory or Death:
Military Decisions That Changed The Course of The American Revolution

Jack Darrell Crowder

Clearfield Company

Copyright © 2023
Jack Darrell Crowder
All rights reserved. This book may not be reproduced, transmitted, or stored in whole or in part by any means, including graphic, electronic, or mechanical, without the expressed consent of the Publisher or the Author for brief quotations in critical articles and reviews.

Published for Clearfield Company by
Genealogical Publishing Company
Baltimore, Maryland

ISBN 9780806359601

Cover illustration: The Battle of Bunker Hill, by Howard Pyle, 1897. Published in Scribner's Magazine, February, 1898. In the public domain.

Books by Jack Darrell Crowder from Clearfield Company:

Women Patriots in the American Revolution: Stories of Bravery, Daring, and Compassion

The First 24 Hours of the American Revolution: An Hour by Hour Account of the Battles of Lexington, Concord, and the British Retreat on Battle Road

Strange, Amazing, and Funny Events that Happened during the Revolutionary War

The Story of Yorktown: Told by the Men Who Were There

FOR

Allie

We will be together again in the next world

Contents

Introduction 5

1 Appointment of George Washington as Commander of the American Army 7

2 British Frontal Assault of Bunker [Breed's] Hill 23

3 The Battle and Siege of Quebec by the Americans 37

4 British General Howe's Hesitation in Attacking Washington in New York 47

5 Washington Makes a Bold Decision and Attacks Trenton 65

6 British Decisions and Lack of Communication Results in a Defeat at Saratoga 77

7 Washington Organizes a Spy Ring 91

8 How Decisions about African Americans as Soldiers Affected the War 101

9 Important Decisions at Valley Forge Save the American Army 107

10 Battle of Kings Mountain: The Beginning of the End 117

11 Washington Appoints Nathanael Greene Commander of the Southern Army 129

12 Yorktown: No Where to Hide 139

Conclusion 157

End Notes 159

Bibliography 169

Index 176

Introduction

"For the want of a nail the shoe was lost,
For the want of a shoe the horse was lost,
For the want of a horse the rider was lost,
For the want of a rider the battle was lost,
For the want of a battle the kingdom was lost,
And all for the want of a horseshoe nail."

---Benjamin Franklin

There have been variations of this proverb around for centuries. Yet each variation has the same meaning. It reminds us that either a small act or an omission, that may seem unimportant, can have grave and unforeseen consequences.

In every war there is usually an event that is considered a turning point, or at the least very important. Most of the time the importance is not revealed until the end of the conflict. The victor will exclaim, "That is the reason we won," while the vanquished uses it as an excuse for losing. Sometimes the importance of the good or bad event is not discovered until many years later, when historians can look back "at the big picture."

Such events occurred during the American Revolution. This book will explore the impact, good or bad, that certain decisions had on events that influenced the eventual outcome of the war. There was not one event that led to the ultimate conclusion of the war. Rather, there was a combination of good and bad decisions that determined who won or lost.

Ranking the decisions would be impossible and open to much debate. To avoid this I have listed them by their date of occurrence, and I know that there will still be disagreement on which events were included and which were omitted.

Please note that any of the quotes used have not been changed, and they will have the original grammar and spelling.

1

Appointment of George Washington as Commander of the American Army

"I found a mixed multitude of people here, under very little discipline, order, or government"

----General George Washington, seeing his army for the first time.

Background:

In the early 1760's most colonists thought of themselves as British. English was the official language, the legal system stemmed from British common law, many towns were named after hamlets in England, and the two countries shared many of the same holidays and customs. Yet, differences between the two peoples began to grow.

The colonists had their own legislatures that were somewhat independent of the King. The colonists could raise troops, and pass local laws. This began to give some of the people the belief that these political powers were their rights. Soon the British Parliament felt a need to curtail the power of the colonial legislatures. After all, the British believed that the colonies were created to serve the needs of the crown, and their colonial subjects should bow to their demands.

When the French and Indian War (1754-1763) took place, King George III went into debt when he provided supplies for his army to defend the British colonies in America. To pay for this enormous cost, the King began to impose taxes on the colonies without their consent. This led to resistance from some of the colonies. British goods were boycotted, which led to tension between the colonists and British soldiers.

On February 22, 1770, an angry mob was protesting at the house of Ebenezer Richardson, a customs service employee. When the mob began throwing stones at the Richardson's home, Ebenezer responded by firing a gun into the crowd. Eleven year old Christopher Seider was hit and later died. Over 2,000 people attended the boy's funeral, where more hatred toward the British was stirred up by the rhetoric of Samuel Adams.

Public outrage continued to boil over and led to the Boston Massacre. On March 5, 1770, British soldiers shot and killed several colonists in a protesting mob that had threatened them. The soldiers were later tried and were either acquitted or given reduced sentences, which further angered the colonists.

In December 1773, the colonial resistance movement struck again in Boston. Members of a radical group, the Sons of Liberty, destroyed the entire shipment of tea sent by the East India Company. They dumped 342 casks of it into Boston Harbor, while many Bostonians looked on.

Parliament responded to this act of defiance in 1774 by passing the Coercive Acts, better known as the Intolerable Acts. These drastic measures ended self-government in Massachusetts, and they closed Boston harbor to trade. The colonies answered the British threat by establishing the First Continental Congress. After much discussion, the Congress sent a "Declaration of Rights and Grievances" to King George. They hoped the King would give in to their demands to avoid further hostilities. Most people in the colonies were opposed to seeking independence. However, a small group of radicals began to encourage freedom from England and the establishment of a new nation.

The British government refused to yield to the demands of the newly formed Continental Congress. Parliament declared that Massachusetts was in rebellion, and the British navy blockaded the ports of the colony. Other punative measures were employed that affected all of the colonies.

The American people began to quarrel among themselves over what actions they should take. Many of the colonists in New England began encouraging armed revolt against England. Some of the people in the middle colonies looked upon the problems with England as a New England problem, and they were opposed to a revolution. Most of the recent emigrants to the colonies were supportive of the King of England. Some merchants saw ruin if they did not break from British rule, while others saw ruin if they did.

In 1775 the American colonies divided into three camps. One group were the Radicals or Patriots, who sought independence from England. A second group were the Loyalists or Tories, who remained loyal to the crown. The third group were neutral and would at times gravitate to one side or the other, depending on how it would benefit them at the moment.

As problems with Great Britain began to rise, Massachusetts saw the need to have special units, who were ready to turn out at a minute's notice when there was an emergency. The Provincial Congress passed a resolution on October 26, 1774, for the formation of minutemen. It stated that the militias in Massachusetts enlist companies to "hold themselves in readiness on the shortest notice from the said committee of safety, to march to the place of rendezvous…"

The minutemen were volunteers, who trained more often and were usually paid an average of one shilling each time they did. They typically served until the emergency was over, which at most times was a term of several days. Many of the minutemen that served in the Battle of Lexington and Concord did so for around five days, and because the threat continued, many enlisted in the militia for eight months. Their officers, like in the militia, were selected by vote, and most of the time the leading citizens were named officers. Men that served in the French and Indian War were also given positions of command. Strangely enough Lexington did not have a minutemen company, but rather they had a militia.

Who were these minutemen? Most were farmers and shop keepers with practically no military experience. The majority of the minutemen were under the age of thirty-five, and some were even teenagers.

Tension began to increase between the colonists and the British, and it reached the boiling point in April of 1775. Men like Samuel Adams were doing everything they could to start a revolt.

Militias were being organized, and arms and ammunition were being hidden away in anticipation of fighting between the Patriots and British. On April 14, 1775, the British Commander-in-Chief and the Military Governor of Massachusetts, General Gage, received orders to disarm the local militias. The King also ordered Gage to capture the offensive Samuel Adams and John Hancock and ship them in chains to England to be tried for high treason.

In a surprise move Gage sent a force of British regulars to Concord to capture the supplies, and at the same time to capture Adams and Hancock who were in the area. This would end talk of a rebellion and prove to the traitors that British rule was not to be taken lightly.

Resistance was met at Concord and Lexington, and men on both sides were killed. More British troops were killed, as they marched back to Boston from Concord. After the battles at Lexington and Concord, the American militiamen surrounded Boston with an army that grew to 15,000 by June. The lines of the American forces extended from shore to shore, but they were too far away to threaten the British. Facing them was the British army of 6,500 regulars, who were commanded by General Thomas Gage.

Regional newspapers called the army outside of Boston the Grand American Army. It consisted of militiamen, who would return home after a few weeks, and enlistees whose service would be up at year's end. Congress was meeting in Philadelphia in the spring of 1775, and they realized that they needed an organized army with an appointed commander.

Some Americans feared that an army in New England, under the command of someone from there, could exert power over the colonies in the south. To avoid having the wrong army under the wrong leadership, many believed that the army and its officers should be taken from all over the colonies. Congress faced a major question....who to appoint as the commander of this new army. There was concern that the current army might dissolve if its present commander, General Artemas Ward a New Englander from Massachusetts, was replaced, and especially if the replacement was from outside of New England. Congress needed a man that could unify the factions in the army, organize the army, and then defeat the British, the most powerful nation in the world.

Congress looks for a leader:

Sometime before June 15, John Adams moved that Congress adopt the army outside Boston and appoint a general to command it. There were several candidates that were discussed to lead the army. The present commander, General Artemas Ward, was the favorite among many members of Congress. John Hancock, the President of the Continental Congress, already had a gorgeous custom made uniform should he be chosen. Hancock had no love for the British, since they had several charges against him for smuggling. Other men considered were Horatio Gates, Charles Lee, Richard Montgomery, and Israel Putman.

Thirty-nine year old Patrick Henry, a delegate to the First and Second Continental Congress, was also considered. He brought some recognition to himself when in a speech he said, "The distinctions between Virginians, Pennsylvanians, New Yorkers, and New Englanders are no more, I am not a Virginian, but an American."[1]

During the meeting John Adams declared that he had but one gentleman in mind for commander of the army, "very well known to all of us, a gentleman whose skill and experience as an officer, whose independent fortune, great talents and excellent universal character, would command the approbation of all America, and unite the cordial exertions of all the Colonies better than any other person in the Union."[2]

George Washington sat nearby listening to John Adams talk. Washington usually kept himself in the background and had made no speeches in Congress. Yet, he had influence, because he was always surrounded by delegates that wanted to consult with him. Washington had heard rumors that he might be nominated for the job, and he had started coming to Congress wearing his military uniform. The uniform was probably that of a special volunteer company formed in Virginia just before he left for Philadelphia. By wearing his military uniform to Congress, Washington advertised his experience in the French and Indian War and of his availability. He had earlier asked Edmund Pendleton to draw up his will, and in his letters to Martha he had stopped mentioning the month he would be coming home.

At the end of his speech, John Adams placed the name of George Washington into nomination for Commander-in-Chief of the Continental Army. Washington, sitting near the door, jumped from his chair at once and rushed out into the hall and into the library.[3]

The appointment of commander was debated in secret deliberation for two days. There were some that questioned the selection of Washington, not based on his ability, but the impact his selection might have on the army outside Boston. They worried if the army would break apart if their current commander General Ward was not chosen, and if the army would follow a leader from a southern colony.

The delegates wanted to obtain a unanimity, and most of the voices in Congress were clearly in favor of Washington. Members in dissent were persuaded to withdraw their opposition, so that unity could be shown. On June 15, 1775, the Second Continental Congress chose George Washington to command the American Army. At the age of forty-three, George Washington had more experience of command than any other American field officer, but he had never won an engagement, and now he would lead the American Army in their fight for independence. Charles Thompson, Secretary of Congress, sent a messenger to summon Washington, who humbly accepted the next day.

By appointing a commander from Virginia, John and Samuel Adams hoped to gather support from the south for the current siege of Boston. Virginia was the largest, most populated, and most powerful colony and critical to the coalition. It would now be up to Washington to hold the army together.

Who was George Washington?

George Washington was born in Virginia on February 11, 1732, and was the first of six children. He also had three half-brothers and one half-sister from his father's first marriage to Jane Butler who died in 1728. The Washington family was wealthy and made its money in land speculation. George did not have the formal education his older brothers had, but he did receive a surveyor's license from the College of William & Mary. He inherited Mount Vernon after the death of his older brother.

George Washington's military experience began in 1752, when he was appointed adjutant in the Virginia colonial militia. In March 1754 he was promoted to Lt. Colonel and ordered by Lt. Governor Dinwiddle to march his 160 Virginia militiamen to the Ohio country. There the twenty-two year old Washington was to reinforce a British outpost at what is now Pittsburgh, Pennsylvania. Before he reached the post, it was captured by the French who renamed it Fort Duquesne.

Washington led a party of forty men and attacked the French at dawn on May 28, 1754. A French force of thirty-five men camped not far from Washington's encampment. Washington attacked the force, and the surprised French had thirteen men killed and twenty-one captured. It was never known for sure who fired the first shot. This surprise attack during peacetime prompted an attack by the French on fortifications built by Washington. The Virginian commander was forced to surrender and accept blame for starting the encounter. Washington and his remaining men were released and they returned to Virginia. This surprise attack by Washington led to the start of the French and Indian War.

The earliest authenticated portrait of George Washington shows him wearing his colonel's uniform of the Virginia Regiment from the French and Indian War. The portrait was painted about 12 years after Washington's service in that war, and several years before he would re-enter military service in the American Revolution. National Archives

Later Washington asked to join the regular British army, but was turned down. Not happy with the attitude of the British officers toward himself and other colonial leaders, and after being passed over for promotion, he resigned his commission at the end of the war and returned home.

The average height of an American during the revolution was five feet eight inches, which was about three inches taller than the average British soldier. George Washington was a towering figure of a man during this time, and stood six feet two inches, 175 pounds, and with large hands and feet (size 13 shoes). He was a strong and powerful man, as demonstrated in a story told by the artist Charles W. Peale, a friend of Washington.

> One afternoon several young gentlemen, visitors at Mount Vernon, and myself were engaged in pitching the bar, one of the athletic sports common in those days. [Pitching the bar was a game of strength, a log-throwing, or pole-throwing, competition similar to the tossing game played by Highland Scots.]
>
> Suddenly Colonel Washington appeared among us. He requested to be shown the pegs that marked the bounds of our efforts; then, smiling, and without putting off his coat, held out his hand for the missile. No sooner did the heavy iron bar feel the grasp of his mighty hand that it lost the power of gravitation, and whizzed through the air, striking the ground far, very far, beyond our outmost limits. We were indeed amazed, as we stood around, all stripped to the buff, with shirt sleeves rolled up, and having thought ourselves very clever fellows, while the Colonel, on retiring, pleasantly observed, 'When you beat my pitch, young gentlemen, I'll try again.[4]

The earliest known description of Washington was written in 1760 by his companion-in-arms and friend George Mercer, who attempted a "portraiture" using the following words,

> He may be described as being as straight as an Indian, measuring six feet two inches in his stockings, and weighing 175 pounds when he took his seat in the House of Burgesses in 1759. His frame is padded with well-developed muscles, indicating great strength. His bones and joints are large, as are his feet and hands. He is wide shouldered, but has not a deep or round chest; is neat waisted, but is broad across the hips, and has rather long legs and arms. His head is well shaped though not large, but is gracefully poised on a superb neck. A large and straight rather than prominent nose; blue-gray penetrating eyes, which are widely separated and overhung by a heavy brow. His face is long rather than broad, with high round cheek bones, and terminates in a good firm chin. He has a clear though rather a colorless pale skin, which burns with the sun. A pleasing, benevolent, though a commanding countenance, dark brown hair, which he wears in a cue. His mouth is large and generally firmly closed, but which from time to time discloses some defective teeth. His features are regular and placid, with all the muscles of his face under perfect control, though flexible and expressive of deep feeling when moved by emotion. In conversation he looks you full in the face, is deliberate, deferential and engaging. His voice is agreeable rather than strong. His demeanor at all times composed and dignified. His movements and gestures are graceful, his walk majestic, and he is a splendid horseman.[5]

George Washington was noted as a modest man. He was having dinner on October 22, 1776, with sixty-one year old Captain Roger Lyon and his wife Mary. The Captain, who was blind, handed a drinking cup to Washington and remarked, "General, the ladies say that you are a handsome man, but I cannot see." Washington took the cup and replied, "Tell the ladies I am afraid they are as blind as yourself."[6]

On January 6, 1759, at the age of twenty-six, George Washington married Martha Dandridge Custis, a widow with two small children. The couple had no children of their own, due to the possibility of George being sterile as a result of an earlier bout with smallpox, or Martha's injury due to the birth of her last child.

The marriage gave Washington control over Martha's estate, and he managed the remaining two-thirds for her children. Almost overnight he became one of Virginia's wealthiest men, and with it he increased his social and political standing.

On August 1, 1774, Washington attended the First Virginia Convention, and he was selected as one of seven delegates to the First Continental Congress. He played a small role in the first Congress. As tensions increased between the colonies and England and because of his military background, Washington helped train the Virginia militia. He also organized enforcement of the Association Trade Boycott of British Goods that was implemented by Congress.

On the day of his election as delegate to the Continental Congress, George Washington wrote, "Dear brother Jack: It is my full intention to devote my life and fortune to the cause we are engaged in, if needful!"[7] It sounds as if Washington was hoping for a military appointment.

Washington assumes command:

On June 16, the day after Congress selected him as the commander of the army, Washington attended Congress in his red and blue general's uniform. He rose from his place at the Virginia table, bowed, and pulled a paper from inside his coat pocket, and began to read his acceptance speech,

> Mr President, Tho' I am truly sensible of the high Honour done me in this Appointment, yet I feel great distress, from a consciousness[3] that my abilities & Military experience may not be equal to the extensive & important Trust: However, as the Congress desire i⟨t⟩ I will enter upon the momentous duty, & exert every power I Possess In their service & for the Support of the glorious Cause: I beg they will accept my most cordial thanks for this distinguished testimony of their Approbation.
>
> But lest some unlucky event should happen unfavourable to my reputation, I beg it may be rememberd by every Gentn in the room, that I this day declare with the utmost sincerity, I do not think my self equal to the Command I ⟨am⟩ honoured with.[8]

After selecting Washington as Commander-in-Chief, Congress granted him five hundred dollars per month for his pay and expenses. Washington refused a salary in his acceptance speech to Congress, "Sir, As to pay, I beg leave to assure the Congress that as no pecuniary consideration could have tempted me to have accepted this arduous employment, I do not wish to make any profit from it. I will keep an exact account of my expenses. Those I doubt not they will discharge, and that is all I desire."[9]

This gesture of receiving no salary impressed several members of Congress. John Adams wrote to Elbridge Gerry, who would later sign the Declaration of Independence,

> There is something charming to me in the conduct of Washington. A gentleman of one of the first fortunes upon the continent, leaving his delicious retirement, his family and friends, sacrificing his ease, and hazarding all in the cause of his country! His views are noble and disinterested. He declared, when he accepted the mighty trust, that he would lay before us an exact account of his expenses, and not accept a shilling for pay.[10]

Delegate Eliphalet Dyer was also impressed, although he did express some concerns about the possible expenses of Washington. He wrote in a letter to Joseph Trumbull on June 17, "His allowance for Wages expences & everything is we think very high, not less than £150 per month, but it was urged that the largeness of his family, Aide Camps, Secretary Servts &c, beside a Constant table for more or less of his officers, daily expresses, dispatches &c Must be very expensive."[11]

Dyer's fears had merit, because after the war Washington turned in his personal expense account to Congress, which was a bill for $160,074. His total expenses, which included his personal expense account and money spent on the members of his headquarters, or his military family as he called them, came to a whopping $449,261.51. Washington was an aristocrat land owner and was used to the finer things, even in war. For example, from September 1775 to March 1776, Washington spent over $6,000 on alcohol to entertain various visitors. Congress approved all his expenses after the war.

Now that the commander of the army had been selected, Congress next appointed the remaining general officers. This was both messy and political. In the past some of the men complained how the British did not always consider talent when they made appointments. Making the same mistake as the British, many times the delegates selected officers not based on ability but for political reasons. Fortunately, Washington was an excellent judge of men, and was able to identify which men would make good officers. The less qualified men were then placed in positions that were not as vital and would cause little harm.

After selecting officers, John Adams wrote to James Warren, the President of the Massachusetts Provincial Congress, expressing the difficulty in the voting for general officers, "Nothing has given me more Torment, than the Scuffle We have had in appointing the General officers."[12]

Publicly Washington showed confidence and determination. However, privately Washington sounded unsure of his ability and was fearful of failure. He realized that he lacked experience and knowledge in commanding a large group of men, and failure would have far reaching consequences on his life. He both wanted to and not to serve in the army as commander

On June 18 Washington faced a task he dreaded, when he wrote his longest surviving letter to his wife. He knew that he would be required to spend a large amount of time away from home, and he wanted to inform Martha that he did not seek this appointment,

> I am now set down to write to you on a subject which fills me with inexpressable concern—and this concern is greatly aggravated and Increased when I reflect on the uneasiness I know it will give you—It has been determined in Congress, that the whole Army raised for the defence of the American Cause shall be put under my care, and that it is necessary for me to proceed immediately to Boston to take upon me the Command of it. You may beleive me my dear Patcy, when I assure you, in the most solemn manner, that, so far from seeking this appointment I have used every endeavour in my power to avoid it.
>
> I could not avoid this appointment, as I did not even pretend to intimate when I should return—that was the case—it was utterly out of my power to refuse this appointment without exposing my Character to such censures as would have reflected dishonour upon myself, and given pain to my friends—this I am sure could not, and ought not to be pleasing to you, & must have lessend me considerably in my own esteem.[13]

Martha was aware that her husband's new job carried a risk. However, one relative wanted to remind her of what could happen, and Martha received a letter from another relative telling her that it was folly for her husband to be drawn into action with the riotous rebels. The relative reminded Martha that if the rebellion failed, he would be arrested as a traitor to the King and probably hanged or beheaded. Martha replied that George always did what was right.

On June 19 Washington wrote to his stepson, John (Jack) Parke Custis, voicing the same concerns about his leadership. He was relieved that John and his family would stay at Mount Vernon and watch over Martha,

> I have been called upon by the unanimous voice of the Colonies to take the command of the Continental Army—It is an honour I neither sought after, or was by any means fond of accepting, from a consciousness of my own inexperience, and inability to discharge the duties of so important a Trust. However, as the partiallity of the Congress have placed me in this distinguished point of view, I can make them no other return but what will flow from close attention, and an upright Intention. for the rest I can say nothing—my great concern upon this occasion, is the thoughts of leaving your Mother under the uneasiness which I know this affair will throw her into; I therefore hope, expect, & indeed have no doubt, of your using every means in your power to keep up her Spirits, by doing every thing in your power, to promote her quiet—I have I must confess very uneasy feelings on her acct, but as it has been a kind of unavoidable necessity which has led me into this appointment, I shall more readily hope, that success will attend it, & crown our Meetings with happiness.
>
> At any time, I hope it is unnecessary for me to say, that I am always pleased with yours & Nelly's abidance at Mount Vernon, much less upon this occasion, when I think it absolutely necessary for the peace & satisfaction of your Mother.[14]

Years later Doctor Benjamin Rush wrote that Patrick Henry told him that he (Henry) was with George Washington and the general expressed a lack of confidence in his ability to lead the army, "Remember, Mr. Henry, what I now tell you; From the day I enter upon command of the American armies, I date my fall, and the ruin of my reputation."[15]

In a letter on June 21, 1775, to Burwell Basset, husband of Martha's sister, Washington again voiced concern about his appointment, "God grant therefore that my acceptance of it may be attended with some good to the common cause & without Injury (from want of knowledge) to my own reputation."[16]

In a letter from George Washington to his brother John A. Washington, June 20, 1775 he once again cast doubts on his abilities. He vowed to do the best he could, and if he failed then the fault would lie with those who appointed him,

> That I may discharge the Trust to the Satisfaction of my Imployer, is my first wish--that I shall aim to do it, there remains as little doubt of. How far I may succeed is another point--but this I am sure of, that in the worst event I shall have the consolation of knowing (if I act to the best of my judgment) that the blame ought to lodge upon the appointers, not the appointed.[17]

Once Washington agreed to take command of the American Army, a committee of three delegates, who were comprised of Richard Henry Lee, Edward Rutledge, and John Adams, drafted Washington's commission on June 29, 1775,

> TO GEORGE WASHINGTON Esquire
>
> WE reposing especial trust and confidence in your patriotism, conduct and fidelity. Do by these presents constitute and appoint you to be GENERAL AND COMMANDER IN CHIEF of the army of the United Colonies and of all the forces raised or to be raised by them and of all others who shall voluntarily offer their service and join the said army for the defence of American Liberty and for repelling every hostile invasion thereof And you are hereby vested with full power and authority to act as you shall think for the good and Welfare of the service.
>
> AND we do hereby strictly charge and require all officers and soldiers under your command to be obedient to your orders & diligent in the exercise of their several dut(ies.) AND we do also enjoin and require you to be careful in executing the great trust reposed in you, by causing strict discipline and order to be observed in th(e) army and that the soldiers are duly exercised an(d) provided with all convenient necessaries.
>
> AND you are to regulate your conduct in every respect by the rules and discipline of war (as herewith given you) and punctually to observe and foll(ow) such orders and directions from time to time as you shall receive from this or a future Congress of the said United Colonies or a committee of Congress for that purpose appointed. This Commission to continue inforce until revoked by this or a future Congress.[18].

Once Washington accepted his appointment, most members in Congress began to write to friends back home praising the man they selected. An example of such letters is typified by the letter that Eliphalet Dyer wrote to Joseph Trumbull on June 17, 1775. In it he mentioned that Washington was lacking military experience, but being from the south was important,

> You will hear that Coll Washington is Appointed Genll or Commander in Chief over the Continental Army by I dont know but the Universal Voice of the Congress. I believe he will be Very Agreable to our officers & Soldiery. He is a Gent. highly Esteemed by those acquainted with him, tho I dont believe as to his Military, & for real service he knows more than some of ours, but so it removes all jealousies, more firmly Cements the Southern to the Northern, and takes away the fear of the former lest an Enterprising eastern New England Genll proving Successfull, might with his Victorious Army give law to the Southern & Western Gentry. This made it absolutely Necessary in point of prudence, but he is Clever, & if any thing too modest. He seems discret & Virtuous.[19]

Just before Washington left for Boston he wrote once again to his wife Martha,

> As I am within a few Minutes of leaving this City, I could not think of departing from it without dropping you a line; especially as I do not know whether it may be in my power to write again till I get to the Camp at Boston—I go fully trusting in that Providence, which has been more bountiful to me than I deserve, & in full

confidence of a happy meeting with you sometime in the Fall—I have not time to add more, as I am surrounded with Company to take leave of me—I retain an unalterable affection for you, which neither time or distance can change, my best love to Jack & Nelly, & regard for the rest of the Family concludes me with the utmost truth & sincerety.[20]

On his way to Boston, Washington and his escorts stopped at New York City, which caused a crisis for the moderate leaders there. William Tryon, the Royal Governor, was returning from England on the same day. An official delegate arranged for Washington to enter the city in the afternoon, and to be welcomed by a military band, along with nine companies of militia, and a cheering crowd. As soon as the city's delegation had rushed him through town, they scurried to the docks to welcome Tryon, who was landing from a British warship in the harbor.

During this trip to Boston, Washington met a messenger hurrying to Philadelphia with news of the Battle of Bunker Hill which had taken place on June 17th. The new commander's greatest anxiety was as to find out how the provincial soldiers had fought. He asked the messenger, "Did they stand the fire of the regular troops?"

"That they did," was the messenger's reply, "and held their own fire in reserve until the enemy was within eight rods."

"Then the liberties of the country are safe!" exclaimed General Washington fervently.[21]

It was on Monday July 3 when General George Washington entered the pasture known as Cambridge Common, where the Continental army was assembled, about half a mile from headquarters. He was surrounded by a crowd of people in carriages, wagons, and on foot. As he rode up, he was escorted by a detachment of cavalry, Generals Philip Schuyler and Charles Lee, two young officers (Joseph Reed and Thomas Mifflin), and two of his slaves.

Washington taking command of the army just before the siege of Boston. National Archives

A friend described General Washington's appearance when he took charge that day, "He was forty-three years old — just as old as Julius Cesar was when he took command of the army in Gaul and made himself great. Just as old as Napoleon when he made the mistake of his life and declared war against Russia. But how different from these two conquerors was George Washington! What they did for love of power, he did for love of liberty."[22]

As the sign of assuming command, he wheeled his horse, drew his sword, and waved it in a saluting manner to the assembled army. When he gazed at his army he was disappointed and shocked. What he saw resembled a mob of men, not an army.

On July 3 he received a warning from the Massachusetts Provincial Congress, when they said that the men lacked, "Regularity, and Discipline" and that the "Youth in the Army are not possess'd of the absolute Necessity of Cleanliness in their Dress, and Lodging, continual Excercise, and strict Temperance to preserve them from Diseases frequently prevailing in Camps."[23]

No two companies dressed alike, except the men of Rhode Island who were commanded by the Quaker General Nathanael Greene. This was the only group of real soldiers who were properly uniformed and equipped with arms, tents, and other supplies. The men from Virginia wore Indian leggings and other garments of backwoodsmen and pioneers, as if they were out on a hunting expedition. As for the rest, they looked like a group of farmers and shopkeepers wearing everything, except uniforms.

Washington found these raw recruits to be men of many minds. There was no discipline, and each man appeared to think of himself as a law unto himself. Instead of being at a battle, they appeared to be taking part in a club outing or a party. They felt that no one had any authority over them, and they could do as they wished. Some of the men thought they had some political influence, so they would come and go as they wanted. They even made a practice of leaving their post before being relieved.

Washington saw officers and other men mingling, as if there was no distinction between the two. Many of the officers were friends and neighbors of the men under their command. This made it difficult to issue orders or command any respect. Washington even saw some officers shaving the recruits. He was also disturbed when he noticed that soldiers from each side talked to each other across the lines. Even though powder was very scarce, groups of soldiers would often fire their guns because they enjoyed the sound, or they took shots at the British who were usually out of range. Washington later discovered that the amount of powder in camp and the surrounding area only amounted to about nine rounds per man.

When General Washington asked the commanders how many men he had in his army, he was met with silence. No one knew the exact number since no roll had ever been taken. The general had originally been told he had 20,000 men, but a few days later the number reported back to him was around 16,000. Only 13,000, were actually fit for duty because 1,500 were too sick to fight, and another 1,500 were absent. The majority of the absent men had farms and family to tend to, so they just simply walked away.

The men were living in a shantytown of huts made of sod, planks, and fence rails, or in tents made of linen or sailcloth. The men were more worried about food for their families back home than they were about the British.

Due to a lack of discipline, hygiene was neglected and the camps smelled of excrement, and the men were not especially clean. Soldiers were known to urinate and defecate in the areas surrounding their camps. Washington even commented to his staff that the New England troops were a dirty and nasty people. But they were really no different than any other groups of undisciplined soldiers.

Soldiers without discipline do not build adequate latrines, practice proper sanitation, or protect their drinking water from contamination. Nor do the officers recognize the importance of camp hygiene. As a result, diarrhea and dysentery were common in camps and greatly reduced the effectiveness of the colonial troops.

New England men were even averse to washing their own clothes, because they considered it to be woman's work. If their wives or any camp followers were not around, then their clothing went unwashed. Washington wrote a letter to his brother John weeks later, and gave his first impression of his new army, "I arrived at this place after passing through a great deal of delightful Country, covered with grass (although the Season has been dry) in a very different manner to what our Lands in Virginia are. I found a mixed multitude of people here, under very little discipline, order, or government."[24]

One of Washington's biggest problems was finding officers to lead the men. He wanted leaders that would enforce the needed discipline to build an effective army. The current officers were at times no more responsible than the troops they commanded. Considering the disorder and confusion in the army, Washington was alarmed when he heard that, at times officers would run during battle, and sometimes disobey orders from their superiors. He was also informed of cowardice by officers at the Battle of Bunker Hill, and he wrote of such cowardice in a letter to John Hancock on July 21, 1775,

> Upon my Arrival & since, some Complaints have been preferr'd against Officers for Cowardice in the late Action on Bunkers Hill. Though there were several strong Circumstances & a very general Opinion against them, none have been condemn'd, except a Captn Callender of the Artillery, who was immediately cashier'd. I have been sorry to find it an uncontradicted Fact, that the principal Failure of Duty that Day was in the Officers, tho. many of them distinguish'd themselves by their gallant Behaviour. The Soldiers generally shew'd great Spirit and Resolution.[25]

Note: This is an account of the above incident involving Captain Callender:

John Callender, a captain, was tried by a court martial on 27 June, 1775 for cowardice and disobedience of orders during the Battle of Bunker Hill. His chief accuser was Maj. Gen. Israel Putman who reported, "that in the late action, as he was riding up Bunker's Hill, he met an officer of the Train drawing his cannon down in great haste ; he ordered the officer to stop and go back ; he replied, he had no cartridges; the General dismounted and examined his boxes, and found a considerable number of cartridges, upon which he ordered him back; he refused, until the General threatened him with immediate death, upon which he re- turned up the hill again, but soon deserted his post and left the cannon. In addition, Callender as a Massachusetts officer apparently did not feel bound to obey Putman, who at the time was a general only in the Connecticut service.

General Putnam declared his opinion, that the defeat of that day was owing to the ill-behavior of those that conducted the artillery, and that one of these officers ought to be punished with death, and that unless some exemplary punishment was inflicted, he would assuredly leave the Army.[26]

[Callender was convicted and dismissed from the army. He wanted to redeem himself so In March 1776, the army was so desperate for men, especially with artillery experience, he enlisted as a private in a volunteer artillery company. At the Battle of Long Island, he took command of his unit cannon after his superiors were killed. He continued to fire even though wounded and was later taken prisoner. Washington learned of Callender's heroism and ordered his court-martial erased and his captain's commission restored. He was exchanged in 1777, and served in the Continental artillery until 1784.]

Luckily for the American army, the well-trained British army in Boston was smaller. It had been purposefully kept small since 1688, in order to keep the King from using it against Parliament. The Americans estimated the British force facing them to be around 11,500 [a little high, it was closer to around 7,000]. The American commanders felt that they would need at least 22,000 men to have a successful attack. Since they only had less than 14,000 fit for duty, an attack was not feasible at the present. Washington had a little time to instill some discipline in his troops, which were described by British General John Burgoyne as a "rabble in arms," and a "preposterous parade."[27]

The impact of George Washington:

In 1775, it was nothing short of a miracle that George Washington was able to turn the mob outside of Boston into an army. General Washington was not the best tactician, but that was only a small part of being a good general. He had to train, instill discipline, organize supply lines, and find a way to pay his troops. He was a master at providing direction and motivation for his men. He was both gentle and brutal, displayed caution and surprise, and he was skillful and resourceful in defense and attack. He had to be and do all these things while fighting the most powerful army on earth.

At times he did not have support of some of his own officers. General Charles Lee once said that Washington, "was a raw general, placed above me for political reasons."[28] General Horatio Gates insulted Washington by sending reports directly to Congress instead of to him, his commanding officer, and Major General Thomas Conway referred to him as a weak general. The three generals even tried to have Washington removed from command of the army.

However, General Washington did have the love, respect, and support of his men. They were willing to stay with him and fight, even when they received no pay for months. In 1776, after losing several battles, the army in full retreat, and the enlistment of many of his men up in a few weeks, Washington did the impossible. He rallied his troops to win victories at Trenton and Princeton and was able to keep his small army together.

Washington was also a good judge of the talents of the men around him. After making Marquis de Lafayette a general, he trusted the twenty year old young man from France to lead men into battle. In 1780 Washington appointed Nathanael Greene as Southern Commander of the Continental Army. This move helped to turn the tide of the war in the south in favor of the Americans. His appointment of Baron Von Steuben at Valley Forge, to train the American troops in the basics of military drills, tactics, and discipline, enabled the Americans to later face the British troops in battle as equals. The baron also established standards of sanitations and camp layouts that made the army healthier.

Washington was a man that did not seek personal glory. In victory he gave credit to his men and officers and was not threatened by taking the advice of others. Also, he was not afraid to make tough and dangerous decisions. One of his best ones was to inoculate his troops for smallpox while encamped at Valley Forge, and it probably saved his army and the revolution.

When Congress appointed George Washington to lead the new army they had no idea that they had probably selected the only man that would be capable of holding the army together for eight years and in the end defeat the British. It is hard to imagine that any other person chosen by Congress could have accomplished what Washington did with so little to start with.

George Washington in continental uniform 1776. Brooklyn Museum

2

British Frontal Assault of Bunker [Breed's] Hill

"The engagement lasted upwards of four hours, and ended infinitely to our disadvantage. The flower of our army are killed or wounded."

----British officer after the battle.

Background:

Boston, located on a peninsula one mile long and one-half mile wide, was surrounded by British warships. After the battles at Lexington and Concord on April 19, the colonial militia consisting of about 16,000 untrained men surrounded the town. Colonial General Charles Lee described the American troops as, "composed in part of raw lads and old men, half armed, with no practice or discipline, commanded without order, and God knows by whom."[1]

The Americans controlled Roxbury Neck, which was the only land access to Boston. They faced a British force of about 6,000 troops under the command of General Thomas Gage, the British commander of North America. Since the British controlled the harbor, they could be resupplied and reinforced without much opposition from the Americans. American privateers, however, were able to capture enough British supply ships, which resulted in food shortages for the citizens and troops inside Boston.

The Charlestown Peninsula was located across the Charles River north of Boston and the town of Charlestown was at the southern end. Located on the peninsula was Bunker Hill, elevation of 110 feet, and to the south was Breed's Hill, elevation of 62 feet. After the battles at Lexington and Concord, British General Gage withdrew his men to Boston and left the Charlestown Peninsula a no man's land.

In May Gage received reinforcements and three excellent generals: William Howe, John Burgoyne, and Henry Clinton. At once the British generals began to plan to break out of Boston. They wanted to take command of the Dorchester Neck, which was the land entrance into Boston. This would give them control of their southern flank and enable forces to take the Charlestown Peninsula and then move into Cambridge driving the Americans away. This attack was to be put into motion on June 18, 1775. The British were very confident of victory, since they faced an army of farmers and shopkeepers.

Map of Boston 1775, United States Military Academy

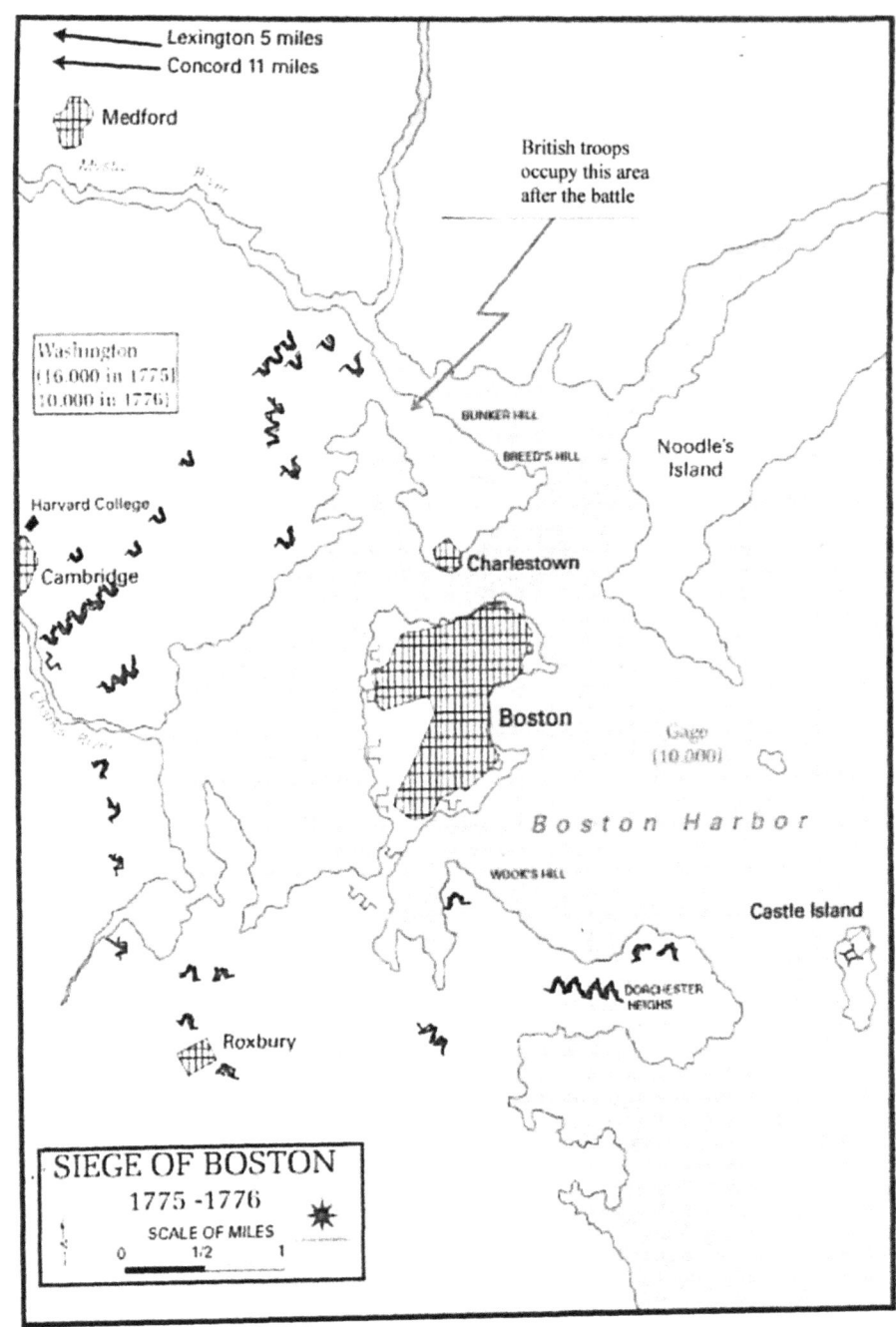

Dorothy Dudley lived in Cambridge and kept a diary during the early years of the American Revolution. She wrote about the British in Boston on June 15, 1775,

> I heard today that when the three British generals with the reinforcement were sailing into Boston harbor they met a ship coming out, and General Burgoyne asked of the skipper, "What news is there?" The reply was that Boston was surrounded by ten thousand country people. "How many regulars [British soldiers] in Boston?" was his next question. "Five thousand." "What!" said the British officer. "Ten thousand peasants keep five thousand King's troops shut up! Well, let us get in, and we'll soon find elbow room."[2]

The American leaders were able to gain information about British activity from people who were escaping from Boston. Unfortunately, General Gage received very little intelligence from deserters of the Americans forces. On June 13, outside of Boston, the leaders of the colonial militia learned from spies that the British were coming out in force to fortify the unoccupied hills around Charlestown. This alarmed the Americans, because these hills would give the British control of the harbor and made it easier to land more troops and supplies.

General Thomas Gage, National Archives

The original colonial response was to occupy Bunker Hill with a force of 1,200 militiamen. This hill was nearest to the neck of land connecting the peninsula with the mainland and the closest to the American forces. The working party that was sent out decided to move closer to Boston and construct the works on Breed's Hill which was a tactical blunder, because it would be easier to cut off if the British landed on the neck in the rear.

Night of June 16:

Around midnight the colonists began to quietly construct a strong redoubt on Breed's Hill and build other fortifications. A cry of all's well was given by patrols at intervals during the night to give assurance that they were still undetected by the British. Breed's Hill was chosen over Bunker Hill, because it was closer to Boston and thought to be more defensible. It would also enable artillery fire to be directed into Boston. As the sun rose on the following morning, the British were shocked to see the Americans fortifying Breed's Hill.

Colonial General William Heath gave the following account in his memoirs published in 1798,

> Just before the action began, Gen. Putnam came to the redoubt, and told Col. Prescott that the entrenching tools must be sent off, as they would be lost; the Colonel replied, "If I send any of the men away with the tools, not one of them would return." To this General Putnam answered, "They shall every man return." A large party was then sent off with the tools, and not one of them returned. In this instance the Colonel was the best judge of human nature.[3]

June 17, 1775 British prepare for an attack:

By daybreak of June 17, when the British became aware of the presence of colonial forces on the Peninsula, General Gage called a war council early in the morning. The staff knew that the Americans must be removed, or Boston and the British fleet would not be safe from attack. The British leaders were not aware, however, that the Americans at this time lacked heavy guns. They only had a few small artillery pieces in camp.

Without gathering further intelligence on the American position, the British hurriedly assembled a council of war to deal with the problem. A majority of the leadership favored occupying the Charlestown Neck, thus surrounding the rebels in the hills and forcing them to surrender by starving them out. General Gage was strongly against this tactic as it was unmilitary and hazardous. He believed the Americans had heavy guns, and these guns would put the British at risk in Boston and the fleet in the harbor, so the guns needed to be removed at once. Also, if they landed behind the rebels, it would place their men between a larger army outside of the neck and an entrenched force. In addition, it was feared that such a move would have brought down fire on the landing party from the high ground in Cambridge.

General Gage decided that a frontal assault on the Americans' positions would be a quick and simple matter. After all, these were not real soldiers they faced but rather a band of rabble that would run at the first sounds of battle. The optimism of a British victory was apparent, when it was decided that just two regiments were needed to dislodge the Americans from the occupied hills. Before the attack on the hills, there would be a feint on Roxbury with a heavy bombardment. It was believed that this would keep reinforcements from being sent to the hills.

It was not until two in the afternoon that they had their troops ready to embark on an assault. This delay enabled the Americans to reinforce their flanks that were poorly defended against attack. About 3,000 of the best troops in Boston were selected for the assault, and would be led by General William Howe and his second in command Sir Robert Pigot. The attack force was assembled, and around noon they began to embark to land at Moulton's Point on the Charlestown Peninsula. The British fleet provided cannon fire to give the troop landings cover. A British officer later reported his confidence, "Our troops advanced with great confidence, expecting an early victory."[4]

Meanwhile, in the American fortifications, knowing that the British would attack, the men were given instructions from veterans of the French and Indian War, "Fire low, aim at their waistbands. Wait till you see the whites of their eyes. Aim at the handsome coats."[5] [These would be officers.] The Americans were organized into three ranks, and one person would always be firing as the others reloaded.

One definite advantage of the Americans was that many of the men were sharpshooters and took careful aim at their targets, just as they would when shooting game in the countryside. The British, on the other hand, did not aim at a specific man but they were trained to lay down a field of fire. The officers were considered gentlemen, and to aim at an individual would be considered murder. As the war progressed, this belief would change.

Abigail Adams was in Boston with her children, while her husband, John, was in Philadelphia hard at work to make George Washington the commander of the American forces outside of Boston. She wrote to him on June 18 about her fears of the battle soon to take place,

> Tis expected they will come out over the Neck to night, and a dreadful Battle must ensue. Almighty God cover the heads of our Country men, and be a shield to our Dear Friends. How [many ha]ve fallen we know not—the constant roar of the cannon is so [distre]ssing that we can not Eat, Drink or Sleep. May we be supported and sustaind in the dreadful conflict. I shall tarry here till tis thought unsafe by my Friends, and then I have secured myself a retreat at your Brothers who has kindly offerd me part of his house. I cannot compose myself to write any further at present. I will add more as I hear further.[6]

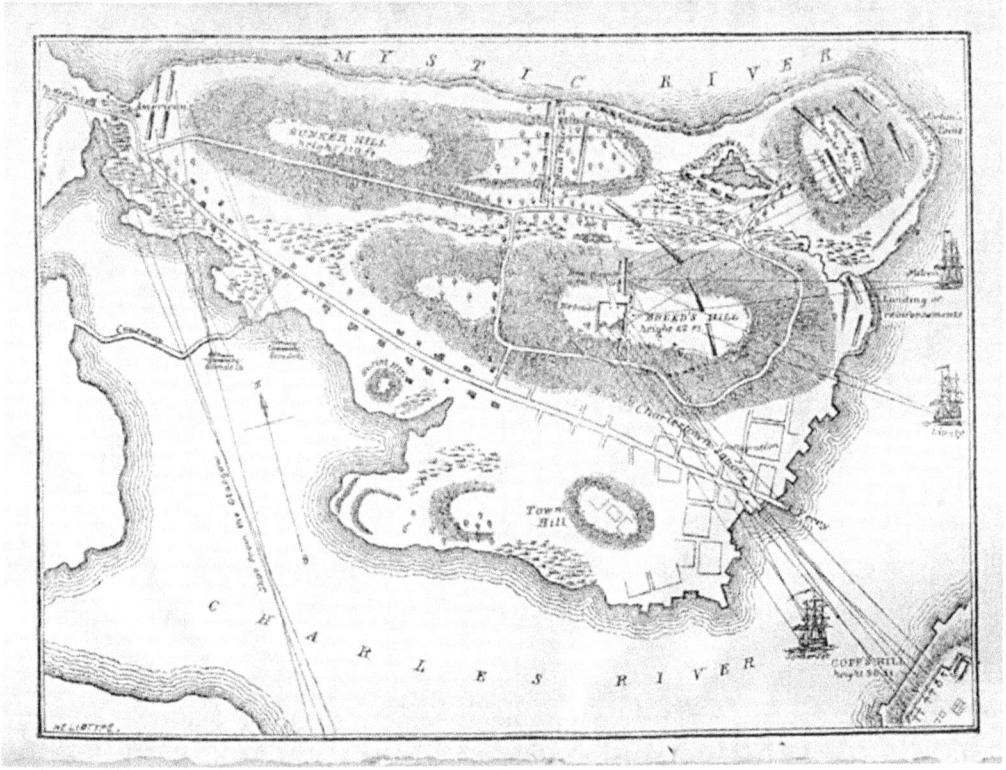

Battle ground showing canon line of fire, U.S. Army

The first attack June 17, 1775:

Howe and his forces embarked about noon and rowed under a warm sun to Moulton's Point. The men came under sniper fire from Charlestown, so a party of British marines, supported by artillery fire, set Charlestown on fire and destroyed many of the 500 wooden buildings. They also hoped that the smoke from the blaze would help to conceal the advancing British troops. However, a breeze carried the smoke away, leaving them with little or no protection. At the same time, a furious cannonade took place at the lines on Boston neck against Roxbury with the intent to also burn that town. Many citizens of Boston gathered on rooftops to watch the battle unfold.

Attack on Bunker's Hill with the Burning of Charlestown, {Public Domain}

General Burgoyne later wrote about the many spectators, "Behind us, the church steeples and heights of our camp [Boston] were covered with spectators, and the rest of our army who were engaged. The hills round the country were covered with spectators. The enemy all in anxious suspense."[7]

General Howe saw that the rebels were being reinforced, so he sent word back to General Gage for more troops. As the men waited for the additional troops, they quietly dined with food from their knapsacks. For many it would be their last meal.

The British troops were also supplied with large tubs of water and "rum by the bucketful," for them to drink before the attack. This was welcomed, because the men were wearing heavy woolen coats and the temperatures were climbing to the upper 90's. The Americans, who had a shortage of water, could only watch the enemy indulge themselves on this very hot summer day. An earlier cannon shot from an offshore ship had destroyed two of their barrels of water.

Before they attacked, General Howe addressed his men, "Gentlemen, I am very happy in having the honor of commanding so fine a body of men. I do not in the least doubt but that you will behave like Englishmen, and as becometh good soldiers. If the enemy will not come from their entrenchments, we must drive them out, at all events, otherwise the town of Boston will be set on fire by them. I shall not desire one of you to go a step further than where I go myself at your head. Remember, gentlemen , we have no recourse to any resources if we lose Boston, but to go on board our ships, which will be very disagreeable to us all."[8]

By three in the afternoon Howe had all his troops assembled in three lines, and they began the assault on Breed's Hill and the adjacent picket fence fortification to the left. [An unknown officer later said they should have advanced in columns, rather than in lines.] When they started moving the field artillery, problems began to develop as the canons became hindered by the muddy fields.

Twenty-one year old Captain Henry Dearborn, of the 1st New Hampshire Regiment, organized and led a local militia troop of sixty men to the Boston area. In an account of the battle he published in 1818 he noted, "The enemy were discovered to have landed on the shore of Morton's point [Moulton's Point], in front of Breed's Hill, under cover of a tremendous fire of shot and shells from a battery on Cop's Hill, in Boston, which had opened on the redoubt at daybreak."[9]

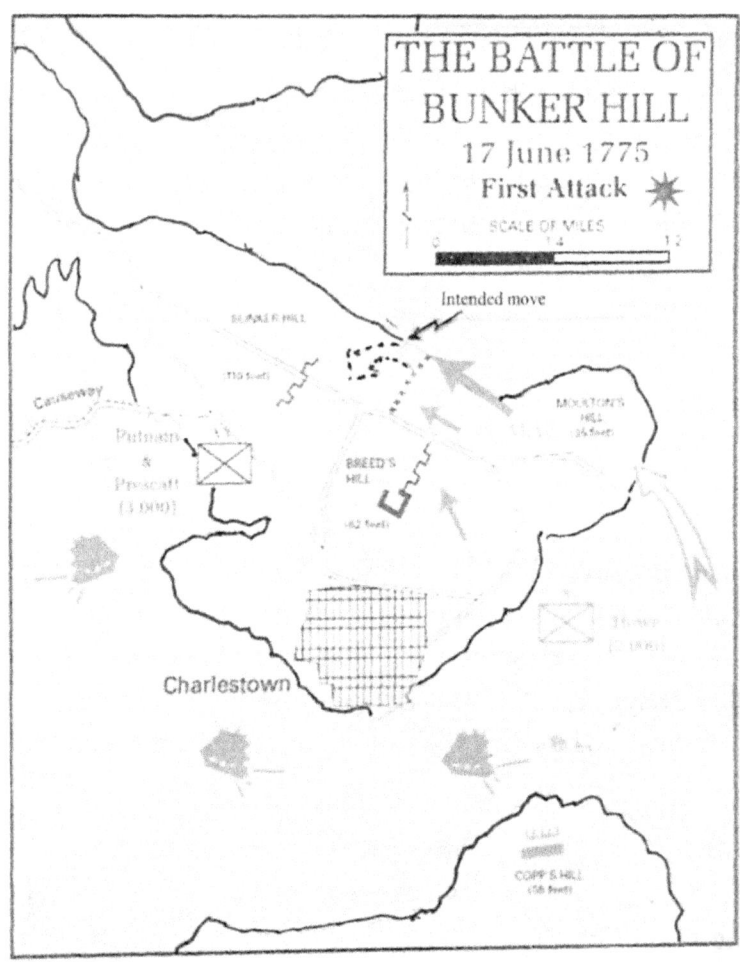

1st attack on Bunker Hill, courtesy of United States Military Academy

As the British lines were marching up toward the hill, their artillery stopped firing. One of the generals inquired why the canons had grown silent, and he was told they had mistakenly brought twelve pound balls for six pound cannons. The few correct sized balls had been used up. The general was told that all they could fire was grape shot, which would be much less effective. The order was given to use grape shot, and a messenger was sent back to Boston requesting the correct sized balls.

The British troops slowly marched in order toward Breed's Hill, while carrying heavy knapsacks that were not needed for the attack. The knapsack and other items they carried amounted to an additional 125 pounds of unnecessary weight. The trek up the hill became even harder to maneuver, due to the waist-high hay that had not been harvested on the hillside of Breed's Hill. In addition, their line of marched was hampered with uneven ground that they could not see due to the tall hay. The hillside also had crisscrossing rail fences that disrupted their line of march.

As they approached the rebel positions, they fired their heaviest volley that flew harmlessly over the fortifications. The British fully expected the rebels to surrender or run without firing back. Many of the rebels were surprised that the British stated firing from seventy to eighty yards out.

Due to a shortage of powder, the rebels were ordered to hold their fire until the British were within forty yards from them. A few colonists discharged their weapons which angered their commander, William Prescott. He vowed instant death to anyone who should repeat it and promised to give the command to fire at the proper moment.[10] When the order to fire was given it sent the entire front rank of the British troops down to the ground. The surprised survivors hesitated and, being largely short of officers still standing, they began to retreat. The rebels had broken the British advance.

One British soldier, who was lucky to survive, later wrote, "As we approached, an incessant stream of fire poured from the rebel lines, it seemed a continued sheet of fire for near thirty minutes."[11]

When the remaining British soldiers retreated, a cry of victory went up from the American fortification. The men congratulated each other on their victory and courage. Many of the men were relieved that they passed the first test of battle and did not break and run. They were also thankful, because they feared that the British would rush them with their bayonets. Some were even hopeful that the British had enough and would not venture another attack.

The 2nd attack June 17, 1775:

Once the retreating British soldiers were safely out of range, they quickly reformed and began to once more move forward toward the waiting Americans. During this attack they faced not only the same obstacles that hampered their last march, but now they had to step over their dead and wounded comrades. As they walked past those wounded, cries went up pleading for help. However, the advancing soldiers were not allowed to break rank and help their dying comrades. By now General Howe had the correct cannonball size and the artillery began to do some damage to the American positions.

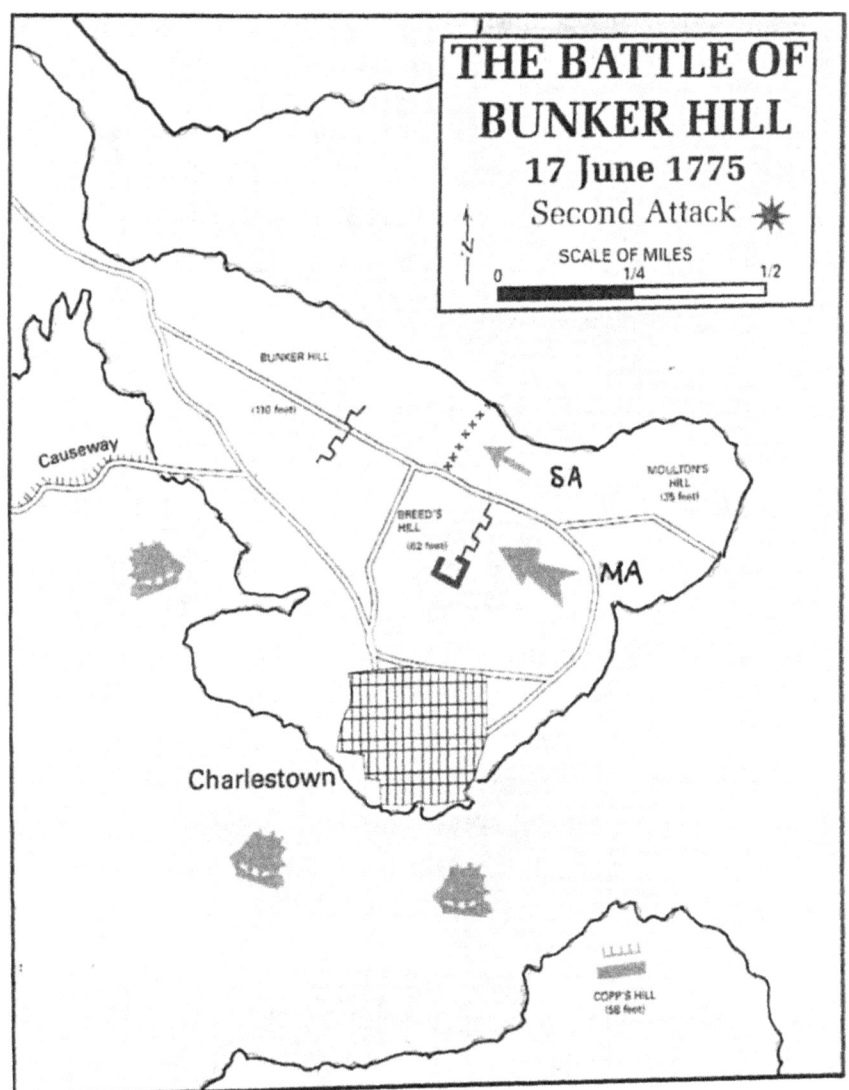

2nd attack on Bunker Hill, courtesy of United States Military Academy

The outcome of the second attack was very much the same as the first. One British observer wrote, "Most of our Grenadiers and Light-infantry, the moment of presenting themselves lost three-fourths, and many nine-tenths, of their men. Some had only eight or nine men a company left, some only three, four, and five."[12]

Again the Americans held their fire and waited until the British got close before they began shooting. The results were the same as the first attack. So many of General Howe's surrounding aids and officers were shot, leaving the general nearly alone. His aid de camp Nisbet Balfour was saved only because, when he was shot, the ball was slightly diverted by his canteen which saved his life. Once again the attack had failed, as the British troops fled the field of battle.

After the second attack, American losses were again slight. Soon confusion reigned in the American lines, due to a lack of command among them. Fear developed as the men began to run dangerously low on powder and shot. Some of the American deserted, leaving only a few hundred men to face a third attack from the determined British troops.

Dorothy Dudley in her diary described the battle on June 17, "We can hear the booming of the cannon and see the smoke arising from Charlestown, which the British have set on fire. It is a terrific battle. Our noble men defend their own works gallantly, and will not yield, we know, till the last moment. It is feared that the want of ammunition will force them to retreat before the greater numbers of the enemy."[13]

Final attack June 17, 1775:

There was a lull of about an hour before the third and final assault. Some of the soldiers thought and hoped that there would not be another attack. Howe and his remaining officers held a council of war to discuss their course of action. Most of the advice he received was to abandon the attack and stop the fruitless butchery of the men. Howe disagreed and said that it was either attack or evacuate Boston. Now that British honor was at stake, Howe had no desire to be beaten by this rebel rabble, and besides the transport boats were back at Boston. They would fight on and conquer or die. Howe had been reinforced by 400 fresh marines, so he ordered a third attack. An additional 200 walking wounded were also convinced to take part. Without these extra men it was possible that the other troops would have refused a third assault.

The Americans had less than 200 tired men left inside the redoubt, with additional troops on the left flank at the fence rail, and some men inside several houses on the slope of the hill. Most of the men only had a couple of rounds of ammunition left. In the redoubt the men out of ammunition vowed to use their muskets as clubs to repel the invaders. Even loose stones inside the redoubt were gathered to use as weapons if needed.

Around five in the afternoon the British troops began to again advance, but this time without their cumbersome knapsacks that contained three days' supply of food, blanket rolls, and anything else not essential. Many of them also removed their heavy wool coats due to the hot temperature. Some of the men that were reluctant to advance were encouraged by the remaining officers with a blow from a sword to their backside. Orders were given to hold their fire and use their bayonets, which should have been used earlier. In addition, the artillery was to sweep the American defenses in support of the advance. This attack would be centered on the redoubt.

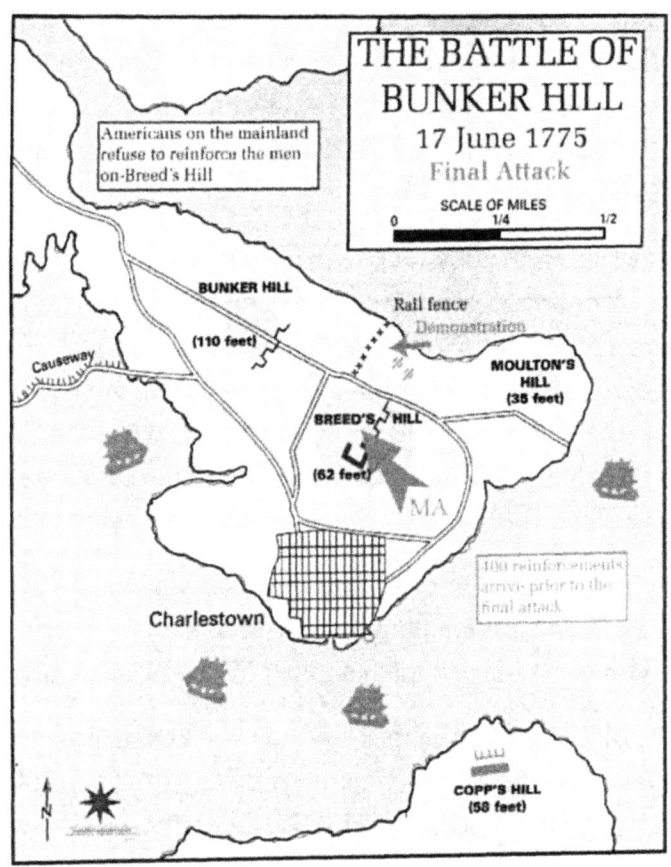

Final attack on Bunker Hill, courtesy of United States Military Academy

The artillery fire and the advancing British, combined with the lack of powder forced the Americans to retreat. Seeking revenge, the British poured destructive musket fire upon them and then attacked with their bayonets, as the Americans withdrew. When the advancing troops saw some of the Americans throwing stones at them, they knew that the battle was theirs. The Americans passed Bunker Hill in an orderly and disciplined retreat, and it was during this time that the Americans sustained the majority of their causalities. Before seven in the evening, the Americans had retreated over the Charlestown Neck to the safety of Cambridge, and left the British in control of the peninsula.

After the battle:

After the fighting ceased, Dorothy Dudley wrote her thoughts about the battle in her diary, "Our enemies rejoice at our loss (and well they may), but their victory is a dear one to them, and one they will not care to buy again at the same price. Eleven hundred of their choicest men, including a great many officers, is no small loss, when they receive in exchange only a little hill overlooking Boston."[14]

Now that the British had control of the peninsula, General Clinton proposed to press on into Cambridge, which could have broken up much of the militia groups surrounding Boston. General Howe, who was a tentative decision maker, declined to continue the attack. He had just sustained heavy losses, including much of his field staff, in the previous three assaults and decided that was enough for one day.

When you consider the heavy loss of life in such a short time, this battle would be one of the bloodiest in the war. The three charges and the pursuit of the retreating Americans took up a little less than two hours. Out of some 3,500 British actually engaged, 226 were reported killed and 828 wounded, or nearly one-third of the soldiers. Whole regiments were nearly obliterated, and over one-seventh of the entire loss was in officers, 157 in all. The casualty count was the highest suffered by the British in any single encounter during the entire war. The Americans, with perhaps 2,200 engaged, suffered 140 killed, 271 wounded, and 30 captured.

General Henry Clinton wrote in his diary about the victory, "A few more such victories would have shortly put an end to British dominion in America."[15] General Nathanael Greene, on the other hand said, "I wish we could sell them another hill at the same price."[16]

Soon after the battle, many Americans felt that the defeat was a military operation that should have never begun. Later, the battle took on a different meaning for the colonists. They realized that the British were not invincible and maybe the militia could win the war. Putting such blind trust in the ability of untrained and undisciplined militia would later prove to be a problem.

One of the British surgeons, Mr. Grant, wrote about the aftermath of the battle six days later, "I have been up two nights dressing our men of the wounds they received the last engagement. The provincials were determined that every wound should prove mortal. Their muskets were charged with old nails and angular pieces of iron, and from most of our men being wounded in the legs, we are inclined to believe it was their design, not wishing to kill the men, but to leave them as burden to us, to exhaust our provisions and engage our attention, as well as to intimidate the rest of the soldiery."[17]

Some of the British officers felt they would have had a more resounding victory, if there had been more troops. Later, General Gage would send a dispatch to London requesting an additional thirty thousand men.

Impact of the battle on the American Revolution:

The British showed a lack of respect for the Americans and were overly confident concerning them. This proved to be a fatal and costly mistake, as one British officer later wrote,

> To great a confidence in ourselves, which is always dangerous, occasioned this dreadful loss. We are all wrong at the head. My mind cannot help dwelling upon our cursed mistakes. Such ill conduct at the first

outset argues a gross ignorance of the common rules of the profession, and gives us for the future anxious forebodings. I have lost some of those I most value. This madness or ignorance nothing can excuse. The brave men's lives were wantonly thrown away. Our conductor has as much murdered them as if he had cut their throats himself on Boston commons.[18]

The Battle of Bunker Hill has been called a "tale of great blunders heroically redeemed."[19] The American command made the first wrong move by moving on to Breed's Hill, which exposed an important part of their force in an indefensible position. Likewise, the British made a mistake by undertaking a suicidal frontal attack on a fortified position. It would have been wiser to land a force behind the Americans and cut off their retreat and with the troops in the front squeezing them in a vise.

Being overconfident, not taking your enemy seriously, and lack of good intelligence could certainly lead to bad decisions. In the beginning, General Gage had been urged repeatedly to take possession of the heights of Charlestown, and he committed a great error in delaying such an important mission. He acted quickly without having the area being reconnoitered.

The army should have landed in the rear of the Americans and cut off their retreat. The force should have been concentrated against the American left wing. Then the troops should have marched up in columns on the first attack, and carried the works by their bayonet. The unnecessary load they bore exhausted them before they got into action. Mystic River was neglected, and navy ships could have taken position at high water in the rear of the Americans and supported their flank at the rail fence.

Instead, General Gage had his judgement influenced by a lack of respect for the America militia, his arrogance, and a desire for revenge for the Lexington and Concord humiliation, so he elected for a frontal assault. He decided that this was the best course of action. It was a mistake for the navy to play a secondary role in the attack.

Not using a bayonet charge may have been a poor decision on the part of the British commander. Marching toward the Americans in slow long lines enabled the sharpshooters to kill more men. A sudden rush with bayonets on the first attack would have frightened the Americans and could have made them break and run. Captain Henry Dearborn was relieved there was no bayonet charge by the British, as he later wrote, "It is a most extraordinary fact that the British did not make a single charge during the battle, which if attempted, would have been decisive and fatal to the Americans, as they did not carry into the field fifty bayonets. In my company there was but one."[20]

If the hills had been taken with the first assault, then reinforcements could have been brought up to pursue the Americans to Cambridge and beyond. This would have given the British room to maneuver, and they could have used the navy canons to disrupt the Americans surrounding Boston. Many of the Americans would have been frightened or discouraged and most likely would have left to return home. If the militia had been brought under control, there would have been no army for George Washington to lead and the revolution might have been crushed. Low morale and fear would have spread across the countryside.

Instead, the Americans were given optimism even with their loss at Bunker Hill. One British officer was aware that the Americans were given hope even in their defeat, "But from an absurd and destructive confidence, carelessness, or ignorance, we have loss a thousand of our best men and officers, and have given the rebels great matter of triumph, by shewing them with mischief they can do us."[21]

When news of the battle reached London, the government concluded that General Gage had made some grave mistakes, so he was replaced as commander in North America in October of 1775. People within the British government had wanted to replace Gage, and the Battle of Bunker Hill provided the incentive push to later do so.

The costly victory also meant that the British troops, for the time being, were prisoners inside Boston and unable to move inland to take part in any other military operations. Determined not to repeat that Pyrrhic victory, the British found new respect for the colonial forces. One British officer even was reported to have said he would rather fight the French regulars.

After Bunker Hill and the battles at Lexington and Concord, the Americans were convinced that the citizen soldiers, when fighting for a cause, were a match for the trained professional soldiers. This gave hope to the colonists and encouraged more support for their cause. They would soon learn that a disciplined and trained army was needed to win this conflict.

The British realized that they would need to prepare for a long war, and more troops and supplies would be required. It would force King George to hire mercenaries, the hated Hessians from Germany. Many months would pass before the British would undertake another offensive action against the colonists.

3

The Battle and Siege of Quebec by the Americans

"The patriotism of the summer of seventy-five, seemed almost extinguished in the winter of seventy-six."

----American private John Joseph Henry

Background:

The First Continental Congress in 1774 and the Second Continental Congress a year later had invited the French-Canadians to join in their meetings. It was hoped that Canada would join in the American struggle against Great Britain and become the fourteenth colony. They believed that the people of Quebec felt the same oppression as the people of Boston. Unfortunately, there was no substantive response to the request of either Congress.

When the American Revolution began, members in the Continental Congress felt that Canada should be included the fight against England. They saw it as a way to generate support for the war and it would prevent an attack from the north. On June 7, 1775, John Adams wrote to James Warren, President of the Massachusetts Provincial Congress,

> Dear Sir, We have been puzzled to discover what we ought to do with the Canadians and Indians. Several Persons have been before Congress who have lately been in the Province of Canada, particularly Mr. Brown and Mr. Price," who have informed us that the French are not unfriendly to us. And by all that we can learn of the Indians they intend to be neutral.
>
> But whether We should march into Canada with an Army Sufficient to break the Power of Governor Carlton, to overawe the Indians, and to protect the French, has been a great Question. It seems to be the general Conclusion that it is best to go, if We can be assured that the Canadians will be pleased with it and join.[1]

In July 1775 there were fears that the British would use Quebec as a launching point for attacks into New York. So, a decision was made to invade Canada and capture Quebec. By invading Canada, Congress hoped to secure their northern border flank, and prevent the British from rallying Indians to raid the colonial frontier, as the French had done in previous wars. The Americans later discovered that most Canadians showed no interest in supporting the American cause, the French Canadians remained indifferent, and the few British subjects supported the British Crown.

The invasion of Canada was to be the first major offensive of the Revolutionary War. The plan of attack was that General Schuyler would take a force of 3,000 men to capture Montreal, and Colonel Benedict Arnold would take another army of 1,500 men to seize Quebec. The men under Schuyler began to march toward Montreal September 16, 1775. However, Schuyler became ill and he was forced to turn his command over to Brigadier General Richard Montgomery on November 13.

Colonel Arnold took his army from Cambridge and would have to march through the wilderness toward Quebec. Some units left September 11, and the remainder left two days later. The march through the harsh wilderness would leave Arnold's troops depleted in numbers, starving, sick, and lacking many supplies. Food was so scarce that the men were forced to eat dogs and shot pouches on their march.

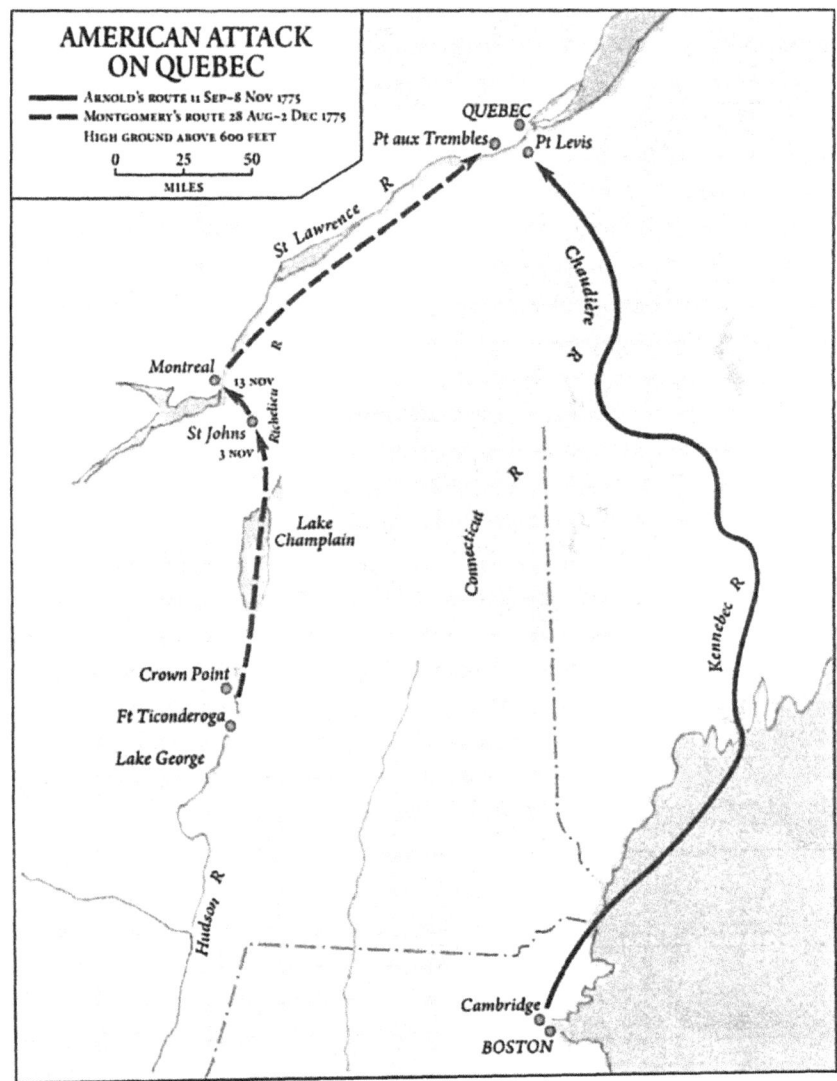

Map showing the routes taken by Benedict Arnold and Richard Montgomery expeditions into Quebec as part of the American invasion of Canada (1775). Map courtesy of the USMA, Department of History.

The March to Canada:

By October 2 Arnold had reached Norridgewock Falls, nearly 200 miles to the north by boats, and soon problems began to develop. Much of the food had spoiled, and many of the men were suffering from dysentery. After making repairs on the boats, they left the falls on the 9th. Traveling was slow because of the sick men, freezing temperatures, and having at times to pull the boats upstream.

On October 11 the army reached the "Great Carrying Place." All their equipment, supplies, and boats would have to be carried over a twelve mile distance spaced by three ponds. Due to a diet of salted meat, the men drank large amounts of stagnant water from the yellow colored ponds. Many of them became very ill and later had to be left behind as the army continued their march. While the men traveled into the wilderness they continued to drink water from murky small ponds which made them ill.

One member of the expedition to Quebec was Dr. Isaac Senter, who was born in New Hampshire in 1753. After the battle of Lexington he joined the Rhode Island volunteers that were marching to Boston. He was appointed surgeon on the expedition to Quebec under Col. Benedict Arnold, and during the march he kept a journal of the events.

Benedict Arnold, National Archives

Dr. Senter wrote about the health of the men,

> Oct Sunday, 15th.- Many of us were now in a sad plight with the diarrhoea. Our water was of the worst quality. The lake was low, sur rounded with mountains, situate in a low morass. Water was quite yellow. With this we were obliged not only to do all our cooking, but use it as our constant drink. Nor would a little of it suffice, as we were obliged to eat our meat exceeding salt. This with our constant fatigue called for large quantities of drink. No sooner had it got down than it was puked up by many of the poor fellows.[2]

During this time the weather had been harsh with heavy rain and at times snow. Soon the men were about to start the most difficult part of their journey, as cases of dysentery and camp fever began to slow the march of the men. There were 1,100 that left on this mission and now they were reduced to 950 due to sickness and desertion, but there was only one death, which was caused by a falling tree. Rheumatism, dysentery, malaria and other ailments, were the inevitable consequences of the hardships and exposure which the men endured. These problems threatened to destroy the effectiveness of the force.[3]

When the British became aware of the American's plan, General Guy Carleton, who was also the Governor, had less than 800 British troops and was forced to declare martial law and call out the militia. On November 11, Carleton decided the best thing for him to do was to march his men to the walled city of Quebec.

Guy Carleton, Library of Congress

The British did not have the manpower to defend Montreal, so they deserted the city and General Montgomery occupied it. On November 28 Montgomery, his army reduced by disease, desertion, and expiring enlistments, left some of his troops at Montreal and St. Johns. He took 300 men and advanced north to Quebec City to join with Arnold.

Dysentery or constipation had become chronic with many of the American soldiers, which were conditions due to starvation and poor drinking water and hindered them in their traveling. Doctor Senter noticed as they began their march, many of the men were so weak they could not stand without support of their guns. The troops were still seventy hard miles from their destination and they were out of food. Doctor Senter wrote in his journal, "In company was a poor dog, [who had] hitherto lived through all the tribulations, became a prey for the sustenance of the assassinators. This poor animal was instantly devoured, without leaving any vestige of the sacrifice. Nor did the shaving soap, pomatum, and even the lip salve, leather of their shoes, cartridge boxes, &c., share any better fate."[4]

Timothy Bigelow was thirty-six and stood over six feet tall. He was a blacksmith back in Worcester, Massachusetts and joined the militia right after Lexington and Concord. After the attack on Quebec he was taken prisoner and later released. He later became a Major and survived the war. During the march he thought this might be his final letter to his wife,

> On that part of the Kennybeck called the Dead River, 95 miles above Norridgewock. DEAR WIFE. I am at this time well, but in a dangerous situation, as is the whole detachment of the Continental Army with We are in a wilderness nearly one hundred miles from any inhabitants, either French or English, and but about five days provisions on an average for the whole. We are this day sending back the most feeble and some that are sick. If the French are our enemies it will go hard with us, for we have no retreat left. In that case there will be no other alternative between the sword and famine. May God in his infinite mercy protect you, my more than ever dear wife, and my dear children. Adieu, and ever believe me to be your most affectionate husband.[5]

On November 9 the American Army reached the St. Lawrence at Pointe-Levis across the river from Quebec with only six hundred of the original 1,100 men. Out of these 600, only 500 were deemed fit for duty. The men arrived about eleven in the morning in snow that covered their shoes. The terrible journey had covered 350 miles, rather than the 180 that Colonel Arnold and General Washington thought it would be. Arnold estimated that he would take 2,000 soldiers to capture Quebec, but he had only 500 battle ready men.

The American troops were described as, "....both pitiful and ridiculous. With their lean forms, half clad in torn and disheveled clothing, and haggard faces unshorn for many weeks, many bare-footed and bare-headed, they made a sorry spectacle."[6]

The American command noticed that there appeared to be confusion in Quebec from lack of leadership. The city was defended by 150 Royal Highland Emigrants, nearly 500 poorly trained militiamen, and 400 marines from two warships that had arrived. Some of the American officers felt that if they attacked the city now, it could be captured. Because the 500 men that were able to fight were in such a weakened state, no attack was carried out.

After several days of bad weather, the Americans crossed the river and arrived at the city of Quebec. Arnold began sending demands for the troops inside Quebec to surrender. The British rejected all demands to surrender and shot at several of the messengers. On Saturday November 18, the Americans were informed by a deserter from the city that the British were preparing their field pieces for an attack. The Americans called a war council, "....an examination of our arms, ammunition, &c. The former were found much deficient in numbers, much in disorder. No bayonets, no field pieces and upon an average of the ammunition there amounted only to about, four rounds per man. Under these circumstances it was thought proper to raise the siege."[7]

The Americans did not have the cannons needed, nor enough healthy troops to take the city, so on November 19 they had no choice but to go back across the river and several miles upriver to Pointe-aux-Trembles. There they waited from reinforcements from Montgomery and prepared for a siege. The men spent the next several days making ladders and pikes to scale the walls of Quebec. The army was now gathered in close, unsanitary conditions that made the troops ripe for an outbreak of disease. Many of the men were sick with pneumonia and sore throats.

Also, on the 19th the outlook for the city improved greatly, when General Guy Carleton arrived from Montreal bringing more reinforcements and much needed leadership. Carleton immediately began to improve the city's defenses. Three days after his arrival, Carleton issued a command that anyone disloyal to the British must leave the city at once, or they would be treated as rebels or spies. This ended any hope for the Americans that there would be any collaboration from anyone inside Quebec, and it also gave the city's defenders additional manpower.

By the end of November, the number of defenders in Quebec had risen to 1,800, and they had enough supplies to last eight months. The defenders were warm, in high spirits, and in good health. The Americans that faced them were fatigued, sick, cold, and hungry.

On the first of December, the ragged army of Colonel Arnold was still at Pointe-aux-Trembles and received some much needed ammunition from Montgomery's army by ship. Later that day at noon two ships appeared that carried Gen. Montgomery and his men. A division of Arnold's men were sent out to welcome the nearly 300 reinforcements. The rest of Montgomery's men were left behind at Montreal under the command of General Wooster to hold strategic points in the surrounding country.

When Montgomery arrived he provided a much needed moral builder for Arnold's troops. Montgomery had captured all the winter uniforms of the 7th and 26th British Regiments. Long white overcoats and other pieces of clothing were passed among many of the American troops, which replaced their light-weight garments. He also brought much needed artillery (not siege artillery) and ammunition.

General Montgomery and Colonel Arnold took their men back in sight of Quebec on December 5. The two men and their officers studied the fortifications to determine if there was any way to breach them. Montgomery sent a messenger with a letter to the city demanding their surrender. The messenger was fired upon, so the general sent a local with the orders to surrender or be attacked. Once again the demand to surrender was met with no success.

General Richard Montgomery {Public Domain}

Twenty-two year old private Caleb Haskell from Massachusetts wrote in his diary on the 6th, "The most of the army has arrived. We are getting in readiness to lay siege to Quebec. The small pox is all around us, and there is great danger of its spreading in the army. There are Spies sent out of Quebec every day, and some taken almost every day, both men and women."[8] Haskell would become sick with smallpox and miss the attack of Quebec City.

The attack on Quebec:

Originally General Montgomery wanted to attack Quebec before British reinforcements arrived in the middle of April 1776. The American leaders knew that they could not maintain a successful siege against Quebec. Their cannons were too small to damage the city walls, the ground too frozen for protective trenches, and a harsh winter was approaching. Also, there was no additional ammunition coming, Continental paper money was worthless in Canada, and many of the enlistments were nearly up for New England troops.

Montgomery began to urge his New Englanders to reenlist until April, but most refused. Montgomery and Arnold agreed that due to the up-coming harsh winter, lack of supplies, and many enlistments about to expire on New Year's Day, the attack must come at once or give up hope of conquering Canada. The fear of smallpox was not only preventing men from reenlisting, but soldiers were starting to desert to the British. Many of the men deserted, because the British could supply them with food, warm clothing, shelter, and perhaps safety from smallpox.

Reinforcements of 3,000 men had been requested from the colonies, but none were promised. Since many enlistments would be up in a few days, it was decided that on the night of December 30, the Americans would storm the walls of Quebec. A small force of less than 800 men, some of them sick, would attack a larger force of well-entrenched soldiers behind massive city walls.

The attack would come as no surprise to the British. Governor Carleton had a network of spies that kept him informed of the situation of the American invaders. The governor was aware of the enlistment situation and desertions, so he was preparing for an attack during the last of December. Hours before the attack on the evening of December 30, a deserter informed British Captain Ainslie of the attack and gave him very misleading information,

> They are three thousand strong, having been reinforced from Montreal; that they have been cloath'd lately; they have plenty of provisions. The Habitants supply them with everything for which "they are paid in hard money — they refuse to take the Congress bills until the Town falls, they'll then accept of them. The small pox still rages among them.[9]

Between four and five in the morning of December 31, the Americans rushed the walls of Quebec during a heavy snow storm. The attack was a colossal failure, as General Montgomery was killed at the beginning of the battle and Colonel Arnold was severely wounded and had to be carried from the field. In addition, hundreds of Americans were killed or captured, which further reduced the already shrinking size of the American Army. The British had only five killed and thirteen wounded.

Despite being wounded, Arnold took command of the remaining army and tried to regroup. At the time he did not have enough men to resume the attack so he began a siege of the city. He was hoping to get reinforcements before the British reinforcements arrived in the spring.

After the failure to capture Quebec, many of the American troops headed home, regardless if their enlistments had ended or not. Montgomery was dead, and Arnold, although wounded, tried to keep the siege going while waiting for reinforcements. He sent word to General Wooster in Montreal of the defeat, and word was sent to the Congress in Philadelphia. Luckily for the Americans, Carleton, who had a large advantage in manpower, decided not to attack the defeated Americans.

Arnold continued to shell the city but did little damage, as Carleton continued to strengthen his defenses. During the winter, American reinforcements were raised by Congress and sent to Quebec. Once they arrived, the men were in poor health and some fell victim to smallpox. Smallpox was still spreading among the troops left with Arnold. He knew in the spring that British reinforcements would arrive.

With his army growing weaker, Arnold wrote to the President of Congress on February 12, 1776, to give them some bad news about the condition of his army, "We have been reinforced with only one hundred and seventy-five men; our whole force is about eight hundred effective men. We have about two hundred sick and unfit for duty, near fifty of them with the small-pox."[10]

The siege had now become a waiting game between the two sides and each waited to see who would be the first to get ample reinforcements. Some began to trickle into the American camp but, as soon as they arrived, most of them succumbed to smallpox and were unfit for duty. By March, 1776, the siege of Boston had finally ended and General Washington had forces available to send to Colonel Arnold. Three regiments consisting of 1,100 men were immediately sent to Quebec.

Retreat from Quebec:

General John Thomas was assigned to take charge of the Canadian invasion, and soon he began to prepare the army for a retreat. On May 6 British reinforcements arrived at Quebec and rapidly launched an attack on the weaken Americans.

The American retreat from Quebec was not orderly, but it quickly became a panic stricken mob running back home and leaving their supplies, dead, and dying. The soldiers that were sick with smallpox, now no longer in quarantine, helped to spread the disease further. The disorganized army made its way to Sorel about forty miles below Montreal. General Thomas died the first of June from smallpox.

General John Sullivan was sent by Washington to take the place of General Thomas, and he promptly ordered a counterattack against the pursing British. When the attack failed, Sullivan took the army back to Crown Point. Washington wrote to the President of Congress on June 14, and told him about a letter he received from General Sullivan, "Genl Sullivan in a Letter of the 2d Inst. informs me of his arrival with the Army at Crown Point. The Army is sickly, many with the small pox, and he is apprehensive the Militia ordered to Join them, will not escape the Infection."[11]

During the retreat death become commonplace among the American troops as one soldier reported, "The army paused while fifteen to thirty men died each day from smallpox, malaria, and dysentery. In foul sheds, lice fought maggots over the sick and the dead, while men yelled, sang, cursed, prayed, and died unheeded."[12]

News of the condition of the Northern Army reached John Adams in Philadelphia, who had been working on the Declaration of Independence. He wrote to his wife on June 26, 1776,

> The smallpox is ten times more terrible than Britons, Canadians and Indians, together. The small Pox! The small Pox! What shall We do with it? I could almost wish that an inoculating Hospital was open, in every Town in New England. It is some small Consolation, that the Scoundrell Savages have taken a large Dose of

it. They plunder the Baggage, and stripped off the Cloths of our Men, who had the Small Pox, out upon them at the Cedars."[13]

The retreat from Quebec to Fort Ticonderoga brought General Gates into conflict with General Schuyler over authority. Schuyler was the commander of the army's Northern Department, which also controlled Fort Ticonderoga, which was under the command of General Gates. The problem was resolved when Schuyler was given command of the whole Northern Department, and Gates replaced General Sullivan and was given command of the Northern Army and the defense of Lake Champlain.

The army arrived at Fort Ticonderoga by mid-July under the command of General Horatio Gates, who had relieved General Sullivan. The campaign against Canada has been a complete failure, and General Gates spent the rest of the summer enlarging the American fleet to protect Lake Champlain from being controlled by the British.

Impact of the attack on Quebec:

The number of men in the Northern Army who died during the expedition to Canada will never be known. Not all died from smallpox, but many died from typhus, dysentery, fevers, lack of supplies, and the harsh environment. Soldier John Joseph Henry summed it up well when he wrote, "The patriotism of the summer of seventy-five, seemed almost extinguished in the winter of seventy-six."[14]

The attack on Quebec was a waste of much needed manpower and supplies. The Canadians were not going to join the Americans, and attacking the city in the dead of winter with a small force of men who were tired, sick, undernourished and ill-equipped, as well as poor timing, led to the defeat in Quebec. The city was a fortress surrounded by thick twenty-five feet high walls with well-placed ramparts. In addition, the British benefitted from superior artillery. This needless attack also cost the Americans one of their better and more popular leaders, General Richard Montgomery.

The Northern Army was nearly destroyed at a time that they could have been a great help to General Washington as he was defending New York form the British. The silver lining to this fiasco was that Washington would later remember what happened in Canada and be forced to make an important and dangerous decision at Morristown in the winter of 1776, and again at Valley Forge in the winter of 1777.

4

British General Howe's Hesitation in Attacking Washington in New York

"Are these the men with which I am to defend America?"

----General Washington about his men running from the British

Background:

In February 1776 General Charles Lee and twelve hundred men were sent to New York to prepare to defend the city threatened by the British. In March after the evacuation of the British in Boston, most of the American troops were sent to New York, while the rest either stayed in Boston or were redeployed to the Northern Army. Later when General Washington joined them in New York, he found he had a force of around 8,000 men.

Congress had decided that New York must be held by the Americans. Washington was not convinced that New York could be held, since he found the circumstances much different than in Boston. When the army surrounded Boston, they had an advantage when winter set in. Now it was spring time in New York, and the British had a large navy around the harbor that could strike at almost any place. In Boston, Washington had the support of the vast majority of the townspeople that were only too eager to supply him with information on the British. New York had a population with a large portion of Tories, who spied on the Americans. Now the British controlled the time and place to engage in battle.

For the first time since the fighting began, the American army was joined by regiments that came from the middle colonies. Shortly, the camps began to see large outbreaks of typhus and dysentery. The new recruits had little or no knowledge of sanitation in large group surroundings, and the camps soon became excessively filthy, smelly, and undisciplined.

General Howe, Public Domain

For the next several months, each side would receive reinforcements. The British would eventually assemble an army, under General William Howe, consisting of about 32,000 men that were supported by a powerful fleet under the command of Howe's brother, Admiral Richard Howe. Washington had nearly 28,000 men, but only around 19,000 were fit for duty. Many of the troops were made up of unreliable militiamen. All of Washington's troops were raw, undisciplined, and had little experience.

April 1776, the start of the New York Campaign:

After the British evacuated from Boston in March, General William Howe went north to Halifax in Nova Scotia. He regrouped and from there he left for New York in June, and at the end of June he appeared in New York harbor with 8,000 troops. More reinforcements followed in the next few weeks. Howe's strategy was to isolate and destroy the rebellion that was growing in New England, and New York was crucial to his plans. The British decided to not launch an attack until all their forces were in place.

Washington arrived in New York in the middle of the day on April 13, 1776. The American army was tired, ragged, and did not look like a professional army as they marched into town. Washington immediately began examining the defenses and found them only half completed. Large groups of the American troops were quartered in vacant buildings and in some of the beautiful old homes. Nearly one third of the people in the city had fled, and the citizens left behind were unfriendly to the rebel troops.

Washington instantly began to improve the defenses of the city. The hundred and twenty-one cannons and nineteen mortars were positioned to repel an attack from the British. Washington stationed one-third of his 18,000 troops on the Long Island side of the East River to protect his left flank. To defend the approach to Manhattan, a division of men under General Nathanael Greene were placed on Long Island's Brooklyn Heights, across the East River from New York City.

On July 3, 1776, General Howe landed 8,000 troops on Staten Island and was supported with 130 ships under the command of his brother Admiral Richard Howe. He decided against landing at Long Island, due to the strength of the American defenses. However, the British troops that landed on Staten Island were well organized and equipped, and the continental regulars on Staten Island took a few shots at them and then ran off. The citizen's militia panicked and switched over to the side of the British.

Washington was in need of reinforcements and in letters appealed to several colonies for additional troops. The Northern Army had retreated from Canada and could offer no help since they were plagued with sickness and lack of unity. According to General Schuyler, "The most descriptive pen cannot describe the Condition of our Army—Sickness, Disorder, and Discord reign triumphant."[1]

Like many soldiers at the beginning of the war, both sides were in a pleasant mood and morale was high. The Americans were still excited about their victory at Boston, and for many of the young men this was their first time away from home. The British troops were anxious to show these upstarts what a real army was like. Their leaders, however, did not share in their confidence or enthusiasm.

Washington realized that he was in a perilous situation. His troops currently outnumbered the enemy, but they lacked discipline, and he feared that many, especially the militia, would break and run at the first sign of battle. He also had large numbers of troops too sick for duty, many with smallpox, and he had little hope of reinforcements.

During the first part of July, General Howe twice sent letters to General Washington trying to open surrender negotiations. Both requests were ignored, because Howe addressed the letters to George Washington, Esq., refusing to acknowledge Washington's rank. On July 20 Washington met face to face with a high ranking British officer, who offered a pardon to all that surrendered. Washington declined, and said that they had done nothing to be pardoned for.

By the end of July, breakdowns in sanitation had become the norm as deaths from dysentery and putrid fever had begun to increase, and the dreaded smallpox was still active. To make matters worse, enemy ships were about to land 14,000 additional troops under the command of Generals Cornwallis and Clinton. It appeared to some that the revolution might be about over.

The British Parliament wanted a quick and decisive victory from Howe, so they gave him the largest British army that had ever set foot on foreign soil. During the summer, ships began arriving in New York, and their troops were camped on Staten Island. By August 12 the British fleet numbered over 400 ships, including seventy-three warships, and there were 32,000 troops camped on Staten Island, all within striking distance of New York City. The long ocean voyage had left many of the men tired and suffering from various sicknesses. This forced General Howe to delay any action against the American forces.

Even with all the problems Washington faced each day, including the looming threat of battle, he took time to write about farming to his distant cousin Lund, who was serving as steward of Mount Vernon,

> There is no doubt but that the Honey locust if you could procure Seed enough, & that Seed would come up, will make (if sufficiently thick) a very good hedge—so will the Haw, or thorn, and if you cannot do better I wish you to try these—but Cedar or any kind of ever Green, would look better; howr, if one thing will not do, we must try another, as no time ought to be lost in rearing of Hedges, not only for Ornament but use.[2]

The Americans were now outnumbered more than two to one. To make matters worse, on August 20 Nathanael Greene, the commander of American forces on Long Island, fell ill with the fever. Greene, who was very familiar with the terrain of the area and the placement of its defenders, was replaced with General John Sullivan, who was not familiar with the terrain or troops' placement.

Washington was aware that Sullivan did not possess some of the more noble traits that Greene had, as he expressed months earlier in a letter to John Hancock, "But he [Sullivan] has his wants; and he has his foibles—The latter are manifested in a little tincture of vanity, and in an over desire of being popular, which now and then leads him into some embarrassments."[3] Four days later Washington had second thoughts, and Sullivan was replaced with Major-General Israel Putnam, who was popular and might boost the morale of the men who were down because of the illness of Greene. Unfortunately, Putnam knew even less about the terrain and placement of the troops than Sullivan.

A little after five in the morning on August 22, Howe began landing men on the south beach at Long Island. A group of Pennsylvania riflemen were stationed on the shore, but as the

British landed, they retreated and killed cattle and burned farmhouse as they moved back. British General Cornwallis took an advanced guard of troops six miles inland and established a camp. The British troops received a warm welcome by many Loyalists in the area.

General Washington received news of the landing and promptly sent some reinforcements. He believed that the real attack would come at New York City, and that this maneuver was just a British diversion.

By mid-day around 15,000 men and forty artillery pieces had reached the shore. Howe knew that he outnumbered Washington's army but he felt some restraint, even though he realized that he could drive the Americans back. Still fresh in his mind were the numerous casualties he took at Bunker Hill, so he delayed attacking.

Howe sent out patrols to probe the American positions. When they encountered any resistance from the Americans, they immediately pulled back. On one occasion American soldiers followed a British patrol, and believing that British soldiers were hiding in three homes, they burned them down. General Sullivan sent a letter to Washington describing the incident,

> This Afternoon the Enemy formed & attempted to pass the Road by Bedford a smart fire between them and the Rifle Men ensued, the Officer sent off for a Reinforcement which I ordered down Immediately, a number of Musketry came up to the Assistance of the Rifle Men whose fire with that of our field pieces caused a Retreat of the Enemy our Men followed them to the House of Judge Lefferds, where a number of them had taken Lodgings drove them out and Burnt the House and a number of other Buildings Contiguous.[4]

Washington, in turn, sent a reply two days later to Sullivan's replacement, General Putnam, rebuking the action against American property by the troops,

> The burning of houses, where the apparent good of the service is not promoted by it; & the pillaging of them, at all times, & upon all occasions, is to be discountenanced and punished with the utmost severity; In short it is to be hoped, that men who have property of their own, & a reguard for the rights of others, will shudder at the thought of rendering any man's situation, to whose protection he had come, more insufferable than his open and avowed Enemy would make it, when by duty & every rule of humanity they ought to aid, & not oppress, the distress'd in their habitations.[5]

General Putnam was in charge of the main defenses at Brooklyn Heights, which was defended by 6,000 troops. There were three main approach roads to the Brooklyn Heights: the Gowanus Road, the Flatbush Road, and the Bedford Road. General Sullivan's men were to defend the Flatbush and Gowanus Roads, with 1,000 and 800 men respectively. Lord Stirling, also known as William Alexander, was to defend the Gowanus Road with 500 men. Washington believed, that by having these men positioned on the roads in the heights, he could inflict heavy casualties on the British before they fell back to the main force on the Brooklyn Heights.

[Note: Lord Stirling was the heir to the Scottish title Early of Stirling, his claim to the title was upheld in Scottish court but overturned in by the English Parliament. He chose to continue to use the title.]

Many military strategists believed that Washington should have withdrawn his forces immediately, when Howe landed on Long Island. They reasoned that Washington did not have the manpower or defense to repel the British invaders. Washington, however, chose to stay either due to his lack of battle experience or for morale reasons. A sudden retreat from the enemy the moment they advanced, after preparations had been made to resist them, would have betrayed weakness and demoralized the army and the country.

The British plan of attack was drawn up by General Clinton and presented to Howe. The plan called for British forces under General James Grant to attack Stirling's position on the right, and the Hessians under General Leopold Philip Von Heister would attack Sullivan's troops in the center. Clinton would take 10,000 men on a night march and flank the Americans in a surprise move through a little known pass. Clinton's force would need to be in position behind the Americans by daybreak.

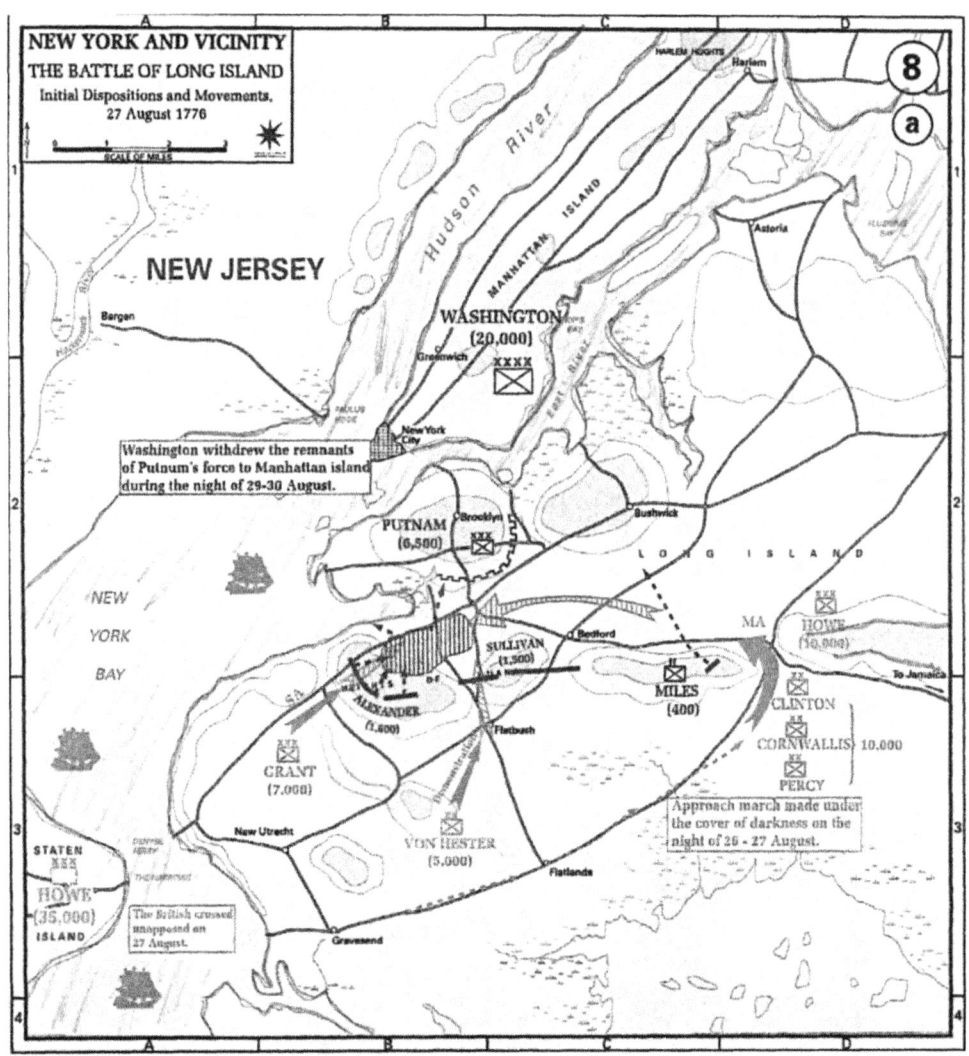

Battle of Long Island courtesy of United States Military Academy

Flanking the Americans:

General Clinton had earlier learned from local Loyalists of an additional road through the heights. The Jamaica Pass was farther to the east, and the American command was aware of it, but because it was lesser known and narrow, they decided to have it patrolled by just five militia officers on horses. There was no need to send men to this pass, since they expected a frontal attack similar to what took place at Bunker Hill. This would prove to be a grave mistake.

General Howe approved the plan and told Clinton to make a night march through the pass on August 26. However, Howe was extremely worried that Clinton would be attacked on his march, but Clinton assured him that there was little chance of that happening. The remaining British troops would make a frontal assault on the three American positions, in order to provide distraction for Clinton.

By the evening of August 26, Washington was now convinced that the main British attack was to take place on Long Island. Just before midnight the 10,000 troops moved out toward the Jamaica Pass. Only the British commanders knew of the secret plan to flank the Americans, as local Loyalists' farmers led the British toward the pass. Clinton led a brigade of troops with fixed bayonets, and he was followed by Cornwallis with eight battalions and fourteen artillery pieces. Behind him was Generals Howe and Hugh Percy with the remaining men, artillery, and baggage. Meanwhile at the British camp, the remaining men were keeping the campfires burning to deceive the unsuspecting Americans.

Around two in the morning on the 27th, the advanced column of British troops reached Howard's Tavern, which was just a few hundred yards from Jamaica Pass. Inside the tavern they encountered the keeper, William Howard and his son.

Howard's Tavern in 1776 by unknown author

Soldiers woke Howard and his son and escorted them to the barroom, where they were met by General Howe and some of his officers. Howe was wearing a camlet cloak over his uniform and asked for liquor for himself and several of his officers. After learning that Howard supported the American cause, Howe told him, "That is alright; stick to your country, or stick to your principles, but Howard, you are my prisoner and must guide my men over the hill."[6] At first William refused, but when told he would be shot in the heart, he agreed.

In five minutes the British were at Jamaica Pass, which was a winding, narrow rocky road, and they took the five American officers by surprise. The Americans did not ride off and there were no shots fired, because they thought the British were Americans. The men believed that the attack would be the customary frontal assault on their positions. After questioning the men, the British were led by William Howard to an old Indian trail that skirted the pass. The British soon turned west on the Bedford Road, and around daybreak they halted to rest and eat. The British were now behind the lines of Sullivan, who was unaware that he was surrounded.

As the men laid in tall grass, they enjoyed a well-deserved rest. They had marched for nine miles in darkness through unfamiliar territory, only stopping at times to quietly clear the road of obstacles that would hinder their wagons. At nine in the morning two large cannons were fired to signal the Hessian troops, facing Sullivan, to begin their frontal attack on his position. Still the Americans were not aware that they were surrounded.

While the main part of the British army was advancing toward Jamaica Pass during the night, the Americans that were preparing for the frontal attack fired the first shots of the battle near the Red Lion Tavern. An American officer later wrote,

> About 120 of our men went as guard to a place on Long Island called Red Lion; about 11 at night the sentries saw 2 men [British scavengers] coming up a water-melon patch, upon which our men fired on them. The enemy then retreated, and about 1 o'clock advanced with 200 or 300 men and endeavored to surround our guard, but they being watchful gave them 2 or 3 fires and retreated to alarm the remainder of the battalion.[7]

Attack on General Stirling:

Later in the morning, the troops under British General James Grant engaged the Americans commanded by Stirling. Grant was holding back, not completely pressing the attack, because his role was to provide a diversion to hold Stirling's troops in place. At nine the British heard the two canons fired in Bedford that signaled Howe was behind the Americans. Grant now pressed his men forward knowing that British forces were approaching in the rear.

The American line under Stirling held against the advancing British, who were still unaware of the British flanking movement. In fact, some of the Americans thought they were winning, since they were holding off Grant's attack. By eleven, Grant was reinforced by 2,000 marines and began to push Stirling back, but as they pulled back they were attacked by the British in their rear. When Stirling realized that he was fast being surrounded, he determined that his only escape was across Brower's mill dam.

The remainder of Stirling's men escaped and made it to the American lines at Brooklyn Heights, only after around 270 men, known in history as the "Maryland 400", covered their retreat. Less than a dozen of these brave men left behind survived and reached the American lines. Stirling stayed behind and fought with the rear guard of the 1st Maryland Regiment. Because of his actions, one newspaper later referred to him as "the bravest man in America," and he was praised by both Washington and the British for his bravery. Stirling was captured and later and was released in a prison exchange.

George Washington watched the fighting and retreat from a redoubt on nearby Cobble Hill, and as he wrung his hands he reportedly said, "Good God, what brave fellows I must this day lose!"[8]

Attack on General Sullivan:

Once the signal was given the Hessians began a cannon bombardment against the American center under General Sullivan. Several Hessian brigades waited in a long line while the cannons fired. Sullivan saw the Hessian troops were not attacking so, believing that Grant's attack was the main thrust, he sent four hundred of his men to reinforce Stirling. Soon the British behind Sullivan's line attacked, and Sullivan discovered that he was nearly surrounded. He left his advance guard fighting the Hessians and took the rest of his men to defend against the British attack in the rear.

To encourage them to fight harder, the Hessians were told that the Americans would give them no quarter. The Hessians overran the American advance guard and vicious hand-to-hand fighting occurred. One British officer wrote of the Hessians fighting against the outnumbered Americans, "The Americans fought bravely, and (to do them justice) could not be broken until they were greatly outnumbered, and taken in flank, front and rear. We were greatly shocked at the massacre made by the Hessians and Highlanders, after victory was decided."[9]

The officer went on to describe what he saw, "The Hessians and our brave Highlanders gave no quarters; and it was a fine sight to see with what alacrity they dispatched the rebels with their bayonets after we had surrounded them so that they could not resist. We took care to tell the Hessians that the rebels had resolved to give no quarters -- to them in particular — which made them fight desperately, and put to death all that came into their hands."[10]

This battle was the first encounter the Hessians had with rebel forces. They quickly developed contempt for the undisciplined and non-professional army. One Hessian officer later expressed his thoughts about the American army, "The rebels looked ragged, and had no shirts on.

When we attacked them courageously in their hiding places, they ran, as all mobs do. These frightful people deserve pity."[11]

The Americans knew they were almost surrounded and began to flee in fear. Sullivan attempted to calm his men and lead them in a retreat. Even with all the chaos around him, Sullivan was able to evacuate most of his men to the American lines at Brooklyn Heights. Unfortunately, General Sullivan was captured by the British.

Washington watched the collapse and killing of Sullivan's command from the American lines in Brooklyn, and determining that the city was safe he crossed over from New York. He was disturbed that he could not send any aid to the retreating troops without weakening his lines and endangering other positions.

When Washington arrived at Brooklyn Heights he brought with him additional troops. One of the soldiers was a sixteen year old raw recruit named Joseph Plumb Martin. Martin had arrived in New York in June, and this was his first exposure to battle. He boarded the boat that would take him to Long Island amid cheers of spectators and shouts of good luck.

Once Martin reached the Brooklyn side, he saw for the first time the horrors of war, which was later written in his memoirs, "We now began to meet the wounded men, another sight I was unacquainted with, some with broken arms, some with broken legs, and some with broken heads."[12]

As the retreating Americans reached the safety of the Brooklyn Heights, Washington could do nothing but watch. The British forces were within two miles of the American line, and Washington faced a terrible disaster. The British forces were fast closing in, and he was hemmed into an area about three miles around with his back to the East River.

The British troops were excited about their victory and wanted to attack the rebel lines at Brooklyn Heights. They probably would have been victorious, but at a high cost. For the past several days each side had made some ill-fated choices, but they were pale in comparison to the decision that Howe was about to make.

Howe believed that he did not have the proper resources to storm the American lines. His artillery had not been brought up, and there were no scaling ladders or axes to cut abatis that surrounded the American redoubts. So, he decided to halt the advance on the Americans and withdraw his troops out of musket range and encamp for the night. Certainly in the back of his mind was the memory of the British soldiers being slaughtered as they advanced on the fortifications at Bunker Hill. So the Americans, unable to retreat any further with their backs pinned against the East River, were given a reprieve. Rather than advance and destroy the American army, Howe decided to save the manpower and lay siege. He hoped that Washington might surrender, since he knew he was trapped with no way out. After all, that would be the traditional gentleman-officer thing to do.

After the battle, General Washington was not sure if his two Generals, Stirling and Sullivan were alive or dead. He expressed his lack of knowledge in a letter to John Hancock on August 29,

> I am sorry to inform Congress that I have not yet heard either of Genl Sullivan or Lord Stirling, who they would observe were among the missing after the Engagement—Nor can I ascertain our Loss, I am hopefull part of our Men will yet get in, several did Yesterday morning—That of the Enemy is also uncertain—The Accounts are various—I incline to think they suffered a good deal—Some Deserters say five Hundred were killed and Wounded.[13]

Two days later Washington had gathered more information and wrote back to Hancock.

> In the Engagement on the 27th Generals Sullivan & Stirling were made prisoners; The former has been permitted on his parole to return for a little time—From My Lord Stirling I had a Letter by Genl Sullivan a Copy of which I have the Honor to transmit—That contains his Information of the Engagement with his Brigade—It is not so full and certain as I could wish; he was hurried most probably as his Letter was unfinished—Nor have I been yet able to obtain an exact account of Our Loss, we suppose It from 700 to a Thousand, killed & taken—Genl Sullivan says Lord Howe is extremely desirous of seeing some of the Members of Congress for which purpose he was allowed to come out & to communicate to them what was passed between him & his Lordship—I have consented to his going to Philadelphia, as I do not mean or conceive It right to withold or prevent him from giving such information as he possesses in this Instance.[14]

[Note: The letter indicates that General Sullivan claimed that General Howe would like to meet with Congress for a conference about ending the strife. Sullivan was paroled and sat up a meeting between Congressional leaders and General Howe at the home of Christopher Billop on Staten Island. The Staten Island Peace Conference took place on September 11, 1776, and reached no agreement. General Sullivan was later released in a prisoner exchange and rejoined the army before the end of the year.]

American losses during the battle were 300 killed, 800 wounded, and over a thousand captured or missing. General Howe reported his total losses at 367, and the Hessians reported only five killed and twenty-three wounded.

Retreat to Manhattan:

Inside their fortification at Brooklyn Heights, the Americans waited for the British attack that never came. Into the night they could hear the cries of their wounded men left on the battlefield, and they could do nothing. At times, stragglers would stagger into their lines, some carrying wounded comrades.

The night of the 27th brought great anxiety to General Washington. His men were dispirited, tired, and had little shelter against the heavy storm that was approaching. He expected that the British might attack the next morning, so he sent orders to move 1,200 more troops from Manhattan to his position. During the night and the next day there were numerous small skirmishes taking place between the two armies. During the afternoon of the 28th it began to rain, and Washington ordered his artillery to bombard the British positions. During the afternoon in the rain, Washington visited every part of his defenses and encouraged his gloomy troops with words of support. Due to the heavy rain, some of the troops in the trenches were up to their waist in water and mud.

Before the sun rose on the 29th, Washington wrote a depressing letter to John Hancock, "The Weather of late has been extremely wet. Yesterday it rained severely the whole afternoon which distressed our people much, not having a sufficiency of Tents to cover them, and what we have not got over yet."[15] By now the British trenches and about 15,000 troops were within 150 yards of around 9,000 Americans. Starting at ten in the morning and into the night the British cannons fired on the America camp.

During a meeting with Washington, General Thomas Mifflin, who had brought reinforcements over from New York, said, "You must either fight or retreat immediately. What is your strength?" When Washington replied that he had nine thousand men, Mifflin answered back, "It is not sufficient, we must therefore retreat."[16] Mifflin asked to be the one to propose the retreat at a meeting with the other officers. This would help shield Washington of any possible damage to his reputation.

Washington called for a Council of War to meet at Philip Livingston's house which stood on Brooklyn Heights. It was apparent to all that attended that the Americans were in a desperate situation, so all the officers voted to abandon Long Island and retreat. One officer, General John Morin Scott, who had large landholdings in Manhattan, was not invited to attend the meeting and later voiced his disapproval. The men knew that their defenses were not strong enough to repel a British attack and felt there was no other choice. Orders were immediately issued to Colonel John Glover to gather his regiment of marines, all boats of every kind, and be ready by midnight for the embarkation from Long Island.

Washington, who had not slept for two days and had been in the saddle all day, supervised the removal of his men and equipment to Manhattan. The men were told to gather all their ammunition and baggage and prepare for a night attack. By eleven that night the wind had died away and the surface of the water was smooth, so both sail and rowboats were able to cross the river without problems.

According to Private Joseph Plumb Martin, wagon wheels were muffled and the troops were strictly told not to speak, or even cough. All orders were given from officer to officer and then to the men in a whisper. They were marched to the boats at the ferry on the assurance that fresh troops were to relieve them from New York. General Mifflin commanded the rear guard, and his men kept the campfires going to fool the British. One errant sound would have quickly alerted the British, yet the undisciplined Americans were able to move their army in silence. This maneuver would have been difficult even for a well trained professional army.

Due to miscommunication, a near disaster was adverted. Mifflin had been ordered by Washington to be the rear guard and protect the retreat, if they were discovered by the British. During the evacuation, Major Alexander Scammell mistakenly ordered Mifflin and his men to join the retreat. As Mifflin's men neared the debarkation area, Washington saw him and asked why he had left his post. Mifflin informed him he was ordered to do so, which Washington quickly pointed out was wrong. Mifflin and his men were sent back to the camp to protect the retreat.

As daybreak approached, the retreat was not complete, but providence intervened and a thick fog rolled in. It was so dense that some men reported they could not even see six feet in front of themselves. By seven in the morning the fog was starting to lift, and all 9,000 men were safely across the East River into Manhattan. General Washington was on the last boat to cross.

During the retreat a woman, whose husband had been taken away because he was suspected of being disloyal to the American cause, sought her revenge. When she saw that the Americans were sneaking across the river she sent her slave woman to alert the British.

Fortunately for the Americans, the slave woman fell into the hands of the Hessians, who could not understand a word she said. They thought the woman might be a spy, so they waited until morning to turn her over to a British officer. The officer sent a British patrol out and discovered that the Americans were gone. As they searched the area they found no Americans but only some supplies and several heavy cannons that had become stuck in the mud. They did manage to see the last boat crossing the river as the fog began to lift. One officer reported, "In the morning, to our great astonishment, found they had evacuated al their works on Brooklyn, without a shot being fired at them."[17] Most of the troops were relieved that the Americans were gone, because they were not looking forward to attacking fortified positions.

The battle of Harlem Heights:

When Washington reached Manhattan, like most of the men, he was tired and had been deprived of a good night's sleep for many days. In fact he was so tired that he did not have the energy to write to Congress about the retreat until August 31, "Inclination as well as duty would have Induced me to give Congress the earliest Information of my removal and that of the Troops from Long Island & Its dependencies to this City the night before last."[18]

The American army began to crumble after the retreat. Many of the new recruits were the first to desert. Washington wrote to John Hancock, "Our situation is truly distressing…too great a proportion of our Troops and filled their minds with apprehension and despair. The Militia instead of calling forth their utmost efforts to a brave & manly opposition in order to repair our Losses, are dismayed, Intractable, and Impatient to return. Great numbers of them have gone off; in some Instances, almost by whole Regiments."[19]

To add to his troubles, Washington found that some of his own troops began to doubt him and to complain that Washington "sold them out," and there were even soldiers who suggested he be replaced. One of his officers, Tench Tilghman, felt that Washington's burden "might be too much for one man." He wrote to Caesar Rodney in Congress, "I fear General Washington has too heavy a task, assisted mostly by beardless boys."[20]

Not everyone shared in the gloom over the loss of Long Island. In Congress Dr. Benjamin Rush said in one of the sessions, "We have lost a battle and a small Island, but we have not lost a State." John Adams added, "The panic may seize whom it will, it shall not seize me."[21]

On September 2 Washington wrote to John Hancock and posed the question, "If we should be obliged to abandon this town, ought it to stand as winter quarters for the enemy?"[22] Washington was asking Congress that if the city was lost, should it be burned. Nathanael Greene felt that most of New York City belonged to the Loyalists, so he encouraged Washington to flee the city and put a torch to it. On September 7 Congress responded back and said they wanted no damage done to the city.

During the day on September 20, five days after the British assumed control of the city, fire broke out and burned until the next day. Nearly twenty-five percent of the buildings were destroyed. Each side accused the other of setting the fire. There were no warning bells, because they had been removed and recast as cannons. Later, some historians suggested it began by accident when the burning of debris from wooden roof shingles spread.

Burning of New York City, Library of Congress

On September 14 Congress told Washington that the army should leave New York City as soon as Washington thought it appropriate. That night Joseph Plumb Martin was on guard duty at the water's edge and keeping a close watch on the British ships anchored in the river. Every half hour the guards would pass the word that "all is well." One time Martin heard someone onboard a British ship respond back, "We will alter your tune before tomorrow night."[23]

The next day, as the British sailor the night before had warned, Howe landed at Kip's Bay on the east side of Manhattan Island with 4,000 British and Hessian troops. This took place between the Americans that were in New York City in the south and the rest of the army in the north at Harlem Heights. Once the American soldiers in the city began to flee, Howe landed 9,000 more men. As before, he hesitated, which would give the American troops time to join the main force in Harlem Heights. Howe pondered his next move, while many of his troops rested and brewed pots of tea.

Washington heard the cannon fire from his post at Harlem Heights, and he jumped on his horse and rode toward the sounds. He soon encountered the retreating Americans and demanded that they stop and fight, which they refused to do and continued to run. In a rare display of uncontrolled emotion, Washington cursed at the men, drew his sword, and threatened to run men through if they did not stop and fight. As the men continued to flee, he was heard to yell, "Are these the men with which I am to defend America?"[24]

Some accounts reported that he waved his pistol threatening to shoot the men, while other stories said he cane-whipped privates and officers alike. Whatever he did, gossip later among the troops turned the event into legend. During the encounter, Washington was just eighty yards from the enemy forces. Fearing that he would be captured or killed by the British, his officers forced the general to join the retreat and seek safety in the fortification at Harlem Heights.

Once the Americans in the south had withdrawn to Harlem Heights, New York City was abandoned. Some of the British units turned south and began to occupy the city. Many civilians in the city came out to greet them as conquering heroes. Some residents paraded around with British soldiers on their shoulders, as the Continental flag was removed, trampled upon, and replaced with the Union Jack.

The British army advanced toward the American lines, and on the 16th the Battle of Harlem Heights began. It was hardly a little more than a skirmish between several hundred light infantry and Colonel Thomas Knolton's militia, who were just forward of the southernmost American lines. The Americans were sent out to observe the British lines, when they ran into an enemy picket. The British unit began to pursue the Americans and blundered into an unfavorable position.

Seventeen year old Private David How had been in the army since Lexington and Concord. After the Battle of Bunker Hill he came to New York and kept a diary of his time in the army. He mentioned the fight with the British, "Some part of our Army Had a Smart fight with the Enimy in Harlem Woods—Our Army Drove them and killed a Grate many on Both Sides."[25] Hopefully, David fought better than he spelled.

After two hours, the British were running short of ammunition and began to pull back toward their lines. Washington stopped the Americans from following them to avoid encountering the large British force. This was Washington's first victory on the battlefield in the American Revolution. Confidence and morale improved with the American troops as a result of the small victory. The British suffered up to ninety killed and over two hundred wounded, while American losses were reported at about thirty killed and one hundred wounded. Both sides claimed victory.

Once again Howe did not press the attack and destroy the American Army. After a month passed, Washington heard that the British were going to try to trap him in Manhattan, so he moved his army to White Plains about thirty miles northeast of New York City. Then, in mid-November the British captured Fort Washington near the north end of Manhattan Island. Besides the loss of the fort, the British seized over 3,000 American troops. Four days later Fort Lee, across the Hudson River from Fort Washington, was captured. Washington was forced to flee to New Jersey.

By the end of December the army under George Washington slowly shrank away with a little over 2,000 men fit for combat. Expired enlistments, desertions, disease, and cold weather plagued his troops. Ninety percent of the Continental Army soldiers who had served at Long Island were gone. If his army was to survive, Washington would need a miracle. It would come on the day after Christmas at a town in Delaware called Trenton.

Battle of Harlem Heights, New York Public Library

Impact of Howe's decision not to continue the attack:

Washington received much praise for his night retreat off Long Island, which was deserved. The retreat, however, was due more to luck than leadership. Had it not been for strong winds that kept the British navy away and the morning fog that covered his retreat, events might have played out differently. Washington was indecisive and inept during this campaign and managed to get his army trapped. He made several bad decisions during this time, but as bad as they were, it did not impact his ability to continue the fight.

At this time Washington was not a professional soldier, but instead an amateur that possessed minimal war experience. He had never led an army of more than 2,000 men and never against an army of European regulars with naval superiority. Even with some success at Boston he remained unsure of his abilities, and at times he was too easily influenced by Congress or his other officers.

However, one of the strengths of Washington was his ability to learn from his mistakes and to better adapt to adversity. He knew what it would take to build a real army, and he was not willing to give up even in the darkest hours. Washington slowly gained the respect and confidence of Congress and, more importantly, of the men under him. There would be other mistakes made, but in a short five years he would be facing the British Army with their backs to a river at a small port called Yorktown.

On the other hand, General William Howe, made two decisions that may well have prevented him from defeating the American army and ending the rebellion. During the campaigns on Long Island and later at Harlem Heights, he had everything going his way. His troop landings, flanking moves, and battle plans all went with clock-work precision. The opening campaign went so well that Washington was practically defeated before the first shot was fired.

Howe's first chance to end the Revolution came when he chose not to continue the attack when he had the Americans on Long Island pinned against the East River. Naval ships could have been deployed earlier to patrol the East River and bombard the American lines. Instead, he declined to peruse the Americans and eventually allowed them to escape.

When the Americans fled to Brooklyn Heights, the grenadiers, in the flanking column led by Howe, showed eagerness to storm the American position and grab the victory. Howe wrote after the battle, "Had they been permitted to go on, it is my opinion they would have carried the redoubt."[26]

British Captain John Montresor, a critic of General Howe's leadership, believed that the general should have taken the attack to the Americans. He later wrote about Howe, "He never pursues his victories."[27] General Clinton also thought Howe made a mistake, but being a good officer would never say so when questioned.

Howe claimed his decision was based on not wanting to attack a fortified position in a frontal attack that might result in a great loss of lives. The vivid memory of his frontal attack earlier at Bunker Hill and the great loss of life, influenced the decision. However, this time Americans were defeated, tired, and their fortifications were not particularly strong. Also, he falsely believed that the American were now trapped and would be happy to surrender.

If Howe had continued advancing against the disorganized Americans, there still would have many of his soldiers killed and wounded. British loss of life could have been greatly reduced, however, if he had used the Hessians to attack the center. He had at least 10,000 of these troops available, and they had suffered very minor losses in earlier fighting. These mercenaries were being well paid [the German government was, not the common soldier] for their work, and they harbored no respect for the fighting ability of the Americans. Hugh Hessian losses would not upset Parliament as much as high British casualties.

Howe, with superior numbers, artillery support, and a quick thrust with a bayonet charge, might have quickly brought the Americans to their knees. Washington and his top men would have been killed or captured, and any of the leaders that survived would have been taken back to England, tried, and then hung. The American Northern Army, still feeling the effects from their disastrous defeat in Canada, were not prepared to continue the fight.

Congress, with the defeat of the American army, would have lost the support of the southern colonies and many in the north. To protect their lives and property, Congress would have been willing to negotiate an unfavorable peace. The rebellion would, at least for the time being, have been postponed. Even if British losses were high, parliament and the British people would have rejoiced at ending the rebellion and re-establishing control over the colonies.

Howe missed his opportunity at Long Island, but he had another chance to achieve the same outcome at Harlem Heights. Once again he became fearful, cautious, and he hesitated, which allowed the Americans to escape.

In October of 1777, Howe sent a letter of resignation to Parliament. Some historians believe he did this, so that he could return home and defend his conduct during the Revolution. His resignation was accepted in April, and he returned to England in May and promptly demanded an inquiry by Parliament into their actions blaming him for the lack of a victory. The inquiry could not confirm any of the charges against him, however attacks against him continued. He was accused by some as undermining the war effort in the colonies to help support the anti-war faction in Parliament.

George Washington emerged from the New York campaign praised, for the most part, on his heroic saving of the Continental Army when he retreated from New York. The New York Campaign could have resulted in the American Army being wiped out, if the British, who had superior numbers, had been more aggressive. From an American viewpoint, the important thing about this campaign was that it proved to Washington, if he was going to win the war, he needed a professional, trained, disciplined, and paid army. He explained his thoughts to John Hancock in a letter on September 25, 1776,

> To place any dependance upon Militia, is, assuredly, resting upon a broken staff. Men just dragged from the tender Scenes of domestick life—unaccustomed to the din of Arms—totally unacquainted with every kind of Military skill, which being followed by a want of Confidence in themselves when opposed to Troops regularly traind—disciplined, and appointed—superior in knowledge, & superior in Arms, makes them timid, and ready to fly from their own Shadows. Besides, the sudden change in their manner of living (particularly in the lodging) brings on sickness in many; impatience in all; & such an unconquerable desire of returning to their respective homes that it not only produces shameful, & scandalous Desertions among themselves, but infuses the like spirit in others—Again, Men accustomed to unbounded freedom, and no controul, cannot brooke the Restraint which is indispensably necessary to the good Order and Government of an Army; without which Licentiousness, & every kind of disorder triumphantly reign. To bring men to a proper degree of Subordination is not the work of a day—a Month— or even a year—and unhappily for us, and the cause we are Ingaged in, the little discipline I have been labouring to establish in the Army under my immediate Command, is in a manner done away by having such a mixture of Troops as have been called together within these few Months.[28]

Would Washington be able to build his professional army, and would the men join and agree to give up their cherished, unbound freedom, and follow strict rules and discipline while serving in it? Could he convince Congress to support a professional "standing army" that many opposed?

5

Washington Makes a Bold Decision and Attacks Trenton

"We have run down the old fox, and we will bag him in the morning."

----British General Cornwallis at Trenton

Background:

In the early part of December 1776, the American Army was expelled from New York and had retreated through New Jersey into Pennsylvania. Ninety percent of the troops that served at Long Island were now gone, while leaving behind troops with little or no battle experience. In addition, troop morale was low, and there was a shortage of new recruits and supplies. To make matters worse, enlistment of many of Washington's men would expire at the end of December.

Charles Willson Peale, a painter in the Pennsylvania militia, was walking among Washington's troops and observed the horrible condition of the men. While observing one man, he gave the following description in his journal, "He was in an old dirty blanket jacket, his beard long, and his face so full of sores that he could not clean it."[1] On first glance, Peale did not recognize that the man he described was his own brother James, a soldier in a Maryland regiment, who fought at the Battle of Brooklyn.

In mid-December Washington sent a depressing letter to his cousin Lund Washington, "The unhappy policy of short enlistments, and a dependence upon militia will, I fear, prove to be the downfall of our cause. Our only dependence now, is upon the speedy enlistment of a new army; if this fails us, I think the game will be pretty well up."[2]

At this time, the small town of Trenton, New Jersey was a British stronghold, and it was under control of four regiments of Hessian soldiers, numbering about 1,400 troops, under the command of the hard-drinking Colonel Johann Rall. Most of the citizens of the town had fled with whatever they could carry, especially since many of the women in town had been raped by the Hessians. Washington had an army of around 2,400 men with infantry commanded by Generals Nathanael Greene and John Sullivan. They were supported with artillery commanded by General Henry Knox.

Washington realized he needed a victory soon to boost the morale of his men and provide an incentive for others to enlist. He devised a plan that would involve moving his men in secret across the icy Delaware River, in the middle of the night, and in the dead of winter. Washington knew the odds of a victory were not great, but a victory just might keep the Revolution going.

Plan of attack:

Washington's plan was to have coordinated attacks from three directions. General John Cadwalader would provide a diversion by attacking the British garrison at Bordertown, about nine miles to the south of Trenton, to block any reinforcements. General James Ewing would take 700 militia, cross the river at Trenton Ferry, and capture the bridge at Assunpink Creek, nine miles north of Trenton, to prevent the enemy's escape.

The main assault group of 2,400 men would be divided into two groups under Generals Greene and Sullivan. Sullivan would attack the town from the south, and Greene from the north would catch the Hessians in a pincer movement. The attack was set for six o'clock, an hour before the sun rose. If the plan worked, there would be follow up attacks on Princeton and New Brunswick.

The plan was not complicated and would not be difficult in good weather conditions. This attack, however, would be carried out at night, in freezing weather, across a river filled with ice, and with a tired, underequipped, and untested army. Much was riding on this difficult decision Washington made.

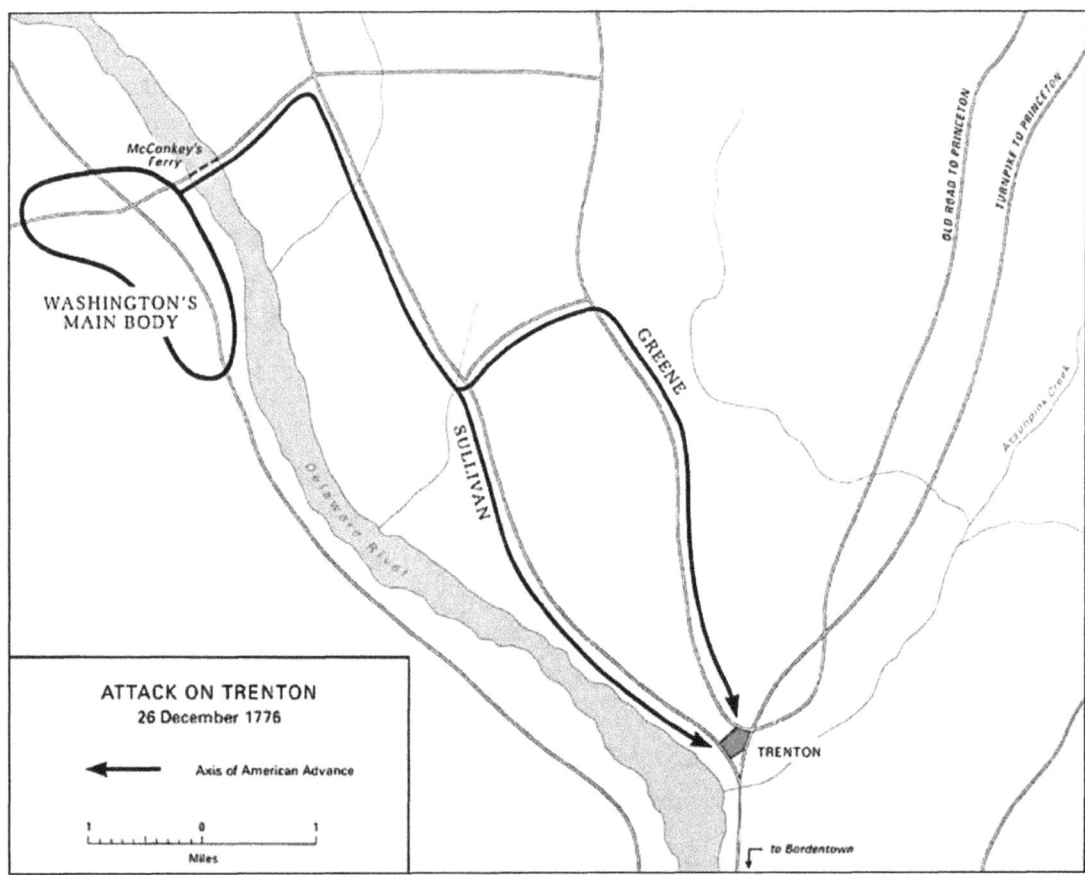

Attack plan on Trenton, Center of Military History

Washington needed intelligence on the enemy forces at Trenton, so he placed a spy in town, John Honeyman, to pose as a Loyalist. Honeywell arranged to be captured by the Americans, give the information to Washington, and then be allowed to "escape". When back in Trenton, he convinced the Hessian commander that the American Army was not capable of launching an attack on Trenton. This did not surprise the commander, Colonel Johann Rall, since he scorned all Americans and thought of their army as "nothing than a lot of farmers."[3]

On December 13 British General Howe was across the Delaware River from Washington, and once again he made a decision that would help the Americans. Sensing that the weather was becoming too cold for fighting and the Americans posed no immediate threat, he suspended military operations until spring. The next day he and General Cornwallis departed for New York, and he sent his army to winter quarters in northern New Jersey and New York. In order to protect the territory he had gained, he set up a series of outposts in New Jersey. Command of New Jersey was given to an average and cocky General James Grant.

Howe was not concerned about leaving, because he sensed that the war was about over. In addition, it was not customary for high ranking British officers to be in the field during winter months. He was also looking forward to spending more time with his mistress, Elizabeth Loring, in New York City.

Washington, not aware of Howe's leaving, was convinced that the British General would march on Philadelphia as soon as the Delaware River froze. This would provide him easy access across. On the 15th Washington received information from General John Cadwalader that Howe had left for New York, "General Howe is certainly gone to New York, unless the whole is a scheme to amuse and surprise."[4] This news was discounted by Washington, since he believed it might be a British trick.

Washington gave a slight hint of a possible attack when he wrote to Jonathan Trumbull, Sr. the day before, "A lucky blow in this quarter would be fatal to them, and would most certainly raise the spirits of the people which are quite sunk in our misfortunes."[5]

By December 20 Washington's reinforcements had arrived, although only half the number he was expecting. His army now numbered about 7,500, but only about 6,000 were fit for duty. People around Philadelphia were trying to raise supplies for the army, while at the same time more Americans were signing oaths of loyalty to the Crown. Two members of Congress had gone over to the British, including Richard Stockton, a signer of the Declaration of Independence, who was then thrown into prison by the British. In New Jersey over 5,000 citizens, believing the war was lost, went over to the British. Washington was learning that if the people couldn't be protected, then you would lose their support.

Washington had not lost hope and was busy going over the plan of attack with his staff. He insisted that the attack remain the strictest secret, because if discovered by the British, he could lose his army and perhaps the entire war.

Washington still believed that the British army was just across the river, "For well convinced I am, that if the enemy go into quarters [winter quarters] at all, it will be for a short season; but I rather think, the design of genl. Howe, is to possess himself of Philadelphia this winter."[6]

On December 21, Washington received a letter from Robert Morris that contained a sentence that must have drained the blood from the General's face, "I have been told today that you are preparing to cross into the Jerseys."[7] Washington must have feared that if a Congressman in Philadelphia knew of the attack, then maybe the British also knew.

Washington was willing to take a chance that the attack was still a secret, so he did not call it off. He quickly sent a letter to one of his trusted aids, Colonel Joseph Reed. He was from Trenton and knew the area well, and Washington wanted to remind him to keep it a secret, "Christmas day at night, one hour before day is the time fixed upon for our attempt on Trenton. For heaven's sake keep this to yourself, as the discovery of it may prove fatal to us, our number."[8]

The Hessians before the attack:

Meanwhile in Trenton, Hessian commander Colonel Rall had been given plans by two of his engineers for the construction of fortifications, since the town contained none. There was concern that the enemy just across the river might attack Trenton, but Colonel Rall, like most of the Hessians, had no fear or respect of the American Army. His reply to his engineers was, "Let them come...We will go at them with the bayonet."[9]

Colonel Rall from Lossing's, *The Pictorial Field-Book of the Revolution, 1852*

Rall had been assured by General Grant, who was left in charge when Howe departed for New York, that there were less than 300 rebels in the area, and that Washington's army across the river was, "almost naked, dying of cold, without blankets, and very ill-supplied with provisions."[10].

The Hessian colonel received several warnings about an attack on Trenton. Because of Hessian brutality, many of the local people that had supported the British came over to the American side. They formed small marauding bands that attacked Hessian and British patrols that ventured outside of Trenton. It had gotten so out of control that when Colonel Rall sent a messenger to General Grant, it was accompanied with a guard of 100 men.

Rall received word from some local Loyalists that the Americans were planning a surprise attack, so the Hessians were ordered on alert and during the day of December 25. Before

Washington began leading his army across the Delaware, a small group of local Patriots, unaware that Washington was planning a later attack, raided one of the Hessian's guard post.

After one Hessian was killed, the Patriots fled back into the woods. Colonel Rall sent his men on patrols out into the woods to look for the rebels. They searched for hours and found no trace of any American soldiers. Colonel Rall called his men back in late that Christmas night, because he thought that there was no danger of attack. He ordered his men to get some rest, and security around the camp was relaxed

Later in the evening, Rall received yet another warning of an attack. To celebrate Christmas, Rall, who liked to drink and gamble, visited the house of Abraham Hunt for an evening of fun. During the evening, a Loyalist farmer knocked on Hunt's door asking to see the Colonel. The waiter who answered would not disturb the Colonel at his party, so the Loyalist gave him a note to give to the Colonel. The note contained information about the movements of the American Army and the attack. The waiter took the note to Rall, who was busy drinking at the card table. Rall folded the note and placed it in his waistcoat pocket. The contents of the note would not be revealed until the end of the successful American attack.

The crossing:

On Christmas day the weather turned menacing. A storm was beginning to gather, the Delaware River had risen, and broken sheets of ice were forming. The plan called for all the troops to be across the river no later than midnight Christmas. Around eleven that night the storm struck with a ferocity.

Crossing the Delaware, Library of Congress

As the men marched to the river, twenty year old Captain James Wilkinson watched and later wrote about the footprints leading down to the river, "tinged here and there with blood from the feet of the men who wore broken shoes."[11]

J. Greenwood, Surgeon Dentist to George Washington, Print of engraving published in the *American Journal of Dental Science*, 1839.

While the boats crossed during the storm, the jagged ice floated swiftly past, at times striking the boats so severely that the men could only handle them with great difficulty. John Greenwood was a sixteen year old fifer that enlisted in May 1775. After the war he moved to New York and years later served as Washington's dentist. During the crossing of the river he traded his fife for a musket, and in his journal he described the conditions,

> I was with the first that crossed, we had to wait for the rest and so began to pull down the fences and make fires to warm ourselves, for the storm was increasing rapidly. After a while it rained, hailed, snowed, and froze, and at the same time blew a perfect hurricane; so much so that I perfectly recollect, after putting the rails on to burn, the wind and the fire would cut them in two in a moment, and when I turned my face toward the fire my back would be freezing. During the whole night it alternately hailed, rained, snowed, and blew tremendously.[12]

When General Washington crossed the river he sat on a box once used as a beehive, while waiting for his horse to be brought across. He was silent, and probably thinking if the dangerous mission would be successful under such conditions. Earlier, he had written a note on a piece of paper that one of the officers had seen. The note contained the simple words, "victory or death," which became the password for the night.

The troops had all passed over the river by two o'clock, and by three the cannons had made it across just as it began to rain. Since they were behind schedule, the attack would now take place after sunrise, which would cause them to lose the element of surprise. Washington knew that this would be the last chance to call off the attack and return back across the river. It was a decision that had to be made immediately and involved tremendous risk whatever was decided.

Several days later Washington wrote a letter to John Hancock about the decision to push on, "This made me despair of surprising the town, as I well knew we could not reach it before the day was fairly broke, but as I was certain there was no making a retreat without being discovered, and harassed on repassing the river, I determined to push on at all events."[13]

While the men, who were not sure where they were going, were marching toward Trenton, Washington was not aware that his plan of attack was falling apart. Because of the weather and ice, General Ewing called his attack off without even trying to cross. General Cadwalader managed to get some of his troops across, but he was unable to get the cannons across so he also gave up. Only one of the three planed attacks was advancing, and it was behind schedule.

Washington had appointed twelve New Jersey men to guide him to Trenton. During the march the storm grew worse, and some men carried lanterns and torches due to the darkness. The roads were slick with ice and snow, and at times the men had difficulty marching up icy slopes. When they finally reached a crossroads called Birmingham, the army divided. They were now just four miles from Trenton.

Washington received a message from General Sullivan to let him know that many of the men discovered that their guns were too wet to fire. Washington sent word to the general to tell his men to use their bayonets. About an hour after the sun rose, the two columns arrived outside of Trenton around eight in the morning.

The attack:

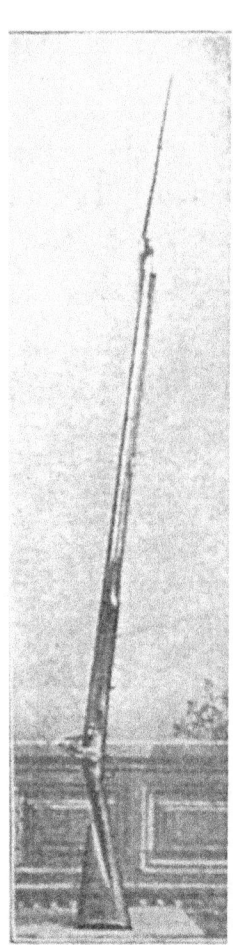

As the Americans were approaching Trenton, they encountered a local man chopping wood. They asked him where the Hessian alarm house was, and, he was only too happy to obliged and give them the location and tell them where to find sentry.

Gun of Amos Scudder at the Battle of Trenton. Amos and his brother, born and raised in the area, guided the advance units to Trenton. From William S. Stryker, *The Battles of Trenton and Princeton.* p. 140.

Just after eight o'clock the two American armies attacked the post, which caused the Hessians to move back toward the town. The Americans advanced at a slow trot through driving snow and converged on the town. Washington moved with them and took a position on high ground, so he could watch the battle unfold.

Later, in a letter to John Hancock, Washington described the open moments of the attack,

> I ordered each of them, immediately upon forcing the out Guards, to push directly into the Town, that they might charge the Enemy before they had time to form. The upper division arrived at the Enemys advanced post, exactly at eight OClock, and in three Minutes after, I found from the fire on the lower Road that, that Division had also got up. The Out Guards made but small Opposition, tho', for their Numbers, they behaved very well, keeping up a constant retreating fire from behind Houses.[14]

John Greenwood, who had been in the army for twenty months, described the attack on the Hessians,

> As we advanced, it being dark and stormy so that we could not see very far ahead, we got within 200 yards of about 300 or 400 Hessians who were paraded, two deep, in a straight line with Colonel Roll, their commander, on horseback, to the right of them. They made a full fire at us, but I did not see that they killed

any one. Our brave Major Sherburne ordered us to fall back about 300 yards and pull off our packs, which we accordingly did and piled them by the roadside. "Now, my boys," says he, "pass the word through the ranks that he who is afraid to follow me, let him stay behind and take care of the packs!" Not a man offered to leave the ranks, and as we never went back that way, we all lost our packs:

> When we were all ready we advanced, and, although there was not more than one bayonet to five men, orders were given to "Charge bayonets and rush on !" and rush on we did. Within pistol-shot they again fired point-blank at us; we dodged and they did not hit a man, while before they had time to reload we were within three feet of them, when they broke in an instant and ran like so many frightened devils into the town, which was at a short distance.[15]

The Americans ran into town, and the Hessians rushed out of their barracks onto the streets. They were met with deadly fire from the Americans, so they broke ranks and retreated to the side streets. They were met there by the troops under Sullivan, and the fighting became house-to-house. The Hessians manned a field gun on one street, and a group of Virginians led by a distant cousin of General Washington, William Washington, seized the gun and turned it on the enemy. During this attack, eighteen year old Lieutenant James Monroe was wounded and was later cited for bravery under fire and given a field promotion to Captain. In 1817 he would become the fifth President of the United States.

Hessian Colonel Rall was awakened from his bed, quickly mounted his horse, and took command. While under fire, he ordered a retreat into an orchard at the southern edge of town where he was mortally wounded. He was taken to the Potts House for treatment, and soon his men in the orchard were surrounded and forced to surrender.

When Rall was disrobed for treatment, the note warning about the attack in his jacket was found. According to some sources the colonel read the message for the first time and remarked, "If I had read this at Mr. Hunt's, I would not be here."[16] He died later that night.

Several of the Americans were expert riflemen and concealed themselves in houses, and through the windows they were able to shoot many of the enemy. Some of the Hessians were unable to fire because their powder was wet, but many of the Americans had kept the firing-pans of their guns dry by protecting them under part of their clothing or under blankets.

The battle lasted less than an hour with twenty-one Hessians killed and about 900 captured. Washington was probably pleased and relieved that the only American deaths were two men that died from the freezing weather during the night on the road. After the battle, a few Americans broke into the Hessian storage of rum and got drunk, which Washington discretely ignored.

Washington was not totally happy with the victory, because he was not able to press the attack on to Princeton. Because Calwalader and Ewing had not joined in the attack, they allowed hundreds of Hessians to escape and sound the alarm. Washington could not continue to Princeton, so he decided that it was best for the men to cross back into Pennsylvania, rest, and regroup. The Hessian prisoners were marched off and later taken to Philadelphia, where they were paraded through the city.

The second crossing of the Delaware proved to be just as difficult as the first. It was dark before all the soldiers had crossed into Pennsylvania, and many units didn't return to their camps until morning. The extremely cold temperatures caused three men to freeze to death in their boats.

Results of the battle:

Colonel Rall took most of the blame for the Hessian defeat. Many criticized him for not taking precautions for an attack and because he ignored intelligence warnings about it. He and his men were accused of being drunk after celebrating Christmas. Rall may have well been drunk after a late night of playing cards and drinking. However, Americans at the battle claim the Hessian solders were not drunk. If they had been drinking to excess, it probably would have occurred earlier on Christmas Eve.

As did other soldiers, John Greenwood claimed that the enemy was not drunk. He wrote in his journal,

> It was likewise asserted at the same time that the enemy were all drunk. I am certain not a drop of liquor was drunk during the whole night, nor, as I could see, even a piece of bread eaten, and I am willing to go upon oath that I did not see even a solitary drunken soldier belonging to the enemy,—and you will find, as I shall show, that I had an opportunity to be as good a judge as any person there.[17]

The British response upon hearing of the defeat was one of shock. General Grant wrote from Brunswick, "I did not think that all the rebels in America would have taken that brigade prisoners."[18] Later in England, Lord George Germain, the Colonial Secretary of State of King George III, wrote, "All our hopes were blasted by that unhappy affair at Trenton."[19]

It was easy for the English to place all the blame for the defeat on Colonel Rall, because he had died and was not able to defend himself. Some of his troops, however, did not blame him. General Cornwallis had his leave cancelled and was ordered to return to New Jersey with an army of 8,000.

Washington wanted to follow up his success the next few days at Princeton to solidify the Patriot gains. The problem he now faced was that the enlistments of many of his regulars in his army would be up at the end of the month. John Greenwood was one of the men whose enlistment was about to expire. He wrote about his thoughts on December 27,

> The next day (December 27, 1776), being two days after our time was out, we received three months' pay,—and glad was I. We were offered twenty-six dollars to stay six weeks longer, but as I did not enlist for the purpose of remaining in the army, but only through necessity, as I could not get to my parents in Boston, I was determined to quit as soon as my time was out.[20]

On December 29 Washington once again took his troops, before enlistments expired, back across the Delaware to Trenton, and he quickly learned that General Cornwallis was marching his army toward Trenton. The next day he gave a passionate appeal to his veteran troops to stay with him for another six months. He promised to pay them a ten dollar bounty if they stayed, which was a generous offer since they were only paid a little over six dollars a month. He told them he was going to attack the British with or without them. Many of the men stepped forward and signed on for another six months.

Washington was making promises that he was not sure he could keep, since he had no money and Congress had not told him any would be forthcoming. Many members of Congress had fled Philadelphia, and Robert Morris was one of the few that stayed. He had been instrumental in raising money and supplies for the army, so on December 31 Washington sent him a letter requesting funds,

> Tomorrow the Continental Troops are all at Liberty [enlistment is up]—I wish to push our Success to keep up the Pannick & in order to get their Assistance have promised them a Bounty of 10 Dollars if they will continue for one Month—But here again a new Difficulty presents itself we have not Money to pay the Bounty, & we have exhausted our Credit by such frequent Promises that it has not the Weight we could wish. If it be possible, Sir, to give us Assistance do it—borrow Money where it can be done we are doing it upon our private Credit—every Man of Interest & every Lover of his Country must strain his Credit upon such an Occasi[o]n.[21]

Morris immediately approached a Quaker friend of his and requested a loan of $50,000. The friend asked what security would be provided, and Morris told him it would be his word and honor. Morris wrote back to Washington on January 1,

> I am up very early this morning to dispatch a supply of fifty thousand Dollars to your Excellency You will receive that Sum with this letter but it will not be got away so early as I cou'd wish for none concerned in this movement except myself are up, I shall rouse them immediately. It gives me great pleasure that you have engaged the Troops to continue, and if further occasional supplys of Money are necessary you may depend on my exertions either in a publick or private capacity.[22]

An engraving by Ole Erekson, c. 1876, of Robert Morris

[Robert Morris was a self-made millionaire who financed the American Revolution, and was a signatory to the Declaration of Independence, the Articles of Confederation, and the United States Constitution.]

On January 1 Cornwallis reached Princeton and left part of his men there and took the remaining 5,500 to Trenton just ten miles away. When he arrived at Trenton that evening, his officers pushed for an attack. Not wanting to attack at night with tired troops, Cornwallis declined and said, "The men had been under arms the whole day; they were languid and required rest; I have the enemy safe enough, and could dispose of them the next morning. I propose that the troops should make fires, refresh themselves, and take repose."[23] Washington was unable to retreat back across the river, because all of his boats were several miles upstream.

His officers tried again to convince him to attack and not miss this opportunity, but Cornwallis refused and added, "We have run down the old fox, and we will bag him in the morning."[24] Once again the American army was trapped, and the British hesitated and allowed them to escape.

During the night the bulk of Washington's army left, with General Knox and 500 men still in camp to keep the fires burning and two cannons firing to let the British know they were waiting for them. Some of the men were loudly engaged in digging entrenchments, so that the British could hear them talking and digging with spades and picks. These 500 men left behind would depart just before the sun rose and join the rest of the army that left during the night.

There would be no "bagging the old fox", because the British found out the next morning that Washington was gone. They thought he moved to the south, but Washington had taken his 5,500 men and cannons on a daring wide sweep around Cornwallis in order to attack the rear guard that was left by him at Princeton.

At sunrise on January 3, the Americans attacked the British at Princeton and soon defeated them. James Read, an officer under Washington, wrote to his wife about the General leading his men, "His greatness is far beyond my description. I shall never forget what I felt at Princeton on his account, when I saw him brave the dangers of the field, and his important life hanging as it were by a single hair with a thousand deaths flying around him. Believe me I thought not of myself."[25]

Once again the British had suffered a defeat at the hands of Washington. Around thirty Americans had been killed along with forty wounded. British losses were nearly a hundred killed, up to seventy wounded, and over two hundred captured.

Washington took his men back across the Delaware River and later to Morristown for winter quarters. Cornwallis and his army were ordered back toward New York, and left all but New Brunswick free of British control. What happen at Trenton and Princeton saved the American Revolution.

Victory at Princeton, National Archives

6

British Decisions and Lack of Communication Results in a Defeat at Saratoga

"I heard often amidst his groans, such words as these, '0 bad ambition! Poor General Burgoyne!"

---- Baroness Reidesel, wife of a Hessian general after the battle

Background:

The American Revolution was fast approaching the two year mark when England decided to try a new plan. The objective was to split the colonies and isolate New England. They believed that the middle and southern colonies were more sympathetic to the British than the troublemakers in New England.

General John Burgoyne's plan, approved by the British War Department, was to join three British armies near Albany, New York and split the colonies. One army under Colonel Barry St. Leger would come eastward from Lake Ontario, and a second army led by General William Howe would march northward from New York City. At the same time, a third larger army under General John Burgoyne would come south from Canada.

1860 Engraving by S. Hellyer of General John Burgoyne. {Public Domain}

In June General Burgoyne left Canada with 8,000 troops, and at that time he issued the Proclamation of Bouquet River. In it he stated that under his leadership he would unleash a horde of Indians who would spread terror across the land and force the colonists into submission.[1] However, Burgoyne's proclamation backfired on him. Rather than terrorize the colonists into submission, it encouraged thousands to enlist in the militia to protect their homes. They would later be among the troops that would defeat Burgoyne at Saratoga.

Immediately, the plan to join the three armies began to fall apart. Colonel St. Leger's army failed to capture Fort Stanwix during a siege, so they turned back. Howe decided to abandon the New York campaign and take his troops by sea to capture Philadelphia and lure Washington into a battle. As a result, Burgoyne marched his army south to face the Americans alone. By the end of August he knew that he would receive no help from the other two armies.

While Burgoyne moved south, he further weakened his army after a victory at Fort Ticonderoga, where he left hundreds of men behind to hold the fort. Then, on August 16 he lost nearly 1,000 men at the Battle of Bennington. The American victory at Bennington encouraged more patriots to enlist, and it proved to be a big morale boost for the people in the region. Burgoyne's army was now thinly stretched and had a long supply line, but the general decided to follow orders and advance toward Albany. At this time, he was unaware that he was the only British army moving toward the area.

Besides losing a large portion of his army, he suffered another loss just as important. After the defeat, most of the Indians that had been traveling with him decided to return to their homes in Canada. The Indians were sick of losses, restrictions, and the refusal of the British Army to share in their limited supplies.

These Indians were vital to Burgoyne because they scouted for the British and supplied them with valuable intelligence on the American army. Without their reconnaissance efforts Burgoyne was essentially marching blindly forward toward the Americans. He would not be aware of their strength or position. Burgoyne was now faced with a decision either to retreat back to Canada and prepare for winter quarters that could be defended, or to follow orders and march on to Albany without any intelligence to prepare him for the Americans. He chose to follow orders and continue his advance. On September he camped near Saratoga, New York.

Meanwhile, the Americans were making a change in leadership. After the loss of Fort Ticonderoga, General Philip Schuyler was removed from command of the American Northern Army and replaced with Major General Horatio Gates (called an old midwife by Burgoyne). Gates had limited abilities, was conceited, and he was purely self-seeking. He engaged in underhanded war against Schuyler, Washington, Arnold, Morgan, Greene, and any other officer that stood in his way. He had found favor with several members of Congress.

Oil painting of Continental Army General Gates, {Public Domain}

Gates was one of the leaders in the Conway Cabal. This was a group of senior Continental Army officers that organized in late 1777 and early 1778 and were in opposition of Washington being the Commander-in-Chief of the army. They were in favor of Washington being replaced by General Gates. The cabal was named after General Thomas Conway, who was an outspoken critic of General Washington.

New recruits were flooding into the American army after their victory at Bennington and the murder of Jane McCrea by Indians which were associated with the British army under Burgoyne. To further boost Gates' army, General Washington sent General Benedict Arnold, who was his most aggressive field commander and a rising star in the army. In addition, 500 riflemen led by Colonel Daniel Morgan were also sent. Morgan's riflemen, as they were called, were some of the best sharpshooters that the Americans had. Their specialty was picking off British officers.

General Daniel Morgan--This is an original by Peale, likely drawn when Morgan passed through Philadelphia in 1794. {Public Domain}

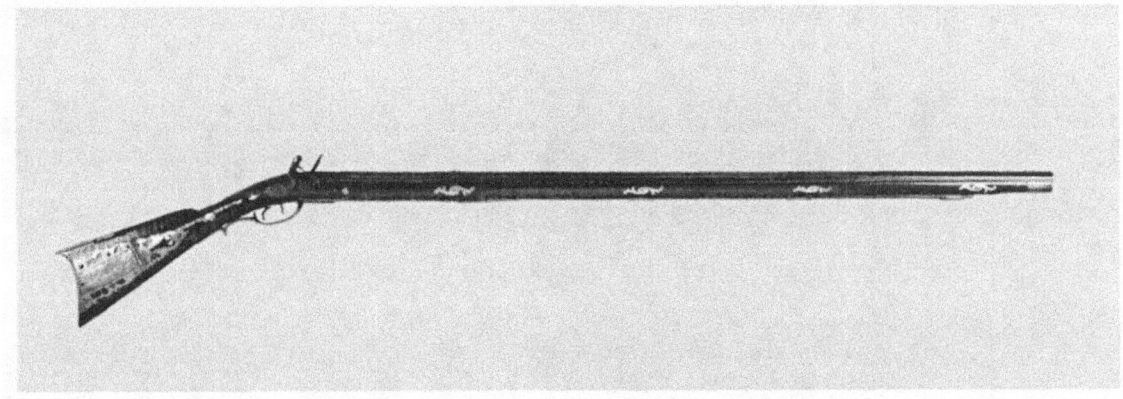

The Kentucky or Pennsylvania Long rifle had an effective range up to 300 yards. It was not designed for war since it did not have a bayonet mount. It measured 54 to over 70 inches long.

Some very accurate shooting by these sharpshooters is described in the Virginia Gazette of September 9, 1775, "Riflemen, bound for Boston, gave an exhibition. A man held between his knees a board five inches wide and seven inches long, with a paper bull's-eye the size of a dollar. A rifleman at sixty yards, without a rest, put eight bullets in succession through the bull's eye."[2]

Burgoyne gave a description of the methods used by Morgan's riflemen during the first battle of Saratoga, "The enemy had with their army great numbers of marksmen, armed with rifle-barrel pieces; these, during an engagement, hovered upon the flanks in small detachments, and were very expert in securing themselves and in shifting their ground. In this action many placed themselves in high trees in the rear of their own line, and there was seldom a minute's interval of smoke, in any part of our line, without officers being taken off by a single shot."[3]

[Note: During the first battle an aide giving a dispatch to Burgoyne was shot by one of the riflemen. The shooter thought the aide, who had laced ornaments on his saddle, was Burgoyne and spread the rumor that the general had been shot.]

On September 7th General Horatio Gates marched north toward the British army. He selected Bemis Heights just north of Stillwater, to establish a base which was about ten miles south of Saratoga. Under the advice of General Arnold, he had his army spend nearly a week building defensive works. On this high ground his forces had a view of the only road to Albany.

September 19 Battle of Freeman's Farm, the first Battle of Saratoga:

On September 13 General Burgoyne took his 6,000 troops across the Hudson River and made camp near Saratoga. Since he had no Indian scouts to provide intelligence on the Americans, he had no idea where the Americans were and what their intentions might be. On the 18th he had advanced just a short distance from the Americans and, due to lack of intelligence, he was unaware that he was outnumbered. He was just four miles from the American lines, and during the day various skirmishes broke out between the two armies.

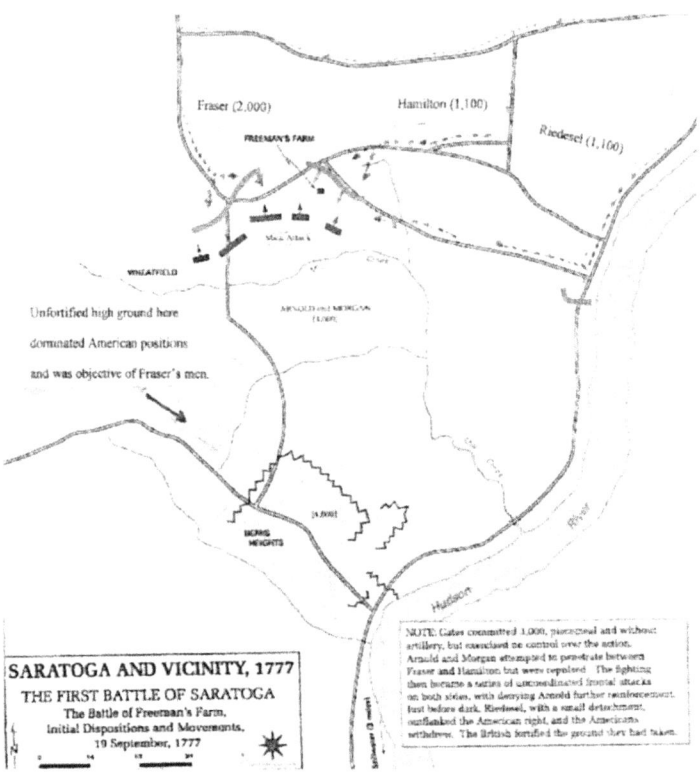

Map courtesy of the United States Military Academy

As the Americans prepared for battle, an uneasiness began to develop between General Gates and General Arnold. Gates was unhappy that Arnold had taken on some of the officers that served under General Schuyler, the man that Gates had replaced. A feud developed between the two men that would fester during the battle, and in the next few weeks it would boil over.

Around ten on the morning of the 19th it was cool and foggy as Burgoyne began to advance toward the Americans. He proceeded with caution in three columns with Baron Riedesel leading the left column, General Hamilton the center, and General Fraser on the right wing with orders to turn the American left flank.

Opposing the British was Gates on the right wing and Arnold on the left facing General Fraser. Both Gates and Arnold realized that their left must not be turned, if they were to remain in control of the heights. Arnold believed that the British would try a flanking movement on the American left. He pleaded with Gates to take action on all fronts. However, Gates chose to hesitate and wait for the expected frontal assault. Arnold argued that he should at least be allowed to take his forces from the heights to meet any British flanking movement.

Gates finally gave in and allowed a reconnaissance in force, consisting of light infantry and Daniel Morgan's riflemen, to advance and cover the left flank. At 12:45 the American riflemen opened fire from the trees on the advance guard from Fraser's troops. The sharpshooters made the British officers the first causalities.

For the next several hours there was fighting and pauses for regrouping by both sides. Shortly after three in the afternoon, Fraser's men threatened to turn the American left flank, which would give the British a victory. Seeing this, Arnold requested additional troops from Gates who gave him Learned's brigade. These additional men allowed Arnold to prevent the left flank from being turned and possibly saved the American army. Luckily for the Americans, their left flank was nearly secured when darkness began to set in. However, the darkness forced the Americans to retreat back to their defenses, which left the British in control of the field.

Twenty-six year old Captain Henry Dearborn wrote about the end of the battle in his journal, "Heavy fire commenced on both Sides, which Continued until Dark. The Enimy Brought almost their whole force against us, together with 8 Peices of Artilery. But we who had something more at Stake than fighting for six Pence Per Day kept our ground til Night, Closed the scene, & then Both Parties Retired."[4]

Major-General Henry Dearborn painted in 1812 by Gilbert Stuart. Dearborn served as Secretary of War under President Jefferson, and as a commanding general in the War of 1812. {Public Domain.}

After the First Battle of Saratoga:

The British claimed the victory since they were holding the field, and that night they slept on their arms at Freeman's Farm. But it was an obvious and disastrous British defeat. The Battle of Freeman's Farm was a British tactical victory but at a large cost of British troops. They had nearly 600 casualties, which was twice what the Americans suffered. British morale was damaged, and their resources were greatly reduced. Burgoyne still did not know the true strength of the American army, and due to his "victory" he was convinced he should continue to move again the Americans.

The next day General Burgoyne was ready to resume the battle, but General Fraser convinced him to wait so that his light infantry and grenadiers could rest. Had Burgoyne pressed the attack he might have been successful, because the American troops were tired and needed to be reorganized. On the 21st Burgoyne called off the attack, after he received a message from General Clinton saying that he probably could join him by the end of the month. Clinton was going to march against American forts along the Hudson River. Since Burgoyne was running low of supplies and men, he decided to wait for Clinton. This decision proved to be a fatal one for Burgoyne. Since he chose not to attack the Americans, but rather to stay and dig in, he also gave up his chance to retreat back to Canada and safety. He was now pinned down, short of food [on October 3 he put his men on half rations], and his army was losing men to desertions and sickness. Burgoyne now had 6,000 men facing about 7,000 American soldiers.

Problems between Gates and Arnold reached a climax in the American camp. Gates sent a report of the battle to Congress and Governor Clinton of New York. His report failed to mention Arnold's role in the battle. Most of the troops involved in the fighting were under the control of Arnold, and the other commanders gave him the credit for the American success. Arnold was the one actively directing the men during the battle, while Gates remained in his tent.

Gates then began countermanding Arnold's orders and humiliating him in front of the troops. Arnold took this treatment for a day or two, until Gates removed Morgan's and Dearborn's corps from Arnold's command without even consulting him. Arnold then went to Gates' tent, and a heated argument developed between the two men. Gates then told Arnold that he was of no consequence to the army and no officer at all, and he would give his command to General Lincoln when he showed up.

After Arnold was relieved of field command, he immediately asked for and received a request to be transferred to Washington's command. Instead of leaving for his new assignment, Arnold went to his tent and stayed there.

For the next two weeks there were clashes between patrols of the two armies. Morgan's sharpshooters constantly took long range shots at the British soldiers, especially the officers. By the first of October it was clear to Burgoyne that aid was not coming from General Clinton, so he called a war council to discuss their options. There were some suggestions calling for a retreat, but Burgoyne felt that it would be disgraceful to do so.

During this time the British entrenched themselves on the field of battle at Freeman's Farm, and most of the few Indians that stayed with the British deserted. The Americans had run so low on ammunition that they had to send to Albany to strip the lead off the windows of the old Dutch houses to make bullets.

During this time, Arnold tried to stir Gates to attack Burgoyne once more. The militia were threatening to go home, and Arnold worried that Burgoyne might be reinforced and make good a retreat. Gates dismissed his suggestion.

The British command decided that an attack, with 2,000 troops would occur on October 7 against the American left flank. Due to desertions and sickness, Burgoyne was going to battle with only 5,000 fit soldiers, while Gates had received a large amount of reinforcements during the two week lull. Gates' army had increased in size from 7,000 after the first battle, to nearly 12,000 soldiers. In addition, Gates had been receiving constant information from British deserters and knew about the dire condition of the British army. Gates was also aware that Burgoyne had earlier sent a plea for help from Clinton.

October 7 Battle of Bemis Heights, the second Battle of Saratoga:

Thirty-eight year old Colonel Timothy Bigelow of Massachusetts, who first fought at Lexington and Concord, wrote to his friend Stephen Salisbury on October 7, 1777. In the letter he described his thoughts just before the battle,

> I arrived in Camp last Saturday, nothing of importance has turned up since, except a small skirmish that happened yesterday between our picket guard and the enemies when the latter was driven to their lines. We had one man mortally wounded, three others slightly. There is great desertions from the enemy, not less than eight or ten, for many days back; mostly German. The enemy are strongly fortifying their Camp. I am much pleased at finding such a perfect union among the different corps of officers. It is the happiest Camp I ever was in. Officers and soldiers put the greatest confidence in the General imaginable. His treatment of the officers and soldiers is quite opposite of that of Schuyler. I should not have written to you, before having something of more importance to communicate had it not been to ask the favor to buy some brown sugar.[5]

Burgoyne was now aware that General Clinton had decided against joining with him. His supplies were growing short and his army was shrinking in size, so Burgoyne felt he had to advance against the Americans at once. On October 7 three columns of troops marched toward the American lines with Baron Riedesel's men in the center, General Fraser on the right, and Major Acland and his grenadiers on the left.

As the British advanced, Gates, who once again became passive, decided to keep his forces inside the Bemis Heights fortifications. Finally, Gates acted and sent Colonels Morgan and

Dearborn to attack the British right flank, General Poor's men to assault the left, and General Learned's men were to hold the center.

Map courtesy of the United States Military Academy

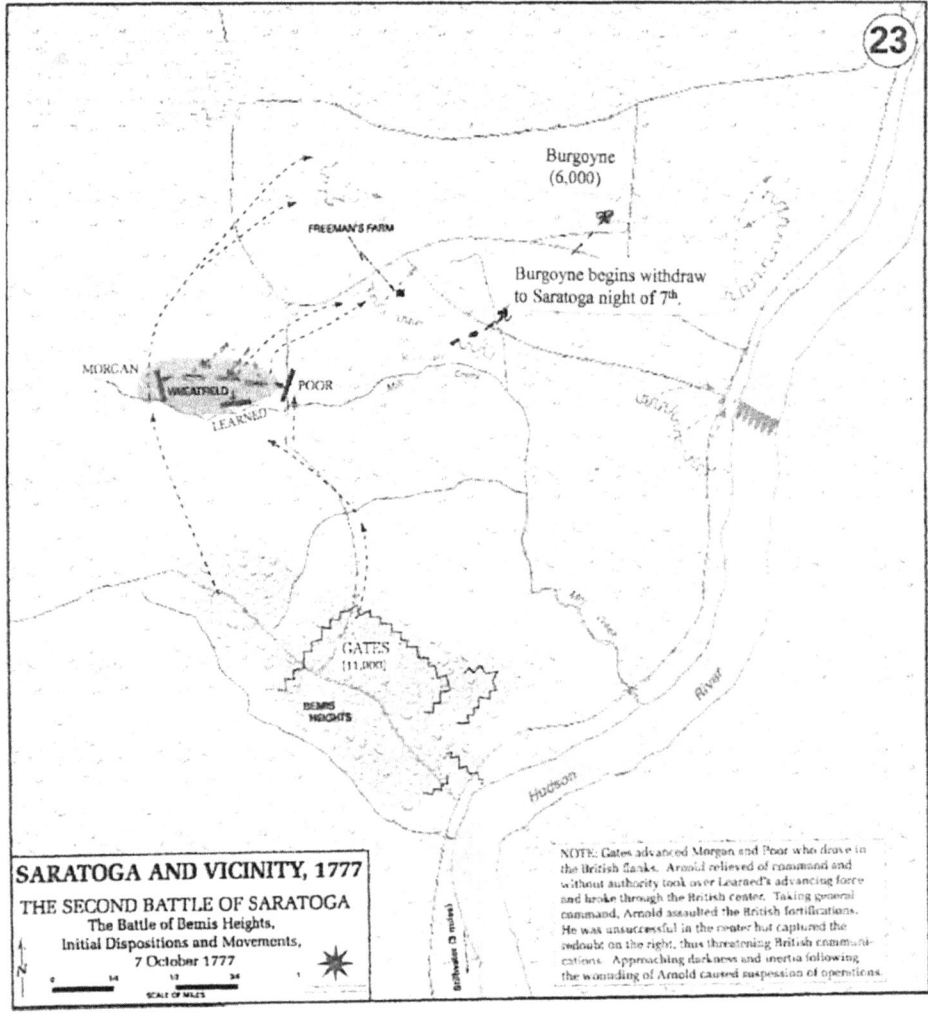

As the Americans began to make gains in the battle, they were able to flank the British center. When Burgoyne saw this, he sent a messenger with orders for Riedesel to retreat. The messenger was killed before the order was delivered, so there was no British retreat.

General Benedict Arnold, who earlier had been relieved of command, could see what was happening on the battlefield and began riding about camp in great indignation. According to some accounts, he may have been drinking freely. Finally, he could no longer resist doing nothing, so he rode to Learned's men to encourage them to press on in battle. At one point in a frenzy, he rode between the fire of the two armies and miraculously escaped unhurt. He may have done this to encourage the troops. However, some possibly thought his actions were those of a madman and not of a brave officer.

Benedict Arnold at Saratoga (Bemis Heights), Oct. 7, 1777, from A Brief History of the United States, Barnes's Historical Series, American Book Company, New York, 1885.

During the battle Arnold saw a high ranking British officer vigorously directing his troops, so he ordered one of Morgan's sharpshooters to shoot the officer. The marksman, who many claim was Timothy Murphy, killed the officer on his third try. The high ranking officer turned out to be the popular General Fraser. The death of their general and the pressure from the Americans forced the British to pull back to the fortifications they had established.

Arnold saw the British troops weakening, and ignoring an order from Gates to leave the field and resume his exile, he remained and encouraged the American troops to advance and secure their victory. During the successful attack on the British fortifications, Arnold had his leg broken by a musket ball and his falling horse. Later, the survivors inside the fortifications surrendered just before nightfall, and Arnold was carried back to headquarters on a litter. To everyone but Gates, Arnold was a hero and instrumental in the American victory.

[Note: Some later claimed that Arnold remained in camp and any orders he gave were sent out by messengers.]

During the night the British found that they had suffered great losses among the officers, due to the rifle fire of the American sharpshooters. While they camped on higher ground, they were constantly under cannon fire. During dusk they held a funeral for the popular General Fraser. The Americans, seeing a gathering of troops and not knowing that it was a funeral, fired several cannon shots at the crowd. The shots scattered dust over the chaplain, Mr. Brudenel, who continued the service.

Baroness Reidesel, who had accompanied her husband during the campaign and watched both battles, was terrified during the second battle. In her memoirs she described the action,

> The noise grew dreadful, upon which I was more dead than alive. About 3 o'clock in the afternoon, instead of guests whom I expected to dine with me, I saw one of them, poor General Frazer, brought upon a hand

barrow, mortally wounded. The table, which was already prepared for dinner, was immediately removed and a bed placed in its stead for the general. I sat terrified and trembling in a corner. The noise grew more alarming, and I was in a continual agony and tremor while thinking that my husband might soon also be brought in wounded like General Frazer. . . . I heard often amidst his groans, such words as these, '0 bad ambition! poor General Burgoyne! poor Mistress Frazer.'[6]

Baroness Riedesel, after the battle she spent the night tending to wounded soldiers. {Public Domain}

Surrender:

Burgoyne had lost over 1,000 men in the two battles and he was now outnumbered by about three to one. He withdrew his shattered army to the north and back to the fortified positions he held on September 16. His army was reduced to less than 3,000 men fit for combat, plus he had only three day's provisions. The Americans had his army surrounded, and after negotiations Burgoyne surrendered on October 14. Gates, being generous, granted the British safe passage back to Europe.

One of the Hessian officers described the appearance of the troops that he surrendered to, "Few of the officers in General Gates army wore uniforms, and those that were worn, were evidently of home manufacture and of all colors. On the other hand most of the colonels, and other officers wore their everyday clothes."[7]

Colonel Timothy Bigelow again wrote to his friend Stephen Salisbury a week after the final battle, and he described how important British General Fraser was to their army. Burgoyne surrendered the day this letter was written,

SARATOGA, Oct. 14th, 1777. Since I wrote, we have almost been in one continual action with the enemy, but not in very close order since the seventh instant, but in close pursuit. We are now all round them and it is common to have thirty to forty, or 50, deserters and prisoners come in for several days past, The Canadians, we are told by the deserters have mutinied and decline having anything to do in the matter and was promised by the General that they should go home in a few days. They lost General Frazer in the action of the seventh, an officer of approved merit who commanded the light troops, in whom they put the greatest confidence, and give it as one reason we took the field, the early loss of that officer. Upon the whole I can hardly realize that the great Burgoyne is reduced to such a destressed situation as you may depend he is at present. How the scene may change I cannot fully determine but from the present situation of things I expect to give you soon a further good account.[8]

This was the fourth battle for eighteen year old Private David How, but he didn't have much to write about in his journal regarding the surrender, "This morning we march To Salletoga with all the Reg And at 10 oClock the British Troops under the Command of Gurl Burgoix All Lay Down there Arms And march to our lines As prisoners of war. This after noon we Draw 4 Days provisions In Order for a march."[9]

The scene of the surrender of the British General John Burgoyne at Saratoga, on October 17, 1777, General Gates, in the middle, accepting the sword of Burgoyne on his left. {Public Domain}

General Gates, not shy about taking credit for the victory, later wrote to his wife, "The voice of fame, ere this reaches you, will tell how greatly fortunate we have been in this department. Burgoyne and his whole army have laid down their arms, and surrendered themselves to me and my Yankees."[10]

However, the surrender did bring some problems for Gates. A number of people believed that if there had been a fighting man at the head of the American army, the British would have surrendered as prisoners of war, and not with conditions.[11]

When Congress heard that the British army would be allowed to return to England, they voided that condition and forced the British to remain in the colonies as prisoners of war. This pleased George Washington because, like Congress, he knew that sending the soldiers back to England would mean that the troops, while on their parole in England, could not serve against America. However, they could serve in India or any British possession that was not American, or on garrison duty in England. Regardless where they were, they would relieve forces which could be sent to America. In this way most of the advantage of the victory at Saratoga would be lost to the patriots. By keeping Burgoyne's men prisoners here, any troops that England sent to replace them would reduce the overall strength of the British Army.

Gates, who held his Commander-in-Chief George Washington in contempt, sent word of the victory to Congress rather than notifying his superior first. Washington heard of the victory by rumors and later by a letter from General Putnam. This breach of protocol and common courtesy increased the hostile feeling between Gates and Washington that had been going on for some time.

Washington, in a letter to Gates on October 30, showed his displeasure about how he was notified of the victory, "I cannot but regret, that a matter of such magnitude and so interesting to our General Operations, should have reached me by report only, or through the channel of Letters not bearing that authenticity, which the importance of it required, and which it would have received by a line under your signature, stating the simple fact."[12]

Although Gates failed to recognize Arnold's contributions to the victory at Saratoga, Arnold had his seniority restored, which had been lost after being passed over for promotion earlier in 1777. General Washington had great confidence in Arnold's capabilities, even if Gates did not.

Impact of the British decisions:

At the end of summer Burgoyne's army was over extended and weakened, and he had a chance to call off the march to Albany and retreat back to Canada and establish winter quarters. Unfortunately, he was not aware that the commanders of the other two armies had abandoned the plan to join in Albany. This lack of communication between the armies would prove to be fatal to Burgoyne as he marched on to meet the American Army.

After the Battle of Freeman's Farm the American troops were tired, and being mainly militia they were disorganized. Even though they outnumbered the British by a little over a thousand men, most of the troops were undisciplined militiamen. If Burgoyne had pressed the attack the day after the Battle of Freeman's Farm, it is very possible that the Americans could have been defeated. At the very least if he did not attack, he could have withdrawn his troops back to the north with his army intact and called it a victory. Instead, he stayed in place and waited almost three weeks.

At the beginning of this pause, the Americans had not received a large influx of reinforcements and were extremely short of ammunition. During the pause, the Americans were able to resupply and add nearly four thousand additional troops. By waiting, Burgoyne's window for victory was closing and his defeat was assured.

If Burgoyne had retreated after the first battle, his army would have been saved to fight another day, and the Americans would have been denied a morale building victory at Saratoga. With no victory, Gates would have been hard pressed to keep many of the militiamen in his army active.

Meanwhile in Pennsylvania, General Washington had lost to the British at Brandywine Creek on September 11, and at Germantown on October 4. Once again, British General Howe's lethargic leadership had allowed Washington to escape.

Washington paid a price for the two losses. From September 1777 to March 1778, he lost one half of his army from battle, disease, desertion, capture, or resignation. With no victory at Saratoga, morale would have reached an all-time low and there would be no help from the French. It was very likely that the success of the revolution would have been in doubt.

If the Revolution had been saved at the Battle of Trenton, then it was established with the victory at Saratoga. What took place at this battle in 1777 is considered to be the turning point in the American Revolution. Twenty-six year old Captain Henry Dearborn wrote of the battle in his journal, "On this Day has Been fought one of the Greatest Battles that ever was fought in America, & I Trust we have Convinced the British Butchers that the Cowardly Yankees Can & when there is a call for it, will, fight."[13]

The biggest impact of Saratoga was international in scope. When the news of the victory reached Europe, France agreed to form a commercial and military alliance with the United States. Later Spain joined against the British to settle some old scores. However, it wouldn't be until the summer of 1781 that the aid of France would become most effective.

Gates received much of the credit for the victory, since he was the commanding general. This encouraged him to conspire with others to replace George Washington as the Commander-in-chief. Gates had sought the position since the beginning of the revolution, because he believed he was better qualified for the job. He would remain a thorn in the side of Washington until the issue was settled with the American loss at the Battle of Camden on August 16, 1780.

Due to his heroics at the battle, Benedict Arnold had his seniority restored. The serious wound he received in the left leg made it two inches shorter that the right leg. After being bedridden for five months, he was still not fit to serve in the field. So Washington appointed him military governor of Philadelphia in June 1778. Arnold possessed a lack of political sense and became involved in many political disputes. He turned bitter about his lack of advancement in the military, and due to failed business schemes he did not obtain the wealth he wanted or felt he deserved.

Then in April 1779 he made his biggest mistake, when he married the wrong person. Eighteen year old Peggy Shippen was a Loyalist sympathizer. She had earlier been courted by British Major John Andre, and she was very interested in politics and social standing. Peggy commanded a great amount of influence over her husband, and in May he began to secretly correspond with Andre. By July Arnold began providing information about American troops to the British. After he was discovered as a traitor, he was made a general in the British Army. At last he felt he had received the promotion and money he deserved.

Once hailed as a hero at Saratoga and a personal favorite of Washington, he had now become the most hated person in the colonies. One patriot, when asked what would become of Arnold if the Americans captured him, said they would, "Cut off the leg that was wounded at Saratoga and bury it with all the honors of war; and then hang his body on the highest tree."[14]

The Hudson Valley was now permanently in American control, and the battle put out of action more than one-fourth of the British forces in America. In England, indignation against Burgoyne grew and led at once to his recall. The Saratoga victory caused the spirit of patriotism to reach its highest pitch, quieted the Tories, and struck worry into the British army.

7

Washington Organizes a Spy Ring

"Washington did not really outfight the British, he simply out spied us!"

----.Major General Beckwith, British Intelligence Officer

Background:

In the 18th century the art of spying was considered to be demeaning, dishonest, and certainly unworthy of a gentleman. It involved deception, cunning, lying, and being just plain sneaky. These characteristics of a good spy violated the code of honor and morals of warfare during this period of time. Spies were usually held in low esteem by the public, and at times, by the people who employed them.

During the French and Indian War, scouts would spy on the opposing side, but they were not considered as spies. They merely observed, undetected, rather than mingle among the enemy posing as a friend. During his experience in the war, George Washington, saw that intelligence could make the difference between victory or defeat in a battle. He wrote to Governor Robert Morris of Pennsylvania on January 1, 1756,

> There is nothing *more* necessary than good intelligence to frustrate a designing Enemy: and nothing that requires greater pains to obtain. I shall therefore cheerfully come into any measures you can propose to settle a correspondence for this salutary end: and you may depend upon receiving (when the provinces are threatened) the earliest and best intelligence I can procure.[1]

In the French and Indian War, Washington was sent as an emissary and a spy, by the Virginia governor, to lead a small expedition into the Ohio Valley to gather information on the French. On December 12, 1763, he wrote in his journal about observing a small French fort, "I could get no certain Account of the Number of Men here: But according to the best Judgment I could form, there are an Hundred exclusive of Officers, of which there are many. I also gave Orders to the People who were with me, to take an exact Account of the Canoes which were hauled-up to convey their Forces down in the Spring."[2]

Later, Washington would remember the value of intelligence gathering that he learned early in his military career. He also learned that faulty intelligence could prove to be detrimental and even fatal in battle.

Early in the Revolution, George Washington realized the need to employ the use of spies in order to level the playing field with the mighty British Army. Washington was willing to lose a little personal honor to achieve victory over the British. Once he began to employ spies, the British also joined the world of espionage to counter the American's actions.

Spies for the British Army were usually paid, and many were deserters from the American side. British spies were more likely to fit the negative image of being dishonorable and selfish. However, the Patriots' spies usually did not receive payment, but rather they were motivated by patriotism and a sense of duty to the cause of freedom. Their image was one of honor, bravery, and love of country. Even though Washington had a vast network of spies working for him, he still maintained respect from the British commanders he faced.

General Washington believed that more could be accomplished by strategy than by bullets. On August 12, 1776, he appointed Thomas Knowlton to organize the war's first spy unit. The 130 man unit would become known as Knowlton's Rangers, which included a twenty-one year old officer named Nathan Hale.[3]

When Washington's army was forced out of New York City and assembled north at Harlem Heights, he realized, in order to save his army and recapture the city, he must have information about the British plans. A call went out to Knowlton's Rangers for someone to volunteer to be a one man army and spy on the British inside the city. Nathan Hale was the only volunteer that came forward.

Hale was sent behind enemy lines on September 12, 1775, to spy on the British. Nine days later he was arrested and questioned, and on September 22 he was hung as a spy. The daily orders on the evening of September 22 contained the following announcement, "A spy from the enemy (by his own full confession) apprehended last night, was this day executed at 11 o'clock in front of Artillery Park."[4] It is not known what activities Hale had been engaged in, or why his identity was discovered.

Early in the Revolutionary War, Washington became a skilled manager of intelligence. He expected his agents to deliver written, rather than verbal reports. His generals were ordered to "leave no stone unturned, nor do not stick to expense" when intelligence was gathered.[5]

As the war progressed, Washington used men, women, and even children as spies. Eight year old Ariel Bradley was sent into a British camp to gather information. He was detained and questioned by British officers and judged to be harmless, so he was set free. Ariel returned back to Washington's camp with the intelligence he was sent to acquire.

Women were very useful and valuable as spies during the war. The British would occupy the homes and farms of Patriots, and the women would listen and watch what went on. They would gather information and then slip away to pass it on to the American Army. The British considered women to know nothing of politics or the military, so the officers would often talk freely around them. Since women posed no threat, they usually could pass in out of British camps freely. However, the British should have known better, because they employed Tory women to spy on the Americans.

Espionage between 1775 and 1777 faced a lot of challenges. The spies involved constantly lived in a state of danger. Many times, these spies experienced failure and defeat, which could mean death. The majority of agents between these years faced their challenges alone. Prior to 1778, intelligence was mainly processed by singular operatives with no support or organization.

Washington finally made the decision to establish the first formal spy network in a letter sent on February 4, 1777, to Nathaniel Sackett, a New York merchant and supplier to the Continental Army,

> The advantage of obtaining the earliest and best Intelligence of the designs of the Enemy—The good character given of you by Colo. Duer—and your capacity for an undertaking of this kind, have induced me to entrust the Management of this business to your care till further orders on this head.
>
> For your own trouble in this business I agree, on behalf of the Public, to allow you Fifty Dollars pr Kallender Month—and here with give you a Warrant upon the Paymaster Genl for the Sum of Five hundred Dollars to pay those whom you may find necessary to Imploy in the transaction of this business.[6].

In the summer of 1777 Washington was in need of intelligence on the British, so he wrote to Colonel Elias Danton to set up a spy network on Staten Island,

> I wish you to take every possible pains in your power, by sending trusty persons to Staten Island in whom you can confide, to obtain Intelligence of the Enemy's situation & numbers -- what kind of Troops they are, and what Guards they have -- their strength & where posted. -- My view in this, is, that his Lordship, when he arrives, may make an attempt upon the Enemy there with his division, If it should appear from a full consideration of all circumstances and the information you obtain, that it can be done with a strong prospect of Success. -- You will also make some enquiry How many Boats are & may be certainly [used?] to transport the Troops, in case the Enterprize [should?] appear adviseable. You will, after having assured yourself upon these matters, send a good & faithful Officer to meet Lord Stirling with a distinct and accurate Account of every thing -- As well respecting the numbers & strength of the Enemy -- their situation &c -- As about the Boats, that he may have a General view of the whole, and possessing all the circumstances, may know how to regulate his conduct in the Affair.
>
> The necessity of procuring good Intelligence is apparent & need not be further urged -- All that remains for me to add is, that you keep the whole matter as secret as possible. For upon Secrecy, Success depends in Most Enterprizes of the kind, and for want of it, they are generally defeated, however well planned & promising a favourable issue.[7]

Washington quickly learned the value of security and the use of spy rings. In 1778, after using various spies and trying to establish a spy ring that had limited success, Washington appointed Major Benjamin Tallmadge as director of military intelligence and ordered him to create a spy ring in New York City, which was the site of British headquarters. This network of spies became known as the Culper Ring.

Benjamin Tallmadge as major of 2nd Continental Dragoons. Public domain

The Culper Spy Ring:

George Washington urgently needed to gather intelligence about British plans in New York. By appointing Benjamin Tallmadge as the Director of Military Intelligence, he had a man who had an understanding of the requirements of espionage and the knowledge of getting intelligence that was accurate. He was also picked for the job, because he was well connected in the New York and Long Island region.

The ring consisted of Abraham Woodhull (alias Samuel Culper Senior), a farmer on Long Island; Robert Townsend (alias Samuel Culper Junior), a merchant in New York City; James Rivington, known as the King's Printer; Caleb Brewster, a whaleboat captain; and Austin Roe, a courier from Setauket. There was also Anna Strong who acted as a neutral wife and relayed messages through hanging clothing, and there were several others who likewise served in the positions of couriers. Washington was the spymaster and oversaw the Culper Spy Ring, and Tallmadge was the main handler of the ring. Tallmadge took the code name of John Bolton and received the reports of the spies. Only Tallmadge and Washington knew the identities of the ring.

The only known sketch of Robert Townsend, Public domain   James Rivington, Public domain

Woodhull became one of Washington's best spies, while knowing all the while that he was one step away from a noose. He would travel to New York City every few weeks on "business." Woodhull would mix with British soldiers, listen for news or gossip, and observe British activities. He would then pass the information to Brewster, who sailed across the Sound and gave the intelligence to Tallmadge. This was the beginning of the Culper Ring.

Soon Woodhull expanded the operation by adding Robert Townsend, given the code name Samuel Culper Junior, to gather information. Townsend owned a share of a coffee house that was popular with British officers and run by James Rivington, who also printed the Loyalist paper *Royal Gazette*. Anna Strong, a friend and neighbor of Woodhull, helped pass along messages.

The ring would pass along information on troop movements, supply problems, naval movements, strength of the enemy, and any military plans. Information could usually be received by Washington in a week or less.

As the war began to wind down, the work of the spy ring diminished. In November 1781, Woodhull married Mary Smith, which caused him to spend less time spying, and Tallmadge had acquired other agents in New York City. Woodhull sent his last report on February 21, 1783, nine months before the British finally left New York City. Woodhull never spoke of his spying to anyone and none of the members were caught. The Culper Spy Ring is still the only known ring of its size and duration during the entire Revolutionary War. The ring's very existence was not discovered until the 1900's and it is still not known how many members it had.

While the ring was in existence, it had many accomplishments. A few are listed here:

1. Intelligence sent on the British plans to raid the port of New London.
2. Washington warned about the British plans to wreck American finances by counterfeiting Continental currency. James Rivington acquired the information and Washington was able to alert Congress of the scheme.[8]
3. Washington was planning for the arrival of the French fleet of Vice Admiral D'Estaing for an Allied attack on New York City. In a letter to Tallmadge he wrote,
    > In your first communication with C——,[Samuel Culper] and you will make it as soon as possible, I shall want to be as perfectly ascertained (as) the nature of the inquiry will ad⟨mit—viz.—⟩The quantity and quality of the ⟨provisions⟩ in New-York—comprehending their whole stock—whether in magazines, or on ship-board. He will be particular as to the kind, and size of the works that are lately formed, or that may be erected—And at all times, keep his attention on the changes of situation or the new positions which may be taken by the enemy. He will tell me what new works are erected on Long-Island, besides those at Brooklyn—and what nature. I wish also to know where their shipping lyes, and if they appear to be taking measures, and what measures, for their security in case of a French ⟨fleet⟩'s entering the harbor.[9]
4. The ring helped to unmask Benedict Arnold as a traitor.

Methods used by the Culper Ring and other spies:

The Culper Ring and other spies used various methods to transmit and keep secret the intelligence they gathered. The Culper ring used a code, created by Tallmadge, to send information to each other. The code consisted of a list of numbers that held specific meanings. For example, the number 10 was code for "absent", while the number 20 meant "affair." In total, there were seven hundred and sixty-three numbers that represented words, names, or places that the Culper Ring found vital to their operation.

Other tools used by spies included invisible inks that responded to fire or acid, as well as the use of cover and disguises. For example, Nancy Morgan Hart, who was tall and muscular, disguised herself as a crazy man and entered Augusta, Georgia to gather information of the British defenses.

This is part of the secret code used by General Washington, Benjamin Tallmadge, Robert Townsend, and Abraham Woodhull, during the Revolutionary War.

USE OF	MEANS	USE OF	MEANS	USE OF	MEANS
e	a	711	General Washington	15	advice
f	b			28	appointment
g	c	712	Clinton	60	better
h	d			121	day
i	e	713	Tryon	156	deliver
j	f			151	disorder
a	g	721	Major Tallmadge	178	enemy
b	h		alias John Bolton	174	express
c	i	722	Abraham Woodhull	230	guineas
d	j		alias Samuel Culper	286	ink
o	k	723	Robert Townsend	309	infantry
m	l		alias Samuel Culper, Jr.	317	importance
n	m	724	Austin Roe	322	inquiry
p	n			345	knowledge
q	o	725	Caleb Brewster	347	land
r	p			349	low
k	q	726	Rivington	355	lady
l	r			356	letter
u	s	727	New York	371	man
v	t			476	parts
w	u	728	Long Island	585	refugees
x	v			592	ships
y	w	729	Setauket	660	vigilant
z	x			680	war
s	y	745	England	691	written
t	z			708	your
341	January	e	1	73	camp
215	February	f	2		
374	March	g	3		
22	April	i	4		
373	May	k	5		
336	June	m	6		
337	July	n	7		
29	August	o	8		
616	September	q	9		
462	October	u	0		
427	November				
154	December				

Code page from *General Washington's Spies on Long Island and In New York.* 1939, page 218 by Morton Pennypacker

Washington himself spread disinformation by having spies exaggerate the size and strength of his troops, when they had conversations with British soldiers. He had his procurement officers make false purchases of large amounts of supplies in order to make the British think that a large force was massing. He would also send military messages, with false information through the regular post, knowing that they would be intercepted. One such event occurred in July of 1780.

Washington learned from the Culper Ring that the British planned to attack a French force that landed in Newport, Rhode Island. He then had information planted with British agents that he was going to attack New York City. He deceived the British by drawing up plans to attack the city, and he wrote letters saying the he would advance on the city as soon as General Clinton's forces were clear of the city and too near Newport to be recalled. The information was given to a courier with explicit instructions on which route he was to take, and Washington knew the courier would be captured. The messenger told Washington that if he took the route he laid out, he would be at risk. Washington looked at him and said, "Your duty, sir, is not to talk, but to obey."[10] As planned, the courier was captured with the documents, and when Clinton read them he called off his attack against the French.

Spies on both sides used hidden letters when they traveled. Small notes with information were hidden in hollowed out quills, buttons, hollowed out silver balls, and sewed into articles of clothing. British spy John Andre had secret papers, which led to the discovery of Benedict Arnold as a traitor, discovered inside his boot.

The Americans also employed code breakers to decrypt British coded messages. In 1775 Washington had Elbridge Gerry, Elisha Porter and the Rev. Samuel West decrypt a letter that uncovered the British spy Dr. Benjamin Church. It is estimated that the British intercepted and decrypted over half of America's correspondence during the war.

Impact of spies on the Revolution:
Washington's decision to use espionage did not win the American Revolution for the Americans, but it certainly helped. At times, the use of spies evened the "playing field" for the American Army and probably saved many lives. Some of the spy operations that contributed to the American victory were lost through time, however. However, a few of the successes are noted.

In 1776 a New York merchant, Elias Nexsen, was asked by the British commander on Staten Island to deliver a letter to Royal Governor Tryon. When Nexsen put the letter in his pocket, he was able to use his finger to loosen the seal of the freshly sealed letter. Nexsen then passed information of the letter on to Washington, which alerted the general of the attack on Long Island.

Also in 1776, not only did spies keep Washington informed of troops movements in New York, but they uncovered a plot to have him kidnapped. In December of the same year, work by the spy, John Honeyman, aided in the defeat of the Hessians at the Battle of Trenton. He had to convince the Hessians that he could be trusted by them, so Washington wrote a deceptive letter to the people of the area,

> To the good people of New Jersey, and all others whom it may concern: It is hereby ordered that the wife and children of John Honeyman, of Griggstown, the notorious Tory, now within the British lines, and probably acting the part of a spy, shall be and hereby are protected from all harm and annoyance from every quarter, until further orders. But this furnishes no protection to Honeyman himself.[11]

During the questioning of Honeyman by Colonel Rall, the spy told the Hessian that "no danger was to be apprehended from that quarter [the American Army] for some time to come."[12] He went on to describe the Americans as in a low state of morale and that there would be no attack.

Even though the Hessians had been on heightened alert for the past two weeks and had received information of an impending attack, they believed Honeyman's story and relaxed security. On the morning of December 26, the Americans attacked and defeated the Hessians.

In 1777, thirty-two year old Moses Harris carried communications between British General's Burgoyne and Clinton. Unknown to the British, Harris was a spy for Washington. Once given a message, he would first take it to the American General Schuyler, who would have it copied, and altered, and then returned them to Moses to deliver. In a small way Moses Harris contributed to the victory over Burgoyne at Saratoga.[13]

An amusing event in May 1778 occurred with American spies that had no effect on the British except to annoy them. British General Howe was preparing to leave for England. He had resigned his command and was being replaced by General Clinton, so the men were giving Howe an extravagant farewell party. Guests had been partying on Knight's Wharf since the middle of the afternoon, and at ten that evening they were being entertained with a fireworks display.

Captain Allan McLane, a scout and spy for Washington, had been in and out of Philadelphia numerous times gathering information. That evening he and his men planned their own party for the British and rode into town throwing kettle bombs that ignited Philadelphia's defenses. It was such a large distraction that prisoners of war were able to make their escape from the Walnut Street jail.[14]

Captain Allan McLane, New York Public Library's Digital Library, {Public Domain}

The guests at the party were alarmed, but the British assured everyone that it was just part of the fireworks, so the celebration continued. Meanwhile, McLane and his raiders made it back safely to Valley Forge feeling very happy with themselves.

In 1779 Pompey, an African slave, volunteered to spy for the American Army at the British fort on Stony Point, New York. Pompey gained the confidence of the British troops there by selling them fresh fruit.

One time he told the officers that he could not come back because he had to work. The officers were unhappy about this, so Pompey agreed to come after dark with the fruit. To do this he needed to know the password, and the unsuspecting officers were happy to share it with him. Each night there was a new password, and for the next nine nights Pompey showed up with his fruit and was able to get into the fort by giving the password.

On the 10th night around midnight, Pompey gave the password and again the gates were opened, only this time Pompey had three soldiers with him. When the gates opened, the three soldiers jumped out of hiding and knocked out the sentry. More American troops were hiding in the shadows, and they rushed inside the gates as even more American troops scaled the back walls of the fort.

The British were taken completely by surprise, and Stony Point was recaptured by the Americans. Pompey, for his role in the victory, was given a horse and excused from all work for the rest of his life.

Spies at Yorktown:

As the French fleet was heading toward Yorktown, Allen McLane was given instructions to learn as many of the British navy's code signals as possible, so that the French fleet could decipher what the enemy ships were communicating to one another during naval engagements. On Long Island, McLane was put into contact with James Rivington, who managed to get hold of a code book and give it to McLane. It was sent to Washington, and then turned over to the French fleet who defeated the British fleet at Yorktown. Once the British fleet was defeated, the French were able to bottle up the army of Cornwallis there.

Also at Yorktown, James Lovell, who designed cipher systems used by several prominent Americans, determined the encryption method that British commanders used to communicate with each other. When a dispatch from Lord Cornwallis in Yorktown was sent to General Henry Clinton in New York, it was intercepted. Lovell's cryptanalysis enabled Washington to gauge how desperate Cornwallis' situation was and it allowed him to time his attack on the British lines. Soon after, another decrypt by Lovell provided a warning to the French fleet off Yorktown that a British relief expedition was approaching. With this information, the French scared off the British flotilla, and sealed the victory for the Americans at Yorktown.

In the spring of 1781, James Armistead was given permission to serve in the Continental Army by his master. He was employed by Lafayette as a spy to gather intelligence of British troop movements. Armistead was sent to the camp of General Cornwallis posing as an escaped slave from the Americans.

On one occasion, he supplied Cornwallis with false information when he delivered a fake document to him that was in a soiled and crumpled condition. He said he found the information on the side of the road, and it contained information about a large number of replacement American troops on the way to Virginia. Cornwallis believed the fake report and kept his troops in a defensive position. This kept Cornwallis from leaving Yorktown and fleeing to the north.

James later sent a report to Lafayette that 60 British ships were anchored in the York River, and that the British were fortifying downstream at Yorktown. This information led General Washington to send a French fleet to the mouth of the York River and blockade the British. The Americans were now able to lay siege to Yorktown, which resulted in the surrender of Cornwallis. When Cornwallis later paid a courtesy call to Lafayette, he was surprised to see James Armistead, who he thought was his servant and spy, in the camp of the Americans. Being the typical emotionless British officer he stared and said nothing.

Engraved portrait of James Armistead from the painting by John B. Martin, ca. 1824

Another deception operation at Yorktown involved Charles Morgan who entered Cornwallis' camp as a "deserter." When he was questioned by the British, Morgan convinced them that Lafayette had sufficient boats to move all his troops against the British in one landing operation. Cornwallis was fooled by the information and dug in rather than march out of Yorktown. Afterwards, Morgan escaped in a British uniform and returned to American lines with five British deserters and a prisoner.

The use of spies helped to keep General Cornwallis at Yorktown, which gave the Americans and French time to surround him and trap his army. The victory at Yorktown assured the American victory in the Revolution. Two years later a peace treaty was signed, and the rest of the British Army left America.

8

How Decisions about African Americans as Soldiers Affected the War

"..."not to enlist blacks, boys unable to bear arms, or old men unable to endure the fatigues of campaign."

General Orders of George Washington, November 12, 1775

Background:

Since there were not enough white men to fill militia quotas, necessity required the colonies to recruit free black men as soldiers during the French and Indian War (1754–1763). Their enlistments were extended through the first battles of the Revolution, and laws prohibiting their serving were overlooked. Thus, black soldiers were inducted, fought bravely and proved their worth in the early fights at Lexington and Concord in April of 1775.

Despite their proven bravery, black soldiers were not included in the overall plan for waging the war and, therefore, General Washington, military leaders, and the Continental Congress decided that the service of black soldiers would not be needed to defeat the British. Black soldiers who had fought bravely were summarily dismissed from military service. The Committee of Safety in Windham, New Hampshire passed the following on April 12, 1776, "All able-bodied men aged twenty-one and above are required to sign a declaration pledging hostilities against the British, with the exception of lunatics, idiots, and Blacks."[1]

This banishment from the regular army was done to appease the southern colonies and gain their support for the cause. Slave owners, especially in the south, were concerned that training and arming black men could lead to an uprising. A group of Carolina slave owners stated, "There must be great caution used [allowing blacks into the military] lest our slaves when armed might become our master."[2]

Unlike the Continental Army, the Navy recruited both free blacks and slaves from the start of the war. They were desperate for sailors, and many blacks were already experienced, since they had served in British and state navies and sailed on merchant ships from both the north and south.

On November 7, 1775, the British Governor of Virginia, Lord Dunmore, had issued a proclamation declaring all "...indentured Servants, Negroes, or others, (appertaining to Rebels) free, that are able and willing to bear Arms, they joining his Majesty's Troops, as soon as may be, for the more speedily reducing this Colony to a proper Sense of their Duty, to his Majesty's Crown and Dignity."[3]

Once the proclamation was issued, thousands of slaves and indentured servants throughout the South escaped from their bondage to join with the British and the promise of freedom. By December 1, nearly 300 runaway slaves were armed and wearing the uniform of Lord Dunmore's Ethiopian Regiment. Across the chest of their uniform were the words, "Liberty to Slaves".

However, the use of blacks as soldiers in the British Army never became general policy. When General William Howe became commander of the British forces in the fall of 1775, he was opposed to black soldiers and dismissed them from service whenever he found them. He issued the following order, "All Negroes, Mollatoes, and other Improper Persons who have been admitted into these Corps be Immediately discharged."[4] The British Army like the American Army would remain white.

It is difficult to determine how many African Americans served with the British Army. They continued to use tens of thousands of blacks throughout the war to build fortifications and roads and drive wagons, which freed the British troops for other duties. The blacks were not particularly pro-British, but they were willing to support whichever side provided them the greatest hope to improve their lives.

This move by the British to promise freedom for the blacks prompted many in the north to push for the abolishment of slavery. As the black population decreased in the north (it dropped from a total of 4.1% to 2.1% from 1780-1790) and the need for slaves lessened, abolition groups began to gain influence. By 1777 in Vermont, where slavery was almost non-existent, they banned slavery outright. One historian noted, "The Revolution triggered the largest emancipation of American slaves outside the ultimate freedom won in the Civil War."

African Americans used as soldiers:

In 1777 things began to go bad for the American Army. They had suffered huge losses, desertions, and recruitment began to dwindle as morale sank. They lengthened the service time to one year for the Continental Army, which also slowed the signing of new recruits. To meet the crisis, Congress called for eighty-eight new battalions from the colonies. Despite paying bonuses and bounties to new recruits, men were slow to enlist. In early January 1777 Congress ordered the states to fill their units by drafting from the militia, or in any other way.

Many of the colonies, particularly those in the north, had trouble filling their quotas. In addition to drafting men, they soon began to recruit black men. Some slave owners were given the option of freeing their slaves and sending them in place of members of their family. Slaves were guaranteed their freedom in exchange for service in the army. New England had the smallest black population of any region, and yet they provided the majority of black recruits. The southern colonies, with the exception of Maryland, still refused to send blacks to fight.

Some slave owners were reimbursed fair market value, if they allowed their slaves to enlist. When the war spread into the south, the Continental Congress urged Georgia and South Carolina, who had large slave populations, to raise slave battalions and they agreed to pay the slave owners a $1,000 for each slave. The slaves would receive no pay, but at the end of the war they would be given $50 and their freedom. Both states rejected the idea, and South Carolina threatened to leave the war if the plan went into force.

Washington was desperate for more men, and he feared that black recruits would give the British an overpowering advantage over the American Army. Also, many American recruits had farms and shops that needed tending, so they did not serve as long as black recruits that did not need to return home.

In January 1777 Washington retracted his early order which barred free blacks from serving. His change in orders may also have been influenced by his abolitionist aids: Marquis de Lafayette, John Laurens, and Alexander Hamilton. Also, it had not gone unnoticed by Washington, that early in the war northern black soldiers had fought bravely.

African-American soldier of the 1st Rhode Island Regiment at the siege of Yorktown. Public domain

Rhode Island was having trouble filling their recruitment quota, so In February 1778, the state government took General James Varnum's idea that he sent to George Washington, which was to enlist slaves in the 1st Rhode Island Regiment. Washington neither voiced an opinion for or against the idea, and in the first few months eighty-eight slaves enlisted. The regiment became known as "the Black Regiment", even though of the 225 men, less than 140 were black.

In May of 1780, when Charleston fell and many of the Virginia soldiers were taken prisoners, the situation was so serious for Virginia, who had the largest slave population, that the legislature began debating the arming and recruiting of slaves, which they later passed. As the war shifted to the south in 1780, more southern black men were allowed to join. By October, even Maryland accepted any able-bodied slave between sixteen and forty, as long as they had the consent of their owner. In the spring of 1781, New York began to recruit slaves.

Georgia and South Carolina still remained opposed to having blacks serve in the military. However, they did have a very small handful of them that served. Other black men did manual labor in the army but were not considered soldiers.

Even though African Americans had joined the fight to free the colonies, prejudice remained in the army. Rather than fighters, many black soldiers were used as waiters for officers, wagon drivers, and laborers for building roads and fortifications. Yet when given the chance, the black soldiers distinguished themselves on the battlefield. They proved to the white Americans that they could fight as well as anyone, and they did not run from danger. Unfortunately, they were not promoted in rank like their white counterparts. The highest rank any black soldier achieved in the integrated army was Sampson Coburn who was made a corporal. During the later years of the war, as much as 10 to 15 percent of the Continental Army was made up of black soldiers.

Since prejudice was still present, why did the black soldiers fight when they knew that victory against the British would have little effect on the conditions of their lives? The answer is more about economic necessity than patriotism. Blacks had been in America as slaves since 1619, but even as free men they were barely able to raise themselves above the economic level of slaves. The army was a vehicle for them to find steady, dignified work, which has been the case for many ostracized groups throughout history. Black men hoped that their status as soldiers would give them a foothold to a better future.

Unfortunately, the gains that African Americans had achieved in the military were erased after the war ended. In 1784 Connecticut and Massachusetts banned all blacks, free or slaves, from serving in the military. In 1792 the United States Congress excluded African Americans from military service, allowing only free able-bodied white male citizens to serve.

By the end of the war over 60,000 slaves had been freed in the United States. The 1790 Federal Census estimated that in the eight northern states there were still a little over 40,000 slaves, and almost half were in the state of New York. In the eight Southern states it was estimated there were over 657,000 slaves remaining.

How did decisions about African Americans serving as soldiers affect the war?

Many of the slaves in the south left to join with the British. Thomas Jefferson wrote that in 1778 nearly 30,000 slaves in Virginia alone were lost to the British. However, later historians believed the numbers that Jefferson gave were highly inflated.[5]

During the campaign of 1780, thousands of slaves escaped in the south to join with the army of Cornwallis. As the British marched north toward North Carolina, one British officer remarked, "All the negroes, men, women, and children…quitted the plantations and followed the army."[6] By the time Cornwallis reached North Carolina, the number of slaves had reached the size of a small army.

During the war, both sides failed to take advantage of arming slaves, and only a few thousand served as soldiers. After the war, many blacks were captured by the Americans and were returned to their owners, or sold back into slavery. It is estimated that around 20,000 blacks left with the British and ended up in Canada, the West Indies, and in Europe. Over a thousand left for Sierra Leone, which was a colony established on the west coast of Africa for former slaves. Many ended up as slaves in the Caribbean and worked on sugar plantations.

There was hardly any military action between 1775 and 1781 that did not involve black soldiers. Eventually, 5,000 African American men fought against the British. These men served in an integrated army, which would be the last one until the Korean War. Yet, this was just a tiny fraction of black men available to fight, who had been welcomed into the American Army.

Both the American and British armies failed to take advantage of the additional manpower that could have been provided, if they had decided to use black slaves and freemen during the Revolution. If just a small percentage of the over half a million population of blacks had been used, the war might have been shortened by the Americans or won by the British.

Washington decided at the beginning of the war that black recruits would not be used as soldiers. Had he decided the other way, he could have easily doubled the size of his army. His aide, Lt. Colonel John Laurens, saw how useful it would be to allow slaves to serve as soldiers. On February 2, 1778, while with the army at Valley Forge, Laurens wrote to his father Henry, a member of Congress, "A well-chose body of 5,000 black men, properly officer'd, to act as light troops, in addition to our present establishment, might give us decisive success in the next campaign."[7]

A 1780 miniature portrait of John Laurens, by Charles Willson Peale.

The use of slaves as soldiers could have tipped the power in favor of the Americans early in the war. Later, when the war shifted to the south, there were nearly a half a million slaves that lived there. If they had been allowed to serve, this could have easily given the Americans an additional 100,000 troops, which would have definitely outnumbered the combined British and Hessian troops.

At the peak of the war, the British strength was around 22,000 regulars, 25,000 Loyalists, and close to 30,000 Hessians. This is less than the number of black troops that could have been used by the Americans. Some historians believed that if South Carolina and Georgia, the two states that refused to arm slaves, had allowed them to fight, it could have shorten the war.

Since the freeing of slaves was in full swing in the north, it's possible that it would have influenced the south to begin freeing theirs. Instead, after the war the number of slaves continued to decline in the north, while in the south it rose. The groundwork was laid to solve the problem of slavery in the future.

9

Important Decisions at Valley Forge Save the American Army

"With regard to military discipline, I may safely say that no such thing existed in the Continental Army."

---Baron von Steuben

Background:

During the first weeks of December, British General Howe tried to lure the Americans into battle but to no avail. Since it was turning cold and the defenses of the Americans were too strong to attack, he gave up and took his men to Philadelphia for winter quarters.

Meanwhile, Washington didn't have a fine city for his winter quarters. In Philadelphia the British enjoyed going to dances, the theaters, and suppers, while just twenty miles away, the Americans were suffering the hardships at Valley Forge. Valley Forge was chosen for winter camp, because it gave Washington a safe position and a large protected valley for his exhausted troops. Also, he would be able to intercept British foraging parties that were in and around Philadelphia.

The suffering of the Americans was largely due to little determined effort to get supplies to Valley Forge. The supply and transport system had broken down after the Quartermaster and Commissary resigned. In addition, many of the officials in both departments were mainly merchants who left, because they found it more rewarding dealing in private trade.

Washington had less than 10,000 men settled in at Valley Forge. During this time he would lose thousands more to disease, desertion, and enlistments expiring. There, the men suffered from not only the harsh winter but a lack of supplies and sickness. The army was short of clothes, shoes, blankets, and food, while forced to live in frigid, drafty, and filthy wood huts. In addition, the men were exposed to a typhus-typhoid type of fever, smallpox, frostbite, "the itch," or scabies, and scurvy.

Washington faced several problems. Securing supplies for his men was a great challenge, because many of the roads were impassable in the winter. Enlistments were soon to expire for many of the men, and desertion rates would begin to climb as winter set in. Lack of proper food, camp filth, and few medical supplies increased the chance of outbreaks of various diseases. The morale of the soldiers was at an all-time low, and there would be little help from a Congress that was in hiding from the British.

Washington was well aware that he had only a short time to solve the problems that faced his army. He wrote to Congress on December 23, 1777, "We have not more than three months to prepare a great deal of business in—if we let these slip or waste, we shall be laboring under the same difficulties all next Campaign."[1]

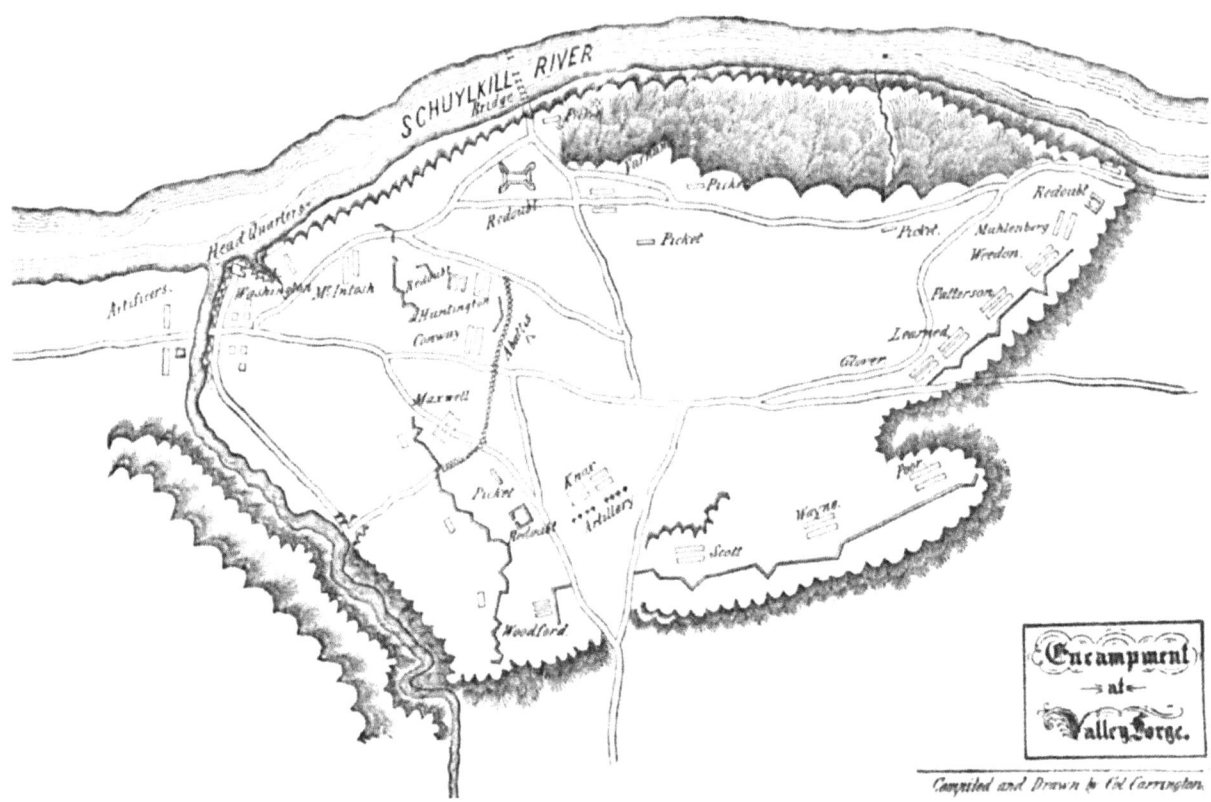

Valley Forge, from Benson J. Lossing, *The Historical Field-Book of the Revolution, Vol. 2*

Howe decides not to attack Washington:

General Howe commanded around 20,000 troops, while Washington had less than 9,000 sick, wounded, and undersupplied troops. By March the American general would lose another 3,000 that died, deserted to the British, or simply left for home, and Washington would be left with less than 4,000 hungry men fit for combat.

If Howe had chosen to attack during this time, he would have likely suffered large losses, but he would have destroyed Washington's army and possibly ended the revolution. Like in previous situations, Howe chose not to fight for the victory, rather he decided to wait and compromise. He believed that by the end of winter Washington's army would be a shadow of its former self, and they would either offer little resistance or give up. By late spring, due to increased enlistments, Washington's army had increased to 14,000 troops, who were better trained and looking for a fight.

Later in a letter, Howe later defended his position to not attack, "The entrenched situation of the enemy at Valley Forge, Twenty-two miles from Philadelphia, did not occasion any difficulties so pressing as to justify an attack upon that strong post during the severe weather, and though everything was prepared with that intention, I judged it imprudent."[2]

Another reason he gave for not attacking was to claim that the grass was not long enough for his horses to feed upon, and that there were bills introduced in Parliament appointing a peace commission to go to America and negotiate a compromise. Also, since Howe had sent his resignation to London in October 1777, he just may have lost his desire for fighting. Regardless, of the reason for not attacking, an excellent chance for victory had once again passed.

Washington decides to inoculate his troops for smallpox:

Early in the war many people believed that inoculation was an insane idea, as that of a man who commits suicide to avoid death. Each of the American Colonies had their own laws on quarantine and inoculation. Since inoculation involved deliberate exposure to smallpox, many people were opposed to it and even banned it in many areas.

In the winter of 1776-77, the threat of smallpox was on the mind of Washington, as he marched his army into Morristown, New Jersey to set up his winter quarters. While the bulk of Washington's army was encamped at Morristown, Washington issued the official order on February 6 to Doctor William Shippen for the entire army to be inoculated. In 1777, more than 100,000 people in North America died as a result of smallpox.

At the winter quarters in Valley Forge in December 1777, many of the troops that had been inoculated against smallpox returned home after their enlistment was up. Therefore, the new troops that Washington had were not inoculated and posed a health risk. He was alarmed that these new soldiers were not inoculated as he had earlier ordered. Washington wrote to General William Heath on December 17,

> After the repeated directions, which I had given to have All the Recruits who had not had that disorder innoculated the moment they were inlisted, I was not less surprized than mortified to find the fine detachment of Men that came forward under Lt Colo. Smith rendered intirely useless for this Campaign by my Orders not being attended to. By the time they reached the Camp the small pox broke out upon them, which obliged me to send the whole into the Hospital, as those who were well were not more than sufficient to nurse the sick.[3]

At Valley Forge in January 1778, smallpox began to break out once again in Washington's army. So, like he did a year earlier at Morristown, Washington had to take a chance and inoculate his men and put his army at the mercy of the British.

Washington wrote to John Trumbull, "I found, upon examination, that between three and four thousand men had not had the small Pox; that disorder began to make its appearance in Camp, and to avoid its spreading in the natural way the whole army immediately inoculated—They have gone through with uncommon success, but are not yet sufficiently recovered to do duty."[4] An angry Washington issued orders that any surgeons that did not inoculate new recruits would be court-martialed. By March his efforts finally paid off, because the cases of smallpox began to lessen.

To accommodate the increase of sick soldiers, hospitals were established at Reading, Bethlehem, Easton, and Lititz. The first permanent army medical hospital was built at Yellow Springs, which was ten miles from Valley Forge. Unfortunately the health conditions in the hospitals were so bad, that hospital duty was considered a dangerous job. Usually the worst soldiers were made orderlies as punishment, which resulted in poor care of the patients.

By late March the soldiers were going through the various stages of inoculation at Valley Forge. Washington, fearing an attack by the British if they learned that much of his army was incapacitated due to inoculation, ordered the doctors to perform inoculation using all possible secrecy. Since he was in need of troops, he had new recruits sent directly to Valley Forge inoculated before they arrived.

Washington allows Baron von Steuben to reshape his army:
Camp Sanitation

During the winter, sanitation around Valley Forge was almost non-existent. The soldiers had trouble keeping themselves clean, much less their surroundings. Outbreaks of typhoid and dysentery spread due to contaminated food and water. A total of nearly 3,000 troops died during the winter, which was the highest mortality rate of any Continental Army encampment.

The soldiers, as they did back home on the farm, relieved themselves wherever they wished. If they did use a latrine, it was usually located outside the mess tent. There was no plumbing or system of trash removal, and dead horse remains laid around the camp, which made the smell in some places intolerable. Washington suggested that the soldiers burn tar or musket powder to cleanse the air. The awful smells in the men's huts would remain until the spring, when Washington ordered that the clay be removed between the logs of the huts, which allowed fresh air to enter.

Officers were supposed to check cabins twice a day for cleanliness, but this was rarely done. After eating, many times the soldiers would throw the remains of food into the corners of the cabins. When a soldier died, his clothing was stripped from him and given to someone else, which possibly spread the disease the man died from. By mid-February nearly 4,000 troops were unfit for duty, and unless something changed, the sickness caused by these conditions would wipe out the colonial army.

With the arrival of Baron von Steuben on February 23, drastic changes were about to take place. He was brought in as a volunteer by General Washington, in order to teach the troops the basics of military drills, tactics, and discipline. When von Steuben arrived and observed the Americans troops, he remarked, "With regard to military discipline, I may safely say that no such thing existed in the Continental Army."[5]

In the summer of 1777 in France, Baron von Steuben met with the French Minister of War and Benjamin Franklin to discuss the Baron coming to America to train the army. However, Franklin could not offer him rank or pay, because Congress was tired of European mercenaries coming to America and demanding high rank and pay to work with the army. Some of these men were given large advances in pay and then they would disappear. So, the Baron agreed to volunteer his services without rank or pay.

The Baron's title had been acquired in the service of a small German state, and he had been introduced as a Lieutenant General on the staff of Frederick the Great, when in reality he had been only a captain. The fraud proved to be harmless, because von Steuben had a broad knowledge of the workings of the military.

Baron von Steuben arrived at Valley Forge on February 23, 1778, looking larger than life. He was surrounded by his aids, servants, personal cook, and a large greyhound named Azor. He was wearing an officer's jacket from the Prussian Army with the front adorned with medals, and he had well-polished black jackboots. On his side were two large, brass-plated flintlock pistols and a long sword. The Americans were impressed by his commanding height, heavy-set body, and aristocratic bearing. One American soldier remarked, "Never before or since, have I had such an impression of the ancient fabled god of War, as when I looked on the baron."[6]

Baron von Steuben, c. 1786, Yale University Art Gallery. Public Domain

Von Steuben was shocked at the condition of the camp and the lack of discipline of the men. With the blessing of Washington, he immediately began to improve the conditions of the army at Valley Forge.

Part of von Steuben's plan to discipline the army also involved camp hygiene. After inspecting the camp, he immediately established rules of basic hygiene. Here are a few of the new rules:

1. Kitchens and latrines were to be placed on opposite sides of the camp. He also expected the latrines to be used and not the outside of the hut.

2. Dead animals and humans were to be removed and burned or buried far from camp.

3. When a soldier died, the straw where he laid was to be burned and his bedding was to be washed and aired before used by someone else. All straw and bedding of the men were to be well aired.

4. Daily inspections of tents were to be carried out to insure they were cleaned. A trench was to be dug to carry rain away from the tent. Eating in the tent was allowed only in bad weather.[7]

Soon after the rules were put into force, health conditions in camp greatly improved by the end of spring. When the warm weather of spring arrived, new clothing for the men had been received, and they were given time to wash their old clothing and bathe in the river.

Drilling the Army

Washington was well aware of the need for uniform training and organization of the army, so he appointed von Steuben as temporary Inspector General. Von Steuben, promptly disregarded the English method of drilling soldiers, which was to use sergeants to teach the men. The Prussian took the musket in his hands, and he himself showed the troops what was needed to be done. The Baron worked from morning until night teaching the men how to advance, retreat, or change front without falling into disorder.

Since von Steuben spoke very little English, Washington appointed a German speaking officer, Captain John Walker, as a translator. In addition, because the Baron also spoke French, Washington appointed Colonel Alexander Hamilton and General Nathanael Greene to translate the drill instructions to the troops from French to English.

At the beginning of the training the Baron showed the Americans he had a sense of humor. On one occasion he wanted to demonstrate his new style of drill that the Americans would use. A company of soldiers from the Pennsylvania Line were organized to follow his orders through the translator. The Baron told Captain Walker that he must translate in English every word he said, as he spoke. The captain tried to tell him why he shouldn't. "You will translate in English exactly what I say," the Baron harshly demanded in German.[8]

Not wishing to disobey him, Walker repeated every order from the Baron in English. Again the Baron gave an order in German, and again it was translated in English. Then, von Steuben looked puzzled as to why the men were not responding to the commands. An aid to General

Washington explained to the Baron that the men selected were all Pennsylvania Dutch, and they spoke only German.

As word about the mistake spread through the ranks, the men, along with General Washington, began to laugh. When the mistake was translated to the Baron, a broad smile began to spread across his face and was followed by a deep belly laugh.

At times the Baron would get angry at the way the soldiers trained, so he would cuss them out in German or French and then have the translators repeat the angry words to the men in English. The men had never been cussed out in three languages, and his salty language made the men feel that the Baron was one of them.

From late winter until early spring, the Baron taught the army a simplified version of the drill formations and movements that the armies of Europe used. He also taught them the use of the despised bayonet, which the Americans had mainly used as a cooking skewer. He attempted to consolidate the small regiments and companies into organized light infantry companies to serve as an elite force of the army.

Von Steuben found the Americans unlike any people that he had previously encountered. They had a strong sense of independence and individualism, and they did not respond with fear and mindless obedience to his orders. In comparing the soldiers he trained in Europe to the Americans he said, "You say to your soldiers [the European], 'Do this' and he doeth it; but I am obliged to say [to the Americans] 'This is the reason why you ought to do that.' And then he does it."[9]

Once the soldiers understood the reason for the order or technique, they not only improved but began to perform superbly and with great confidence. Steuben taught the officers the most approved military science, which they learned very quickly. By the end of spring, the American Army became a disciplined body which could march, deploy, and maneuver on equal terms with any army in Europe.

Steuben also created an effective staff which Washington did not have, and he wrote a new book of tactics adapted to American conditions, which would be used by the army for many years. Steuben also improved how the officers cared for their men.

The men were pleased with the work von Steuben was doing. Washington's aide, John Lauren, wrote to his father on April 1, 1778, "Baron Steuben is making sensible progress with our soldiers. The officers seem to have a high opinion of him, and discover a docility from which we may augur the most happy effects."[10] Washington was also pleased with the Baron, because on May 5, 1778, he made him the official Inspector General of the Army with the rank and pay of a Major General.

On May 27, 1778, von Steuben introduced a plan to organize the infantry, artillery, cavalry, and engineers. He formed a system of accountability for public property, which resulted in large savings for the government.

By the end of spring the Baron had accomplished his task. The American army was healthier, more organized, and better trained. In June the British Army marched out of Philadelphia toward New Jersey. The Baron's work would soon be put to the test, when the outnumbered Americans faced the British at Monmouth Court House, New Jersey on June 28, 1778.

Two decisions that changed the course of the war:

Washington's first decision:

The most feared disease in colonial America was smallpox. It was highly contagious, and if a person survived they could suffer other physical problems and even be permanently disfigured. Not all people exposed to it got sick and some became only mildly ill. Other diseases ran through the American Army due to poor sanitation practices. It is estimated that during the war around 6,800 soldiers died in battle and at least 17,000 died from disease.

Washington had seen what smallpox could do to his army and his battle strategies. The threat of smallpox had kept Washington from attacking Boston. Instead of a quick victory over the British he was forced to engage in a long siege. Eventually, the British withdrew from Boston but with their army intact.

While the siege of Boston was going on, Washington sent an army to capture Quebec, which he hoped would convince Canada to join with the American cause. Unfortunately the plan failed, partly because smallpox ran through his army, and the fear of the disease helped to demoralize the men and discourage recruiting and re-enlistments.

Smallpox and other diseases also affected the New York Campaign. Smallpox did not strike in Washington's camp like it did with the army outside of Quebec. However, it did keep Washington from getting needed reinforcements, since the Northern Army at Quebec was decimated and recruitment was low due to the fear of smallpox.

During the winter of 1776-1777, Washington inoculated his army against smallpox, but the enlistment of those men had expired, and the men he brought to Valley Forge were not inoculated against the dreaded disease. At Valley Forge he lost men due to desertion and disease. If smallpox swept through his camp, he would lose his entire army.

Washington faced an enormous decision; loss of much of his army to smallpox, or inoculate. Washington knew that if he inoculated his troops against smallpox it would take several months to complete since it had to be done in groups. There was also the risk that the disease could get out and spread through his camp. Moreover, if the British discovered what was happening, they could attack while a third of his army was recuperating from inoculation. Each decision carried the risk of losing his army.

One of the most important decisions of the war was when Washington decided to inoculate his troops at Valley Forge and to order new recruits to be inoculated. Luckily, he was able to keep this from the British and preserve his army.

At this time, the morale of the soldiers was at an all-time low, and many of them believed they had been abandoned by Congress. Then, Washington made another important decision, when he appointed Baron Von Steuben to instill discipline in his army.

Washington's second decision:

When Washington's army reached Valley Forge, they were in a horrible state. After suffering several military defeats, moral was low, they were sick, and it appeared that by spring they would cease to be an effective fighting force.

Baron von Steuben, with his exaggerated credentials, was first introduced to Washington through a letter from Benjamin Franklin, who had met him in France. Upon the recommendation of Franklin and the French War Minister, Washington was willing to take a chance on this volunteer from Europe.

Von Steuben not only gave the army much needed military training, but he made great strides in improving the sanitation of the camp. His efforts changed an army that was close to defeat that winter, to one that emerged in the late spring a healthier and better trained force.

The army was able to attract new recruits, because smallpox was no longer a major threat, and by the time the army left Valley Forge, it was over 14,000 strong. Thanks to the training by von Steuben, the troops were anxious to face the British in battle to prove themselves.

In their first major engagement with the British at Monmouth Courthouse on June 28, 1778, the Americans faced a larger British army and fought them to a draw. This raised morale in the army and convinced the soldiers that they could go toe-to-toe with the British as equals in battle. This would be the last major battle fought in the north.

Von Steuben's army reforms that winter were far reaching. He trained the men in the use of the bayonet, which was especially important in the Battle of Stony Point in July 1779. The Americans attacked the British fort at midnight and defeated them in a surprise bayonet charge.

Before von Steuben took control, no accounts had been kept of arms, which resulted in the loss of from five to eight thousand muskets each year. Soldiers were allowed to take home their weapons as keepsakes, and new recruits were issued new ones. Under the watchful eye of von Steuben, in his first year the number of lost muskets fell to less than twenty.

The Baron was able to adapt his training in warfare to the conditions of American warfare that was practiced. In woodland fights with Indians, the Americans found it necessary to work in loose columns among the trees, separate, and reunite in a brief notice. Steuben was able to fashion out of this a kind of light infantry adapted for this type of skirmishing.

There was no man in America capable of doing what Baron von Steuben did during the winter of 1778 at Valley Forge. Washington was probably the only commander in the American army not afraid to admit that his army had a problem and to have the courage and confidence to appoint this stranger to solve the problem. Washington decisions at Valley Forge may have saved the Revolution.

10

Battle of Kings Mountain: The Beginning of the End

"All the Rebels from hell could not drive me from it."

----Tory leader Patrick Ferguson at the top of Kings Mountain before the battle

Background:

Up until this time, most of the fighting had been in the north. Since the war was at a stalemate there, British strategy was to take the fight to the south. Southern ports could be captured, which would hamper the influx of supplies needed by the Americans. There were more Tories in the south who would fight for the British. Also, large groups of recent immigrants lived there and would still be friendly to England.

Late in 1778 the British captured the port city of Savannah and controlled the coastline of Georgia. In May 1780 they captured Charleston, and their victory, at the Battle of Camden in August 1780, gave them control of much of South Carolina. The British victory at Charleston was the worst defeat for the Americans in the Revolution. General Lincoln surrendered his army of over 5,000 to the British. Many of the American prisoners later died on British prison ships. Sensing victory in the south, General Clinton divided his army and sailed to New York City. He left behind General Cornwallis and his army of over 8,000 men to capture the south. The plan of Cornwallis was to take both North Carolina and Virginia. He emphasized the point when he stated, "Unless we take North Carolina, we must give up both South Carolina and Georgia and retire within the walls of Charleston."[1]

The war in the south developed into a bitter struggle between neighbors and families. At times the savagery in battles between the Patriots and Tories even shocked the British and Hessian troops. The hatred between the Patriots and the Tories went deeper than that of the Patriots and the British. Each side saw its position in the war as sacred, and for fellow Americans to go against it was an act of betrayal that could not be matched. Both sides harassed each other, stole or damaged the property of the other side, and killed family members of the opposition. The following story typified the strong feelings each side had toward each other.

On July 3, 1778 a bloody battle took place between Tories and Patriots in Wyoming, Pennsylvania. Some of the Tories and Patriots were friends and neighbors before the war. As a result, their emotions and hatred ran deep and anytime they fought each. Only a handful of the Patriots survived the battle, the Patriot leader was Colonel Butler and he related the following event.

One of the soldiers, Giles Slocum, had escaped after the battle and was hiding in some bushes on a small island in the Susquehanna River just below the battlefield. There he was witness to the meeting of the Pensell brothers, John and Henry.

John was a Tory and Henry was a Patriot. Henry had lost his gun, and upon seeing his brother John, fell to his knees and begged for his life to be spared. John looked at his brother and called him a damned rebel, and he began to load his weapon while Henry continued to beg for his life. Henry told John that if he would spare him, he would serve him for the rest of his life.

John finished loading his gun and Henry said to him, "You won't kill your brother will you?" John replied, "Yes I will as soon as look at you, you are a damned rebel." John then shot him and afterwards went up and struck him four or five times with a tomahawk and scalped him.[2]

In the spring of 1780, British Major Patrick Ferguson was sent by his commander to raise Tory volunteers in the south. Ferguson's appearance was not commanding. He was of middle stature, slender body, but he did have great personal magnetism and he was described by many as a born commander and absolutely fearless in battle. He soon had new troops organized, drilled as riflemen, and skilled with the bayonet. He was the only British officer in his force of over 1,000 men. With his army he began to terrorize areas in South Carolina, North Carolina, and Georgia.

During the morning of August 18, 1780, two hundred American militiamen, under the command of Colonels Isaac Shelby, James Williams, and Elijah Clarke, were hoping to catch a Tory camp by surprise at Musgrove's Mill. The battle lasted around an hour and resulted in a Patriot victory. After the battle, the Americans were forced to retreat back over the Appalachian Mountains with British Major Ferguson and his militiamen in hot pursuit.

Anonymous miniature of Patrick Ferguson, c. 1774-77, {PD-1923}

Ferguson and his men nearly caught the Americans, since they were just thirty minutes behind them. However, they had to give up the chase because their mounts were near exhaustion, and they were not sure how far ahead the Americans were from them. So, Ferguson turned back and established a base camp at Gilbert Town in southwestern North Carolina.

The Americans regroup:

Patrick Ferguson learned from spies that a large group of backwoodsmen were gathering from "over the mountain" to oppose him. He thought a threat by him would strike terror in the hearts of the mountain men in the area. He sent a message to them through a released prisoner, Samuel Phillips, who was a relative of militia Colonel Isaac Shelby. Ferguson told Phillips to say, "If they did not desist from their opposition to the British arms, he would march his army over the mountains and hang their leaders, and lay their country waste with fire and sword."³

When Colonel Shelby received the threat, he met with Colonel Sevier to discuss it. The two men decided that the thing to do was to raise all the men they could and attempt to surprise Ferguson by attacking him at his camp, before he prepared to attack them.

The men that Shelby and Sevier gathered to fight were frontiersmen and their sons. They were from the mountains of southwest Virginia and today's northeast Tennessee, and they were known as "Overmountain Men." These men were accustomed to a rugged and dangerous life. When their freedom was threatened, they would come out of the hills to fight. They fought for themselves and would come mounted and equipped at their own expense. Up in the hills they were cut off from the rest of the world and knew little of the war that had been raging in the northern colonies.

The call went out for Patriots to meet, by September 25, at Sycamore Shoals, in what is today the far northeastern part of Tennessee. Men from Virginia and North Carolina led by William Campbell, Benjamin Cleveland, Charles McDowell, and others joined the "Overmountain Men." Robert Campbell, an ensign in one of the companies wrote,

> In the fall of the year of 1780, when the American cause wore a very gloomy aspect in the Southern States, Cols. Arthur and William Campbell, hearing of the advance of Col. Ferguson along the mountains of the State of North Carolina, and that the Whigs were retreating before him, unable to make any effectual resistance, formed a plan to intercept him, and communicated it to the commanding officers of Sullivan and Washington Counties, in the State of North Carolina. They readily agreed to co-operate in any expedition against Col. Ferguson. Col. Arthur Campbell immediately ordered the Militia of Washington Co., Virginia, amounting to near four hundred, to make a ready march under command of Col. Wm. Campbell, who was known to be an enterprising and active officer. Cols. Shelby and Sevier raised a party of three hundred, joined him on his march.⁴

Artist Lloyd Branson's *Gathering of Overmountain Men at Sycamore Shoals* before the Battle of Kings Mountain. From *Andrew Jackson and Early Tennessee History* 1915.

On the morning of September 26, the rebels left Sycamore Shoals and began a march to the southeast, which would eventually take them to Kings Mountain over 100 miles away. After marching for five days and covering more than ninety miles over the mountains and sometimes through an early snow, the Overmountain Men joined up with members of the North and South Carolina Militia at Quaker Meadows.

On October 2 they made camp near Pilot Mountain, which was less than twenty miles north of Gilbert Town. The officers met for a conference during the evening, and it was decided that there should be a military head for the entire force assembled. Colonel Shelby argued to elect Colonel William Campbell, because he was a man devoted to the cause and he commanded the largest regiment. At first Campbell asked that his name be withdrawn but later agreed to accept the position. It was also agreed that they would seek a permanent commanding officer from headquarters. But for now Colonel Campbell was in charge of an army of over a thousand men.

It was believed that Ferguson was in Gilbert Town, so they began making preparations for the battle. There was no movement of the troops at this time due to the constant rain. Also, during this time two Patriot deserters, James Crawford and Samuel Chambers, reached Patrick Ferguson and warned him of the large militia force that was marching toward him. They made it clear to Ferguson that he would need to fight on the defensive and not as the aggressor. On October 1st Ferguson sent a letter out to the inhabitants of North Carolina,

> Gentlemen: Unless you wish to be eaten up by inundation of barbarians, who have begun by murdering an unarmed son before the aged father, and afterwards lopped off his arms, and who by their shocking cruelties and irregularties give the best proof of their cowardice and want of discipline—I say, if you wish to be pinioned, robbed and murdered, and see your wives and daughters in four days abused by the troops of mountain men—in short, if you wish, or deserve to live, and bear the name of men, grasp your arms in a moment and run to camp.
>
> The Black Water men have crossed the mountains; McDowell, Hampton, Shelby and Cleveland are at their head, so that you know what you have to depend upon. If you choose to be degraded forever and ever by a set of mongrels, say so at once, and let your women turn their backs upon you, and look out for real men to protect them.
>
> Pat. Ferguson, Major 71st Regiment[5]

For some reason Ferguson waited for three days before he began to leave Gilbert Town. Finally, he ordered his men to begin a retreat to General Cornwallis and his army in Charlotte, which was nearly seventy miles to the east. He sent word to Cornwallis that he was taking the road that led north of Kings Mountain, and he suggested that reinforcements be sent to meet him.

The Patriot militia reached Ferguson's camp on October 4 at Gilbert Town, and found that the Tories had already left and were marching east toward Cornwallis in Charlotte. So, that night they decided they needed to make a desperate attempt to overtake Ferguson, before he could reach the safety of the British army. In order to catch him, they decided to select all the men who had good horses and were best with a rifle. Around nine that evening, about 910 men left camp and began to march in pursuit of Ferguson. The men left behind were told to follow as fast as possible.

The pursuing Americans did not stop until late in the evening of the 6th, when they reached Cowpens about twenty miles from Kings Mountain. They ate supper, fed their horses, continued toward Ferguson in a hard rain, and rode until noon the next day.

Meanwhile, in the British camp Major Ferguson was not certain of a victory against the oncoming army of mountain men. The morning of the 6th he sent a dispatch to General Cornwallis asking for help,

> My Dear Lord: A doubt does not remain with regard to the intelligence I sent Your Lordship. They are since joined by Clark and Sumter, and of course are become an object of some consequence. Happily their leaders are obliged to feed their forces with such hopes and so flatter them with accounts of our weakness and fear that if necessary, I should hope for success, but, numbers compared, that must be doubtful.
>
> I am on my march toward you, my route leading from Cherokee Ford north of King's Mountain. Three or four hundred good soldiers, part dragoons, would finish the business. Something must be done soon. This is their last push in this quarter, etc.   Patrick Ferguson[6]

Patrick Ferguson would not receive any help from the British for several reasons. Toward the end of September Colonel Banastre Tarleton, along with other officers in the cavalry, had been taken seriously ill with the fever. Cornwallis was afraid to send troops to Ferguson without Tarleton in command. He later did request that Tarleton go to the aid of Ferguson, but Tarleton declined saying he was still too sick. Cornwallis was hesitant to aid Ferguson and leave Tarleton and his many sick troops undefended, and risk capture. If Tarleton and his men were captured, it would mean that Cornwallis would not only lose one of his best commanders, but he would also lose the recon information that Tarleton provided. So, Patrick Ferguson was left to face the mountain men alone.

With little rest, the Patriots continued their march on the 7th, and after traveling a mile they learned that Ferguson was only seven miles from them at Kings Mountain. Colonel Sevier's advance guard had captured several Tories who were out spying, and they gave the Patriots the position of Ferguson's camp and the location of his picket guard. The leaders held a council of war, decided that their plan of attack was to surround the enemy, and then attack on all sides simultaneously.

Without firing a shot, the Americans soon captured a Tory outpost. They were about a quarter of a mile from Ferguson's position, when they were finally discovered. When Ferguson was told that the mountain men had arrived, he ordered his men to take their positions and wait for the attack. The upcoming battle would be the largest battle of the war consisting of all American participants.

This battle would be particularly bloody for several reasons. It was fought between two opposing militias, and both were made up of fathers, sons, brothers, uncles, and cousins, who were serving together and in some cases against each other. Hatred between Tories and Patriots had been intensifying for many years. Each side felt that they were defending their homes and families. Four months earlier, at the Battle of Waxhaw, American troops under Colonel Abraham Buford had tried to surrender, and many of them were slaughtered as they begged for quarter by Tarleton's cavalry. Both militias entered the battle full of hate and vengeance.

The Battle of Kings Mountain

Kings Mountain took its name from the King family that lived at the foot of the range. The portion of Kings Mountain where the battle took place did not rise more than 100 feet above depressions drained by adjacent streams. The sides of the mountain were covered with trees spaced far enough apart, so that troop movements would not be hampered. The summit where Ferguson made his camp was bare, narrow, and stony with an outline like that of a canoe paddle. The camp was in an area about 500-600 yards long and 60-70 yards wide.

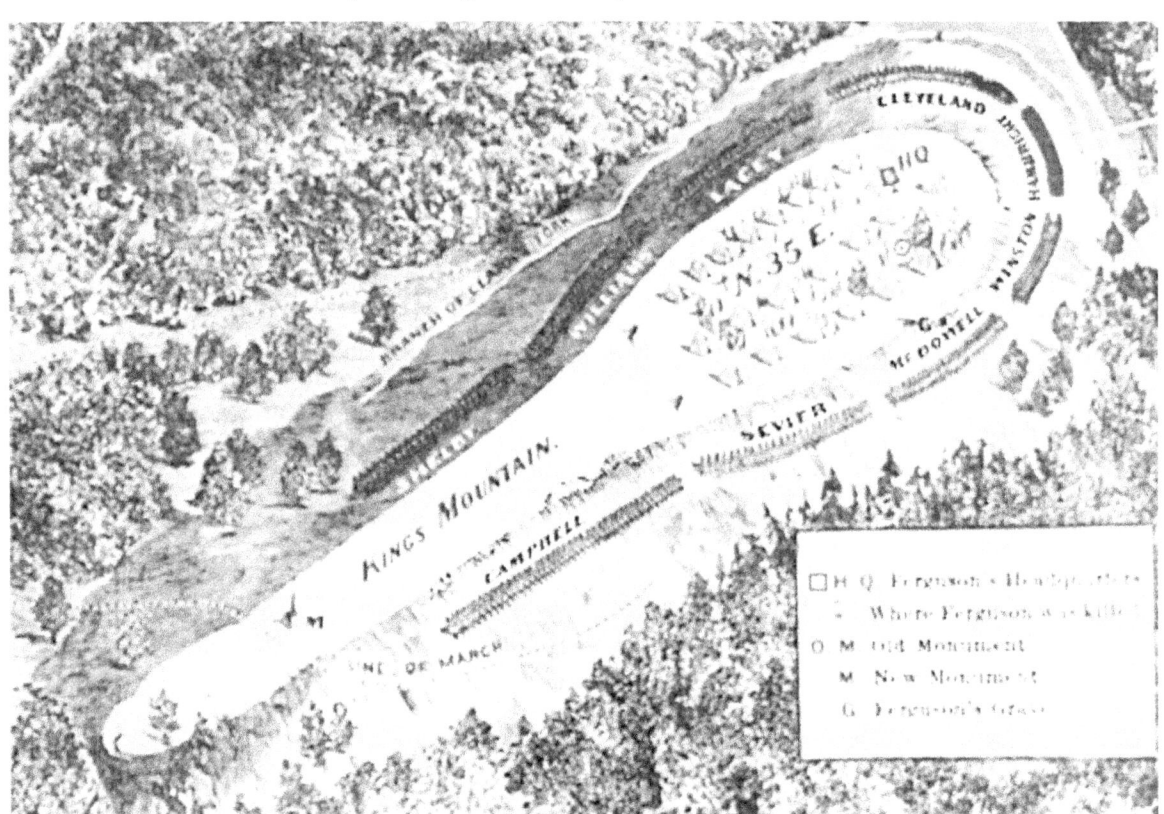

Battle of Kings Mountain taken from the book "Kings Mountain and Its Heroes" by Lyman C. Draper, Peter G. Thomson, Publisher, 1881.

There were ample trees that Ferguson could have cut down to make defensive breastworks. Instead, he placed his wagons and baggage along the northeast ridge, where his headquarters was located. He may have chosen not to make defensive preparations, because he was hoping that reinforcements would arrive in time.

However, Ferguson was convinced that his position on top of Kings Mountain was a good choice. Before the battle he remarked, "All the Rebels from hell could not drive me from it."⁷

The top of Kings Mountain as it appears today, looking toward the narrow part of the battlefield. Note that the area to the right and left of the path is not very wide before it starts to descend down the mountain. Photo by author

About two in the afternoon on October 7, the Americans began to encircle Ferguson's men on the top of Kings Mountain. They were told that the signal for attack would be loud frontier war-whoops. All were reminded to keep low and use the trees and rocks for cover, as they advanced up the mountain. Seventeen year old James Collins was about to take part in his first battle, and he recorded his thoughts in his journal,

> Near two o'clock in the afternoon we came in sight of the enemy, who seemed to be fully prepared to give battle at all risks. When we came up, we halted, and formed in order of battle, Shelby happened to be in command that day as every colonel took command day about. The men were disposed of in three divisions—the right was commanded by Cleveland and Sevier, the left by Campbell and Williams, and the center by Shelby and Hamright. The enemy was posted on a high, steep and ragged ridge, or spur of the mountain, very difficult of access, with a small stream of water running on each side: along each stream was a narrow strip of flat ground. The plan was to surround the mountain and attack them on all sides, if possible. In order to do this, the left had to march under the fire of the enemy to gain the position assigned to them, on the stream on the right of the enemy, while the right was to take possession of the other stream; in doing this they were not exposed, the cliff being so steep as to cover them completely. Each leader made a short speech in his own way to his men, desiring every coward to be off immediately; here I confess I would willingly have been

excused, for my feelings were not the most pleasant—this may be attributed to my youth, not being quite seventeen years of age—but I could not well swallow the appellation of coward. I looked around; every man's countenance seemed to change; well thought I, fate is fate, every man's fate is before him and he has to run it out, which I am inclined to think yet. I was commanded this day by Major Chronicle and Capt. Watson.[8]

Around three in the afternoon, the Americans began moving up the side of the mountain in Indian fashion. They took advantage of every rock and tree to fire behind, as they advanced. Major Ferguson soon ordered his first bayonet charge against the forces of Shelby and Campbell, which caused the Americans to retreat. Before the battle the Tories had whittled down handles of their butcher knives, so that they could be inserted in the muzzles of their rifles and serve as bayonets.

When the Tories rushed down the side of the mountain, the Patriots began to fall back. Colonel Campbell called for his men to halt their retreat and attack the enemy. The mountain men stopped the retreat, turned, and reloaded their rifles. With Colonel Campbell in the lead, they pushed the enemy back up the mountain. Three times the Patriots were attacked and driven back down the mountain, and each time the Patriots charged back.

Tory Captain Alexander Chesney, who served under Ferguson at the Battle of Kings Mountain, later wrote in his diary,

> So rapid was the attack that I was in the act of dismounting to report that all was quiet and the pickets on the alert when we heard their firing about a half mile off. I immediately paraded the men and posted officers. During this short interval I received a wound which however did not prevent me from doing my duty; and going towards my horse I found he had been killed by the first discharge.[9]

Many of the volleys from Ferguson's men were missing their mark by passing over the heads of the Patriots. The mountain men, on the other hand, were taking a deadly toll with their rifles. They shot from cover, which allowed them to be more accurate. A marksman in the valley had an advantage to one on the hill. The men on the hill often shot too high, when they were above their targets.

During the battle, Patrick Ferguson seemed to be everywhere encouraging his men to fight. He could be seen racing from one side of the hill to the other on his white horse, while blowing his silver whistle. He carried the whistle in his wounded left hand that had been shattered at the Battle of Brandywine. Ferguson would rush to his troops, whenever they began to be driven back, offering them encouragement and blowing the whistle for them to advance.

Attacking from all sides, the Americans began to reach the summit, and Ferguson could not be everywhere. His men began to fall under the relentless and accurate fire of the Americans. The Tories were out in the open with no cover available for protection, surrounded, and outnumbered.

By three thirty in the afternoon, Colonels Sevier, McDowell, Shelby, and Winston's men reached the summit without being charged by bayonets, they rushed to support Campbell's men.

Campbell's men reached the summit, while Ferguson was directing a bayonet charge at the troops of Colonel Cleveland.

James Collins had survived three bayonet attacks by the Tories and later wrote,

> We were soon in motion, every man throwing four or five balls in his mouth to prevent thirst; also to be in readiness to reload quick. The shot of the enemy soon began to pass over us like hail; the first shock was quickly over, and for my own part, I was soon in a profuse sweat. My lot happened to be in the centre, where the severest part of the battle was fought. We soon attempted to climb the hill, but were fiercely charged upon and forced to fall back to our first position; we tried a second time, but met the same fate; the fight then seemed to become more furious. Their leader, Ferguson, came in full view, within rifle shot as if to encourage his men, who by this time were falling very fast; he soon disappeared. We took to the hill a third time; the enemy gave way; when we had gotten near the top some of our leaders roared out, "Hurra, my brave fellows! Advance! They are crying for quarter."[10]

Sevier and Shelby united their forces at the summit and drove the enemy to one end of the ridge. At times, the combat became hand-to-hand and personal. The Tories were being slaughtered, yet Ferguson would not think of surrendering. Some accounts of the battle reported that some Tories began to show some flags of surrender, which Ferguson would ride up and cut down with his sword.

As the battle raged on, Ferguson had two horses shot from under him. When finally killed, he was in the direction of Sevier's men. James Collins had survived the ascent to the top of the mountain and described what he saw,

> By this time, the right and left had gained the top of the cliff; the enemy was completely hemmed in on all sides, and no chance of escaping—besides, their leader had fallen. They soon threw down their arms and surrendered. After the fight was over, the situation of the poor Tories appeared to be really pitiable; the dead lay in heaps on all sides, while the groans of the wounded were heard in every direction. I could not help turning away from the scene before me, with horror, and though exulting in victory, could not refrain from shedding tears,--"Great God!" said I. "Is this the fate of mortals, or was it for this cause that man was brought into the world?"[11]

Toward the end of the battle there were several white flags of surrender being raised, without the sanction of a commanding officer. Charles Bowen shot one man off his horse that raised a flag. Major Ferguson had knocked flags from several of his men, and even Captain De Peyster had a flag of surrender knocked away after the death of Ferguson. In the heat of battle many of the Patriots continued to fire without comprehending the meaning of the flags going up and then down. After the battle, some of them even said they did not know what a white flag meant. So, firing continued while men were trying to surrender. These Patriots were from the backwoods, and some were not familiar with the rules of war.

According to Mills' *Statistics of South Carolina,* "When the British found themselves pressed on all sides, they hung out white handkerchiefs upon guns and halberds. Few of the Americans understood the signal, and a few that did, chose not to know what it meant; so that, even after submission, the slaughter continued until the Americans were weary of killing."[12]

Lieutenant Joseph Hughes wrote in his pension application in 1833,

> General Williams [James Williams was a Colonel at the time] of S. Carolina was killed after the British raised their flag to surrender by a fire from some Tories. Col. Campbell then ordered a fire on the Tories & we killed near a hundred of them after the surrender of the British & could hardly be restrained from killing the whole of them.[13]

After the fighting, some of the Tory officers were looking for an American commander in order to surrender their swords. They were surprised when the Americans pointed out Colonel Campbell to receive the honor. The Colonel did not look like a leader, because he was walking around in his shirt sleeves and open collar.

Once the fighting had stopped, people in the countryside began to appear to see who had won the battle. Some of the women arrived, stayed, and acted as nurses to care for the injured. Unfortunately, some came to scavenge the dead bodies for treasures.

The soldiers had to sleep on the battlefield that night amidst the dead, the groans of the wounded, and the cries for water. Patriot John Spelts recalled,

> The groans of the wounded and dying on the mountain were truly affecting—begging piteously for a little water, but in the hurry, confusion and exhaustion of the patriots, these cries, when emanating from the Tories, were little heeded.[14]

Thirty-seven year old Colonel Arthur Campbell wrote an interesting observation of the battle,

> It has been remarked why so small a number of the Americans were killed at Kings Mountain, compared with the loss of the enemy. Our officers accounted for it in this way: The Tories occupied much the least space of ground, and of course were more thickly planted than the extended circle of the Americans around them, so that the fire of our men seldom failed doing execution; besides, when the Virginia regiment reached to the other end, without returning a shot; and when they were driven into a huddle by meeting the fire of Col. Williams division, they received a heavy fire before our troops could be notified of the surrender.[15]

Importance of the battle:

The battle lasted a little over an hour, and the American victory led to the destruction of the Tory influence in North Carolina and forced the retreat of General Cornwallis. It was a victory for the people that were willing to fight and die without pay, at their own expense, and without the expectation of any reward. The number of casualties in the battle varied from source to source. The Patriots had twenty-six to thirty-five killed with twice that number wounded, while the Tories suffered 290 killed, 163 wounded, and over 660 men captured.

British Colonel Tarleton later wrote in his book that the victory "weakened the army of Cornwallis, was the total ruin of his militia, and presented a gloomy prospect at the start of his campaign in the south." The victory proved to be the beginning of the end of British rule in the colonies. One year later Cornwallis would surrender to George Washington at Yorktown.

This loss crushed the spirit of the Tories and weakened beyond recovery the influence of the British in the Carolinas. Cornwallis had hoped to move with ease from one Carolina to another and then conquer Virginia, now he was left with no choice but to retreat.

If the Tories in North Carolina had intended to rise up and join the British, they were now utterly discouraged. They had seen their own army under Ferguson defeated and with many killed and captured. They saw their British protector, Cornwallis, marching in panic to South Carolina.

Washington Irving wrote, "The battle of King's Mountain, inconsiderable as it was in the numbers engaged, turned the tide of Southern warfare. The destruction of Ferguson and his corps gave a complete check to the expedition of Cornwallis."[16]

Colonel Shelby wrote about the battle to Governor Sevier of Tennessee on February 24, 1810,

> It was an enterprise undertaken from pure and patriotic motives, without the aid of the Government, at a time that tried the souls of men. In its consequences, the salvation of North Carolina, inasmuch as it obliged Lord Cornwallis to retreat out of the State with the whole British army, and he could not advance until he was reinforced from New York. Besides, in the great scale of our national affairs, it was the very first perceivable event that gave a favorable turn to the American Revolution.[17]

Impact of the British decisions leading up to the battle:

Days before the Battle of Kings Mountain, there were several very poor decisions made by the leadership of the Tories and British. The first was made by Tory leader Patrick Ferguson. When he was at Gilbert Town, knowing that a Patriot force was marching to him, rather than leaving at once for the safety of Cornwallis, for some reason he chose to wait for three days to march. This was ample time to allow the Patriots to get close enough to him, which later forced him to make a stand against them.

The next bad decision Ferguson made was his selection of Kings Mountain for his final stand against the Patriots. He knew many of his men were untested in battle, so he may have picked this site because they would not be able to run once the battle began. The top of the mountain was not defensible from attacks from all sides at the same time. Advancing troops had plenty of protection from the trees, while the top had few trees and offered no protection for the Tories. In addition, Ferguson failed to build any strong defensive breastworks along the ridge. Instead, he hoped that reinforcements from Cornwallis would arrive in time and save him.

The worst decision involved Cornwallis. He had an ample amount of men and could have sent a relief force to rescue the Tories. Since Tarleton was ill and could not lead the rescue force,

Cornwallis did not trust anyone else to command the troops. So, he chose to lose 1,000 militiamen, which left him with little hope of being able to replace them.

In his book after the war, Tarleton was quick to blame Cornwallis for not sending Ferguson reinforcements in time,

> Near the end of September, Major Ferguson had intelligence of Clarke's having joined Sumpter, and that a swarm of backwoodsmen, by an unexpected and rapid approach to Gilbert Town, now threaten his destruction. He dispatched information to Earl Cornwallis of the superior numbers to which he was opposed. A detachment did not march in time from Charlottetown to yield him assistance.[18]

Cornwallis responded to Tarleton's comments in a letter he sent to the Bishop of Lichfield and Coventry on December 12, 1787,

> Tarleton's is a most malicious and false attack; he knew and approved the reasons for several of the measures which he now blames. My not sending relief to Colonel Ferguson, although he was positively ordered to retire, was entirely owing to Tarleton himself; he pleaded weakness from the remains of a fever, and refused to make an attempt, although I used the most earnest entreaties. I mention this as proof, amongst many others, of his candour. I know it is very foolish to be vexed about these things, but yet it touches me in a tender point.[19]

In the response, Cornwallis said that he ordered Ferguson to retire, but he does not say when that order was sent or whether Ferguson received it. A letter from Cornwallis, dated September 23, was found in Ferguson's baggage after the battle. There was no order for retreating, and it gave the impression that Ferguson was safe.

Sir Henry Clinton, the British Commander- in -Chief in America, blamed Lord Cornwallis for detaching Ferguson without any support of regular troops, when his Lordship had previously stated that Ferguson's hopes of success of his Tory militia "were contrary to the experience of the army, as well as of Major Ferguson himself," and "that his Lordship should, after this opinion, not only suffer Colonel Ferguson to be detached without support, but put such a river as the Catawba between him and Ferguson. It was a matter of wonder to Sir H. Clinton and all who knew it."[20]

11

Washington Appoints Nathanael Greene Commander of the Southern Army

"Greene is as dangerous as Washington. He is vigilant, enterprising, and full of resources. With but little hope of gaining any advantage over him."

---British General Charles Cornwallis

The "Fighting Quaker":

Nathanael Greene was born on August 7, 1742, in Warwick, Rhode Island. His father, a Quaker preacher, discouraged book learning, dancing, and other activities. Nathanael managed to convince his father to hire a tutor, who taught him mathematics, the classics, law, and other various subjects. After the death of his father in 1770, he and his brother inherited the family foundry, and Nathanael began to collect a large library that included books on military history.

When England began to impose economic policies on the colonies, Nathanael began his opposition to British rule. Also during this time, he started to stray away from his father's Quaker beliefs, especially regarding serving in the military. This soon led to his suspension from Quaker meetings. In 1774 Nathanael helped form the Kentish Guards, which were organized to protect East Greenwich from the Tories.

At thirty-two, Nathanael was 5'10", a handsome man with a sharp mind, and he had a strong resolve. At times he was impulsive, and he could be very sensitive to criticism. Greene was strongly built with broad shoulders. However, he was also susceptible to health problems. When there was an outbreak of smallpox, he was inoculated which left him with a slight blemish in his right eye, but fortunately it did not affect his sight. He suffered from asthma, which cost him many sleepless nights. Nathanael, after a childhood accident, had a stiffness in his right knee, which caused him to limp. Once a dance partner remarked to him that he danced stiffly, and Greene replied, "Very true, but you see that I dance strong."[1]

General Nathanael Greene, National Achieves

While Greene was serving in the guard, he was told that his stiff leg disqualified him from being an officer and perhaps even a private. He responded in a letter, "I was informed the gentlemen of East Greenwich said I was a blemish to the company. I confess it is my misfortune to limp a little, but I did not conceive it to be so great; but we are not apt to discover our own defects."[2]

He was allowed to remain in the guard as a private, but he needed a musket. So, Nathanael went to Boston and purchased a musket and while there he encouraged a British deserter to return home with him and be a drill instructor for the Kentish Guard. It soon became obvious that Greene had the knowledge and ability to be a leader of men, so his limp was overlooked and he was appointed commander of the Rhode Island Regiment. Since he had risen in the ranks from a private, the men saw him as one of them and quickly accepted him as their commander. In the summer of 1775 the regiment marched to Boston and joined in the siege.

The rise of Nathanael Greene:

Washington arrived in Boston on July 1775 and took command of the new Continental Army. Congress appointed sixteen generals to serve with Washington, and Greene was the last name on the list. Washington divided the army into three grand divisions, and he placed Greene in command of seven regiments in the left wing under the command of General Charles Lee.

When the British were forced to leave Boston, Washington moved his army to New York, and he left Boston under the command of Greene. In April 1776 Greene rejoined Washington in New York, and that September he saw combat for the first time at the Battle of Harlem. Later, Greene commanded troops at the battles of Trenton, Princeton, Brandywine, and Germantown.

While Greene was at Valley Forge in the winter of 1777 to 1778, Congress, under the suggestion of Washington, offered the appointment of Quartermaster General to Greene, who promptly turned it down. He thought that the position offered no honor or reward, as he later wrote to Washington, "Nobody ever head of a quartermaster in history."[3]

Washington asked him to reconsider, and he reluctantly accepted the position due to Washington's urging. Greene told Washington, "Your task is too great, to be Commander-in-Chief and Quartermaster at the same time. I will serve a year."[4] Greene only accepted with the understanding that he retain his place in the line and his right to command in action.

Greene took part in the Battle of Monmouth in June 1778, and the next month he was given temporary leave as Quartermaster General, so he could take part in an attack on the British in his home state of Rhode Island. He continued serving as Quartermaster General and taking part in several battles, until he resigned his position shortly after fighting in the Battle of Springfield on

July 23, 1780. After Benedict Arnold turned traitor, Greene was briefly appointed to serve as Commandant of West Point.

Nathanael Greene is given command of the southern army:

The war had shifted to the south, and by fall 1780, the Americans suffered two shocking defeats. During the previous May, General Benjamin Lincoln, the commander of the southern army, had surrendered his army of over 5,000 troops at Charleston, and later General Horatio Gates suffered a humiliating defeat on August 16. Gates, still vain about his success at Saratoga, never learned how little he was responsible for that victory, and so he falsely assumed he would have an easy victory over Cornwallis.

Gates, with nearly twice the number of troops, was soundly defeated by British General Cornwallis at Camden, South Carolina. At the end of the fighting, Gates was seen rapidly riding away from the field of battle in disgrace. When the news of the defeat reached Washington's headquarters, Alexander Hamilton mockingly wrote of Gates' flight, "Was there ever an instance of a general running away, as Gates has done from his whole army? And was there ever so precipitous a flight? One hundred and eighty miles in three days and a half! It does admirable credit to the activity of a man at his time of life."[5]

With these two defeats, it appeared that the war was lost in the south. After the defeat of Gates, Washington made a decision that would change the course of the war in the south, when he appointed General Nathanael Greene as commander of the Southern Army.

When Greene was serving as Quartermaster General, Washington knew that he was not happy with the assignment since he desired a field command. At the time, Washington had written to Greene, "If it points to a resignation of your present office, and your inclination leads you to the southward, my wish shall accompany it; and if the appointment of a successor to General Lincoln [the present commander of the Southern Army] is left to me, I shall not hesitate in preferring you to this command."[6] Washington had kept his promise.

For more than five years, Greene had been at Washington's right hand. He had been in every battle in which Washington had commanded, with the single exception of White Plains. Greene had become the chief subordinate, in whom Washington placed his main reliance. Washington had grown to appreciate fully the merit of such a steadfast officer, and he had the most complete confidence in Greene's judgment and ability. However, this intimate association was about to come to an end.

Greene was to be transferred to where he was to act on his own responsibility. For the greater part of the next year Washington was to be inactive, and the fighting and marching were to be done under Greene's sole command. In a letter to Greene, Washington gave him the freedom to conduct the campaign in the south using his own judgement, "I rely upon your abilities for everything your means will enable you to effect."⁷

While Greene was traveling south to assume his new command, his spirits were lifted when he learned that the American militia had defeated British Loyalists at the Battle of Kings Mountain. The advance of Cornwallis into North Carolina had been checked by the victory at Kings Mountain, but the war in the South had only just begun.

Greene assumed command of the southern army under the most unfavorable circumstances. The British controlled much of Georgia and South Carolina, which included their governments. Cornwallis was a commander of exceptional ability with a superior army. Greene's army was weak, morale was low, and they were poorly equipped.

He was constantly under the apprehension that his ragtag army would disband. Since most of his army were volunteers, the men would often leave without permission and be gone for several weeks. In order to stop this, soon after he arrived Greene ordered that the next man guilty of this sort of desertion should be shot. He described his army in a letter to General Knox, "The so-called Southern army was rather a shadow than a substance, having only an imaginary existence."⁸

The British controlled the ports of Savannah and Charleston, and now their confidence was so high that General Clinton divided his army and sailed to New York City. He left behind General Cornwallis who had over 6,000 troops and a cavalry commanded by Banastre Tarleton, who had never been defeated. Victory over the rebels in the south now seemed a real possibility.

Nathanael Greene loses every battle he fights in and wins the south:

Many historians claimed that General Nathanael Greene engaged in guerrilla warfare against the British, because his army was highly mobile and he liked to use mounted troops. This is not completely true, although he did approve of guerrilla tactics while he rebuilt his army. Greene used mounted guerrillas, such as Francis Marion, as spies and as a means to harass the British. The previous commander, General Horatio Gates, disapproved of using guerrilla fighters such as Marion, the celebrated "Swamp Fox."

Marion was a very effective leader, even though he did not look the part. One British officer that encountered him described him in a letter as a, "....swarthy, smoke-dried little man, with scarce enough of threadbare home spun to cover his nakedness." On the other hand, Nathanael Greene had a great amount of respect for the ability of Marion when he said, "As a partisan officer, the page of history never furnished his equal."⁹

Nathanael Greene actually engaged in conventional warfare against the British. He avoided putting his army at any great risk, even though he could afford casualties better than the British.

Greene knew that even if he lost a battle, it would cost the British more men than they could replace. So, the American army began to play a cat-and-mouse game with the larger British army of Cornwallis. Greene only began his offensive when his army was significantly larger than the British Army and his logistical situation was as stable as possible. He desired to have a "flying army," who would be lightly equipped, mobile, and as familiar as possible with the country they traveled.

Greene fought two battles, several small ones, and a siege in South Carolina. Each was considered a technical loss as men judged victory in that era, but each bled the British Army of men it could not afford to lose, while American losses were replaceable. South Carolina had a high percentage of Loyalists compared to the rest of the colonies. However, South Carolina fielded twice the number of Patriot military forces than the Loyalists. As a result, Greene was able to replace his loses more effectively than Cornwallis.

When Greene took command of the army, Gates had earlier sent Daniel Morgan with a small force to probe British defenses. Instead of recalling Morgan, Greene sent him more men and thus divided his forces. Dividing your army in the face of superior numbers was a risky move for Greene to take. Morgan now had roughly 600 men, and Greene was left with 1,100 Continental troops to face more than 6,000 British soldiers.

Shocked that Greene divided his army, Cornwallis was forced to divide his forces, and sent Colonel Tarleton to follow Morgan, while his main force faced Greene. Making this decision left Cornwallis in no position to invade North Carolina.

So for the time being, Greene probed and maneuvered to put his army in position to give himself every possible advantage in combat, such as assuming a defensive posture, gaining the high ground, or making certain his line of retreat was clear and established. His objective was to have Cornwallis follow him, which would draw the British many miles from their supplies and reinforcements.

Battle of Cowpens January 17, 1781:

General Daniel Morgan and British Colonel Tarleton met in a major battle at Cowpens, South Carolina on January 17, 1781. The size of the American forces is disputed and ranged between 600 to 1,900 troops, while the British fielded over 1,500 troops.

Knowing that the undefeated Tarleton would be overconfident, Morgan placed the militia in the middle of his line to encourage Tarleton to attack there. Morgan instructed the militia to fire two volleys and retreat back to a line of experienced troops out of sight in the rear. His plan was simple; to draw Tarleton into a trap.

Shortly after sunrise, Tarleton's men emerged from the woods and with little preparation quickly attacked the American center. Tarleton knew from experience that the militia would break and run, which on this occasion they did. The American center line stopped retreating, turned, and mounted a bayonet charge, while other troops began to encircle the British. The British, drawn into the trap, panicked and began to surrender. After an hour the battle was over, and Tarleton managed to escape only by the speed of his horse. The retreating British left eighty-six percent of their men killed, wounded, or captured. It was later reported that when Tarleton reported the disaster to Cornwallis, the General placed his sword tip on the ground and leaned on it until the blade snapped.

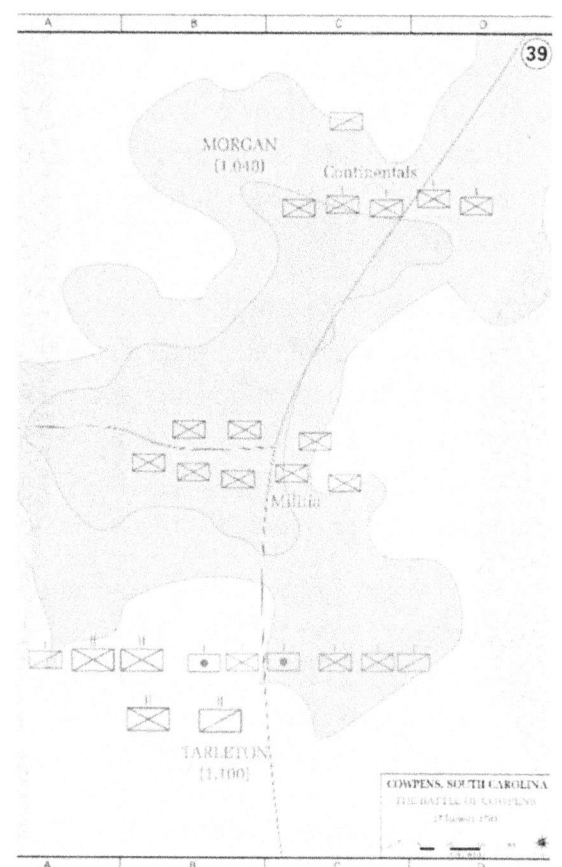

The Battle of Cowpens Map courtesy of the USMA, Department of History

Cowpens today looking toward the American positions. It has been kept close to how it looked at the time of the battle. The field of battle itself was open woodland, sloping to the front, and well adapted for skirmishing, while sufficiently clear of under growth for the movements of mounted men, Tarleton says, "there could be no better." Photo by author

William Seymour, a Sergeant Major in the Delaware Regiment, recorded his thoughts about the battle in his journal, "This victory on our side can be attributed to nothing else but Divine Providence, they having thirteen hundred in the field of their best troops, and we not eight hundred of standing troops and militia."[10]

After the battle, Cornwallis pursued Morgan, so he burned some of his own supplies in order to travel faster after Morgan. Greene joined forces with Morgan, and the combined army retreated into North Carolina, which drew Cornwallis even further from his supply lines. He hoped to wear out the British by constantly tempting them with the prospect of a battle, as he constantly avoided one. Greene was able to get his army safely across the Dan River into North Carolina, which was just moments ahead of the British. With his army exhausted, Cornwallis broke off the pursuit and camped.

An interesting story occurred during the retreat by Greene. After riding most of the day, the general stopped at an inn to rest. When he was asked about his health, Greene replied, "Fatigued, hungry, alone, and penniless." The hard journey had left the general in low spirits.

Mrs. Elizabeth Steele, the hostess of the inn, chanced to overhear these words but said nothing. When Greene was seated at a table, she entered the room, closed the door, and took from under her apron two bags of coins, which she had saved for emergencies. "Take these," said the woman, offering them to him, "You will want them, and I can do without them." Greene accepted the money with thanks and continued his journey with a lighter heart. Such was the patriotism of the women during the Revolution.[11]

In a letter to Greene, Washington fully supported his retreat from Cornwallis, "You may be assured that your retreat before Lord Cornwallis is highly applauded by all ranks, and reflects much honor on your military abilities."[12]

Alexander Hamilton later wrote of Greene's retreat, "The art of retreating is perhaps the most difficult in the art of war. To have effected a retreat in the face of so ardent a pursuit, through so great an extent of country; through a country offering every obstacle; affording scarcely any resource; with troops destitute of everything, who a great part of the way left the vestiges of their march in their own blood: to have done all this, I say, without loss of any kind, may, without exaggeration, be denominated a masterpiece of military skill and exertion."[13]

Battle of Guilford Court House:

In early March, Greene had received reinforcements from North Carolina and Virginia, which increased the size of his army. Greene's forces now consisted of about 4,400 troops with over half being militia. Cornwallis had about 2,200 battle hardened troops, many of which had been fighting since 1776. On the 14th Greene led his army to Guilford Courthouse in North

Carolina to face Cornwallis in battle. He used the same tactics that Morgan used at Cowpens, which was placing the militia in the center, firing a few shots, and then fleeing.

This battle was important for both generals. Cornwallis needed a victory over Greene to persuade the people of North Carolina to remain loyal to the Crown, and to assure them that he could protect them from the Patriots. On the other hand, Greene needed a victory to show North Carolina that he could save them from the British. If he lost, his newly arrived militiamen would probably desert him.

Battle of Guilford Courthouse Painting. Greene is leading on horseback just before the American bayonet charge. Public domain

The battle lasted only ninety minutes. The British were outnumbered more than two to one, and yet they defeated the American force. In doing so, however, Cornwallis lost a quarter of his men, while Greene lost around seven per cent. The Americans withdrew intact, which accomplished Greene's primary objective. The loss ratio was such that Cornwallis never sought battle with Greene again.

William Seymour wrote in his diary, "Lord Cornwallis, however, afterwards confessed that General Greene had the honor of the field, and likewise the best of the battle, if he did but known it."[14]

Cornwallis was right, and Greene did not realize that he had done well in the battle. In his letters to Washington and Congress he expressed regret that he had lost the day. Greene was worn out and was near the limit of his physical endurance. For the past six weeks he had not taken time to change his clothes, and for days before the battle and several days after it, he had barely slept even four hours a night.

One night during this time, Greene was making the rounds and found a colonel asleep who was in command of a large outpost. He asked the drowsy soldier how he could sleep when he was near the enemy, and might be attacked at any time. The soldier replied, "Why, General, we all knew you would be awake."[15]

Much was written about the British "victory" at Guilford Courthouse. Greene wrote after the battle, "The enemy gained his cause, but is ruined by the success of it." Tarleton regarded it, "the victory as the pledge of ultimate defeat." In England, Charles Fox in the House of Commons said, "Another such victory would ruin the British Army."[16]

After the battle, Cornwallis retreated with his army to Wilmington, North Carolina and was followed by Greene's troops. In late April, the British army, who were weakened and exhausted, marched north to Yorktown. Washington ordered Lafayette to go south to join with the forces of von Steuben to pursue Cornwallis. This freed Greene to turn south and engage the troops under Francis Rawdon for control of South Carolina and Georgia. After several battles, which were tactical losses, Greene gained control of most of the south by September 1781. By the end of 1781, British control in the south was limited to the seaports cities of Savannah and Charleston.

Washington's decision to appoint Greene Commander of the Southern Army wins the war in the south:

Nathanael Greene had lost every battle he led troops in, despite of having the larger army. Yet, he defeated the British in the south. Greene baffled the British over and over again. He gained from his losses greater advantages than his opponent gained from their victories.

The cause of each loss was not due to the individual qualities of the troops or their leader, rather to factors beyond the control of Greene. A large portion of his troops lacked experience, discipline, served for a short period of time, and had little training.

Due to his perseverance, tactics, and leadership, the man once considered unfit to be an officer was now considered to be the second best American general behind only George Washington. Washington was aware of this fact, because he said that in the event of his death during the war, General Greene should be appointed his successor in the chief command.[17]

Greene's ability was also recognized by his adversary, General Charles Cornwallis, who remarked that Greene, "is as dangerous as Washington. He is vigilant, enterprising, and full of resources. There was little hope of gaining any advantage over him."[18]

Since he could not depend on the militia, which was the majority of his army, he was forced to give personal supervision to everything. He slept very little, partly due to his asthma, and spent his waking time checking on his troops, while rarely relaxing. After the battle of Eutaw Springs, he wrote to the Committee of War, "I have been seven months in the field without taking off my clothes."[19]

If Gates had not been so soundly defeated at Camden, it is unlikely that Greene would have been given command of the Southern Army. If Cornwallis had continued to go unchecked in the south, there probably would have been no Yorktown victory, and the outcome of the war would have been much different.

At the close of the war, the states of South Carolina and Georgia showed their appreciation to General Greene. South Carolina presented him with an estate valued at over fifty thousand dollars, and Georgia gave him an estate near Savannah worth over twenty-five thousand dollars.

12

Yorktown: No Where to Run

"General Washington and the army, are gone to take Lord Cornwallis in his mouse trap."
---William Clajon secretary to General Horatio Gates

Background:

As the year 1781 began, General George Washington warned anyone that would listen that his army was tired and the supporters of the war had grown discontent. In a letter to John Laurens dated January 15, 1781, he wrote, "The people are discontented, but it is with the feeble and oppressive mode of conducting the war, not with the war itself."[1]

John Adams feared that France, faced with growing debts and the lack of progress in the war, might stop her support within the year. It appeared that if there was not a major American victory in 1781, the fate of the country would be decided at a conference table consisting of the great European powers.

After six years, the war in the colonies was also growing unpopular back home in England. The British controlled only a handful of coastal cities in America, and around the world they were in a war with Spain and France. Prominent men such as Horace Walpole, 4th Earl of Oxford and a former member of parliament and a man of many letters, began to become critical of the war. In a letter to the Countess of Ailesbury on July 10, 1779, he wrote, "We could not conquer America when it stood alone; then France supported it, and we did not mend the matter. To make it still easier, we have driven Spain into the alliance. Is this wisdom?"[2]

It was clear that one side needed to score a knock-out blow and seize the victory. Both Cornwallis and Washington saw that this knock-out would come in Virginia in 1781.

In January of 1781, Washington ordered Lafayette to take a force of troops south to link up with soldiers commanded by Baron von Steuben. In Virginia on June 18, Lieutenant Ebenezer Denny of the 4th Pennsylvania Regiment joined the troops under the command of General Lafayette. In his journal he wrote the following description of his new army,

> The Marquis [Lafayette] had marched two or three days to meet us. His men look as if they were fit for business. They are chiefly all light infantry, dressed in frocks and over-alls of linen. One day spent in washing and refreshing, in fixing arms, carriages &c, and served out ammunition. Move toward Richmond, where Lord Cornwallis with the British army lay. Heard that his lordship was employed burning and destroying warehouses of tobacco, all public store-houses, &c. Passed through Richmond toward Williamsburg after the enemy, joined by Baron Steuben with some new levies.[3]

After the Battle of Guilford Courthouse, the army of General Nathanael Greene, which had been pursuing Cornwallis, turned to go further south into South Carolina and Georgia to challenge British commander Francis Rawdon for control of those two colonies. This left General Lafayette and his army of about 3,000 troops to face Cornwallis in Virginia. By the end of June, Cornwallis was marching toward Williamsburg with a reinforced army of over 7,000 troops. He was followed by Lafayette, whose forces had increased to 4,500 men.

A series of British blunders or poor decisions:

In June of 1781 the focus of the war in the south was in Virginia. There were over 7,000 British troops there, and some of the leadership on both sides believed that the war could be decided there. General Washington, however, was focused on capturing New York City, and British commander Sir Henry Clinton was determined to prevent it.

The two British commanders, Cornwallis and Clinton, faced several large problems. One was that the two men were not very fond of one another and constantly engaged in petty squabbling. At times, Cornwallis failed to keep Clinton informed of his movements while in the south. In fact, he did not even tell Clinton of his march into Virginia until late in May of 1781.

Another problem was on numerous occasions, due to changing conditions, a letter sent to one was irrelevant by the time it reached the other person. Also, Clinton was sending many letters by different messengers, so they arrived at various times and in no particular order. This set the stage for a series of confusing orders from Clinton.

Fear of the enemy took hold of Clinton early in June, when he learned through intercepted letters that New York was threatened with a siege by General Washington. He immediately called upon Cornwallis for 3,000 troops to be sent to him.

If Cornwallis had sent the 3,000 troops to Clinton, it would have given the Americans a superior number of troops over the British in the south. Aware of this, Cornwallis made excuses why he was unable at the time to send the additional troops to Clinton. General Clinton's decision to reinforce the northern army, at the expense of the army of Virginia, was based upon an overestimation of Cornwallis's strength and an underestimation of Lafayette's command.

Clinton was aware that the French fleet was sailing for the American coast, and he assumed that once it arrived at New York, Washington and his French allies would attack him. Clinton wanted Cornwallis to select a spot in Virginia, where he could easily embark some of his troops to return to New York and reinforce Clinton. He directed Cornwallis to take a strong position on the Chesapeake. He first ordered him to Portsmouth and then later to Yorktown to build fortifications for a deep water port.

When General Clinton learned that nearly 3,000 reinforcements were being sent to him from Europe, he countermanded the orders for Cornwallis to send troops to New York. Clinton wrote to him on June 19, "I shall not, as I have already told you, press you for the corps I wished to have sent me, at least for the present."[4]

While General Clinton was sending conflicting dispatches during the summer to General Cornwallis, Washington continued to probe the New York area. During this time there were several skirmishes between the British and American armies.

On July 3 with nearly 900 troops, General Benjamin Lincoln attempted to take the British garrison by surprise and capture Kingsbridge. This bridge controlled the access to New York City from the mainland. The attempt failed, but concern about another move by Washington to take the city encouraged British General Clinton to again call for reinforcements from Cornwallis in Virginia.

Then on July 20 a runner arrived at the camp of Cornwallis at 1 o'clock with a dispatch that reversed all of Clinton's previous demands for troops. The letter was dated the 11th of July,

> I cannot be more explicit by this opportunity than to desire, that if you have not already passed the James river, you will continue on the Williamsburg Neck, until she [the dispatch frigate] arrives with my dispatches by Captain Stapleton. If you have passed, and find it expedient to recover that station, you will please to do it, and keep possession until you hear further from me. Whatever troops may have been embarked by you for this place, are likewise to remain until further orders; and if they should have been sailed, and within your call, you will be pleased to stop them. It is the Admiral's and my wish, at all events to hold Old Point Comfort, which secures Hampton road.[5]

Americans put pressure on the British:

On July 6 the French and American armies met at White Plains, which was about thirty miles north of New York City. The Americans needed help from the French, and without it their revolution most likely would be lost.

The two leaders, Washington and Rochambeau, discussed where to launch their joint attack. Washington wanted it to be New York, because with their combined forces the British would be outnumbered three to one. Rochambeau did not agree. He said an attack on the Chesapeake area was a better option, since the French fleet was going to sail from the West Indies under Admiral De Grasse and return by mid-October. The Admiral was pleased to be leaving the port in the West Indies during this time, because the memory of three large hurricanes in the Indies during the late summer and early fall were still fresh in his mind. In addition, De Grasse felt the Chesapeake area with a deep harbor was better suited for his large vessels.

Meanwhile back in the south, thirty-two year old Josiah Atkins of the 5th Connecticut Regiment was marching with the army of General Lafayette. He kept a journal from April until mid-October of 1781. He recorded an entry about germ warfare used by British General Cornwallis,

> Within these days passed I have marched by 18 or 20 negroes that lay dead by the wayside, putrifying with the small pox. How such a thing came about, appears to be thus: The negroes here being much disaffected (arising from their harsh treatment), flocked in great numbers to Cornwallis. This artful general takes a number of them (several hundreds) inoculates them, and just as they are growing sick, he sends them out into the country where our people had to pass and repass. These poor creatures, having no care taken of them, many crawled into the bushes about and died. This is a piece of Cornwallisean cruelty. He is not backward to own that he has inoculated 4 or 500 in order to spread the smallpox through the country and to send them out for that purpose. Which is another piece of his conduct that that wants a name. But there is a King far above the British King, and a Lord superior to their lords.[6]

After marching around in central Virginia, Cornwallis moved to Williamsburg by the end of June. Generals Lafayette and Wayne followed Cornwallis closely during this time, as they waited for the right moment to attack. On June 30, 1781, Cornwallis was in Williamsburg and wrote to Sir Henry Clinton,

> LaFayette's Continentals, I believe, consist of about 1700 or 1800 men, exclusive of some twelvemonths' men, collected by Steuben. He has received considerable reinforcements of militia and almost 800 mountain riflemen under Campbell. He keeps with his main corps about eighteen or twenty miles from us, his advanced corps about ten or twelve, probably with an intention of insulting our rear-guard when we pass James River; I hope, however, to put that out of his power by crossing at James City Island, and if I can get a favourable opportunity of striking a blow at him without a loss of time, I will certainly try it.[7]

On July 4 Cornwallis left Williamsburg and was going to cross the James River on his way to Portsmouth. Since Portsmouth was a city with a harbor, Cornwallis thought that if he moved his army there, it would appear to Lafayette that he was leaving Virginia. This might lure Lafayette into attacking him, while he was vulnerable crossing the James River at Green Spring. This would become the largest open field battle of the war in the state of Virginia.

The British General believed that if he could set a trap and lure the Americans into it, he would be able to defeat them and end the war in the south and maybe even the entire war. In a letter that was intercepted he remarked, "The boy [Lafayette] cannot escape me."[8]

On the morning of the 6th of July, Cornwallis sent his horses and baggage across the James River at a narrow inlet of water not more than two feet deep. To cover the crossing, the army camped in an area that was protected by ponds in the center and on the left by a marsh. Should Lafayette attempt to attack the crossing, his troops would have difficulty in deployment.

It was now time to set the trap. Cornwallis hid his main army on the north bank of the James River to lay and wait for Lafayette. Colonel Tarleton gave money and promises to a Negro and a dragoon to pose as deserters and go to the camp of General "Mad" Anthony Wayne. Once there, they were to tell the general that most of the army was across the river, and only a rear guard lagged behind. Lieutenant Colonel Tarleton years later wrote about the deception,

On the morning of the 6th, the foragers from the cavalry were ordered into the front, who reported that the enemy were advancing. Lieutenant-colonel Tarleton, after the party returned, gave money and encouraging promises to a negro and a dragoon, to communicate false intelligence, under the appearance of deserters. These emissaries were directed to inform the Americans, that the British legion, with a detachment of infantry, composed the rear guard, the body of the King's troops having passed James river.[9]

Wayne took the bait and launched his 800 men against the British pickets. The skirmish lasted for several hours, as the British slowly retreated and drew Wayne deeper into the trap. Cornwallis did not want to spring the trap just yet, until Lafayette committed his troops to the battle. If the British moved too early, then "the boy" would again escape him.

Meanwhile, Lafayette was watching the battle and was about to send in his troops. But, he grew suspicious and decided instead to send a small detachment to reinforce Wayne. This small force made Cornwallis think that his entire army was coming to rescue Wayne.

Around 5 o'clock Wayne's men forced the British back to where they reached an abandoned gun left in the road. When the Americans reached the gun, it was a signal to Cornwallis to release his hidden men into the battle. Lafayette, from his advantage point, could see that the Americans had entered a trap, and there was no way he could stop Wayne from walking into it.

The appearance of the main British army was a complete surprise to the Americans. In an instant, Wayne went from what was going to be an easy victory to the possible annihilation of his 800 man army. The Americans were now outnumbered five to one and were about to be surrounded. If Wayne ordered a general retreat, it would essentially mean every man for himself, and his entire army would probably be killed and captured. The solution that Wayne came up with was a stroke of daring and genius. General "Mad" Anthony Wayne ordered his cannons to fire a blast of grape shot at the British, and then he had his men attack the British with fixed bayonets.

An unknown writer for the *New Jersey Gazette* later wrote, "Madness — Mad Anthony, by God, I never knew such a piece of work heard of — about eight hundred troops opposed to five or six thousand veterans on their own ground."

The bayonet charge stunned the British, and halted their advance long enough for Lafayette to bring reinforcements up to cover a fighting retreat by Wayne. Since the sun was beginning to set, Cornwallis decided not to pursue the retreating Americans.

Josiah Atkins of the 5th Connecticut Regiment was a member of the brigade that reinforced Wayne's troops. With great pride he recorded the following account of the battle in his diary,

> Our officers and soldiers, like brave heroes, began the attack with, at first, but a handful of men. The contest began at five and lasted until dark. The riflemen, some of them, 'tis said, stayed and skirmished with the enemy in the woods all night, so that they have not found time nor opportunity to pick up their dead. Our party consisted only of the brigade of infantry and one brigade of Pennsylvanians and a few riflemen. The enemy were more than six times our number. Our loss of men cannot yet be ascertained.
>
> The enemy gained the ground, but have no cause for glory—their dead from all appearances being many. We retired five miles that night to rest and get some refreshments of which we stood in much need. Six

hundred men have attacked and stood the fire, sword, and bayonet of the force of an army of 5,000, yea, of the whole army under Lord Cornwallis. Where we were often broke, often formed, several times almost surrounded; and yet all came off again in heart! Our General, the Marquis had two horses shot under him, yet he is not daunted.

I cannot forget this memorable action! So few as a 1000 men should attack the whole British force and lose no more, even when we were several times cut off and scattered to and fro. The fatigues of the day I can't describe, and being weary before we began! Our general gave us great applause. He assured us that he himself was eye-witness to our two regiments attacking the whole army with spitit.[10]

The British reported seventy-five men killed or wounded. Since Wayne's sharpshooters targeted officers, five British officers were killed. The Americans could have had several hundred casualties, if not for the boldness of General Wayne. They reported twenty-eight killed, and the battle was a setback for the Americans. However, it did not harm the reputation of the popular Lafayette, and General Wayne's reputation was enhanced even more because of his daring bayonet charge.

After the engagement at Green Spring, General Cornwallis retired to Portsmouth, on the south side of the James River, and began to fortify himself there. He was unhappy with the width of the waterways in Portsmouth, so he decided to dig in at Yorktown and Gloucester Point across the York River. By the 1st of August he left Portsmouth, landed at Gloucester, and began to prepare his defenses. His decision to fortify Yorktown gave the British a disadvantage because it was low ground, and they always preferred to command the high ground. Also, with his back to the sea, it could make a retreat by Cornwallis difficult.

Yorktown was located on a long peninsula eight miles wide between the York and the James Rivers. The harbor was deep and two miles wide. The James River wound more than twenty miles inland and was navigable only by small ships.

On the opposite shore of Yorktown was Gloucester Point, where a piece of land projected deep into the river. Gloucester Point was fertile country and it provided forage for the cavalry and would most likely be the point of junction for the promised relief from General Clinton. Both of these posts were occupied by Cornwallis. The communication between Yorktown and Gloucester Point was commanded by the batteries and by some ships of war, which lay in the harbor.

At Yorktown the York River narrowed and was deep enough for the British men-of-war ships, and there were marshes on both of the town's flanks. This would make the attack on the town by land more difficult. Gloucester, just a mile across the river from Yorktown, could house a gun battery and fort. Also, if American land forces threatened Yorktown, the British could escape across the river into Gloucester.

Cornwallis believed he had the best soldiers in the world, because he had Tarleton's Legion, a large group of Hessians, and the Royal Navy to protect him. When he considered these advantages, he could not believe that he could be trapped at a base of his own choosing. While setting up defenses at Yorktown, Cornwallis never anticipated the possibility of a siege.

The location made a good naval station which would need to be defended, but otherwise it was a poor selection by the British. Lafayette, knowing that Cornwallis may have made a bad move by going to Yorktown, wrote a letter to General Washington on July 31, "Should the French fleet now come in Hampton Road, the British army would, I think, be ours."[11]

Through much of the summer General Clinton wrote about the danger the heat posed for the British troops. He began to believe that the solution to the heat was for Cornwallis to secure a defensive base around the Chesapeake Bay and send many of his troops to the north. Not only would this save the soldiers from the oppressive heat, but it would give Clinton more troops to face George Washington.

Cornwallis did not initially agree with Clinton's thoughts. He believed he needed not only the troops he had but more troops. Cornwallis did not show any concern for the heat until he landed in the Yorktown area in August. During that time he began to complain about the heat and the bad conditions he was encountering around the Chesapeake Bay.

However, heat was not the only problem facing Cornwallis at Yorktown. Malaria was all over the south, especially along the coast. Many in the south were resistant to it, because they had been infected many times. The people of African descent also had genetic traits that helped them to be resistant. On the other hand, the British troops had no resistance to the disease and many soon became infected.

On August 2 George Washington sent a letter to Count de Barras requesting that Count de Grasse sail toward New York rather than the Chesapeake Bay area. Washington was still hopeful that New York City would be where his next attack would take place.

On August 5 French Admiral de Grasse sailed from France to America, and the British allowed him to leave without interfering. The British were not aware of the Admiral's destination, so they had no reason to attempt to stop him. Admiral de Grasse had written to the French commander in America, Rochambeau who commanded 7,000 French troops under Washington, that he would be in Chesapeake Bay by the end of August.

Once Washington learned the French navy would not be going to New York, he turned his attention toward Cornwallis in Virginia and prepared his troops to march there. The plan was that de Grasse and the French fleet would take possession of the Chesapeake Bay and the rivers. This would cut off the retreat and stop reinforcements from reaching Cornwallis. At the same time, the troops under Washington, Rochambeau, and Lafayette would surround Cornwallis and either destroy him or force him to surrender.

General Washington wanted to keep Clinton's army in New York City pinned down, so he decided to keep his change of plans a secret except from a few officers. He wanted to move his army toward the south in such a way that it would appear as if he was still planning an attack on the city of New York. Then, at the last moment he would move toward the south, and Clinton would not have enough time to react and aid Cornwallis.

Toward the end of August, Hessian soldier Stephen Popp was concerned that the British were not in a good situation when he wrote in his journal, "Trenches dug and lines thrown up in Yorktown, but there are reports that we are in a very bad situation."[12]

Washington managed to convince General Henry Clinton that New York City was where he planned to attack, as he prepared to take his army south to Virginia. This was the showdown that Cornwallis and Washington had been waiting for to take place. The fate of the young nation of the United States would soon be decided. When Clinton finally realized Washington's plan, it was too late for him to stop the Americans from marching to the south.

On August 28 Admiral de Grasse arrived at the mouth of Chesapeake Bay with a fleet of twenty-four ships carrying 1,700 guns and 3,100 soldiers. He anchored there, and his French troops landed at Green Springs and joined with the army of Lafayette. French frigates lined up to block the James and York Rivers.

When Washington learned of de Grasse's arrival in the Chesapeake, he became very excited. As Rochambeau arrived at Chester, he saw General Washington, who was usually very stoic, dancing around on the dock and waving his hat. When Rochambeau stepped ashore, Washington grabbed him in a bear hug and whirled him around the pier.[13]

In August the British fleet, under Sir Thomas Graves, was sent from New York to meet the French fleet at Chesapeake Bay. When the French arrived there the British underestimated their size, and in the afternoon of September 5th the two fleets prepared to fight. Because of a failure of British tactics and confusion in commands, the British fleet broke off the fight after heavy losses. Since they were outnumbered by the French, they later chose to withdraw to New York. Cornwallis was now surrounded with little chance for escape.

When King George III heard of the British naval defeat, he said to the Earl of Sandwich, "I nearly think the empire ruined."[14] The King was not aware that by the time the news reached him of the defeat of the British fleet, Cornwallis had already surrendered his army to the Americans.

Heat, illness, and a shortage of food was taking a toll on the British troops at Yorktown. Daily desertions had become common place. British officers informed Cornwallis that they believed they could hold out for only a few more weeks, unless they received aid from General Clinton in New York.

General Clinton knew that Cornwallis was in a very dangerous situation. He raised the hopes of Cornwallis, when he told him that he was making preparations to send him a relief force. Cornwallis welcomed this news, but he was concerned that the aid would come too late.

The allied army that would soon face Cornwallis at Yorktown was made up of three parts: American Continental, American Militia, and French auxiliaries. Most of the 3,000 militia were from Virginia and North Carolina. The allied total number of troops was over 18,000. Cornwallis had around 8,000 British and German troops.

Washington arrives and begins a siege:

When General Clinton finally learned that Washington was going south, he was unable to mobilize quickly enough to assist Cornwallis. He was also unwilling to detach a large percentage of his troops that faced the Continental soldiers that Washington had left around New York.

Clinton later wrote about hearing of Washington marching to the south, "Early in September, to my surprise, (for I still considered our fleet as superior) hearing that Mr. Washington was decidedly marching to the southward."[15]

By September 28 the entire allied force was now at Yorktown, and Washington met with his officers to discuss if they should attack, or lay siege to the British positions. The Americans had no experience with siege warfare, but fortunately the French were very experienced. Washington approved the plans for the siege, upon advice from both French General and chief engineer, Du Portail, and General Rochambeau. Washington's pride was not involved, and he did not have to be persuaded to yield to the French's suggestions on how to go about squeezing Cornwallis into surrendering.

To prevent Cornwallis going across the York River and escaping at Gloucester, Washington immediately sent Duc De Lauzun's cavalry and infantry to Gloucester to reinforce the 1,200 men under the command of George Weedon.

The British began to prepare for a siege by cutting rations by a third. Food was scarce for the horses and the several thousand slaves that were used to construct fortifications. Soon dead horses littered the British camp, and starving slaves were released toward the American lines. Cases of smallpox began to break out, especially among the slaves that built the British fortifications. Help from General Clinton in New York was promised, but would it arrive in time?

In his diary, Joseph Plumb Martin wrote about one of the greatest inconveniences the American troops faced in camp,

> We were on duty in the trenches twenty-four hours and forty-eight hours in camp. The invalids did the camp duty, and we had nothing else to do, but to attend morning and evening roll calls, and recreate ourselves as we pleased the rest of the time, till we were called upon to take our turns on duty in the trenches again. The greatest inconvenience we felt, was the want of good water, there being none near our camp but nasty frog ponds, where all the horses in the neighborhood were watered, and we were forced to wade through water in the skirts of the ponds, thick with mud and filth, to get at water in any wise fit for use, and that full of frogs. All the springs about the country, although they looked well, tasted like copperas water, or like water that had been standing in iron or copper vessels.[16]

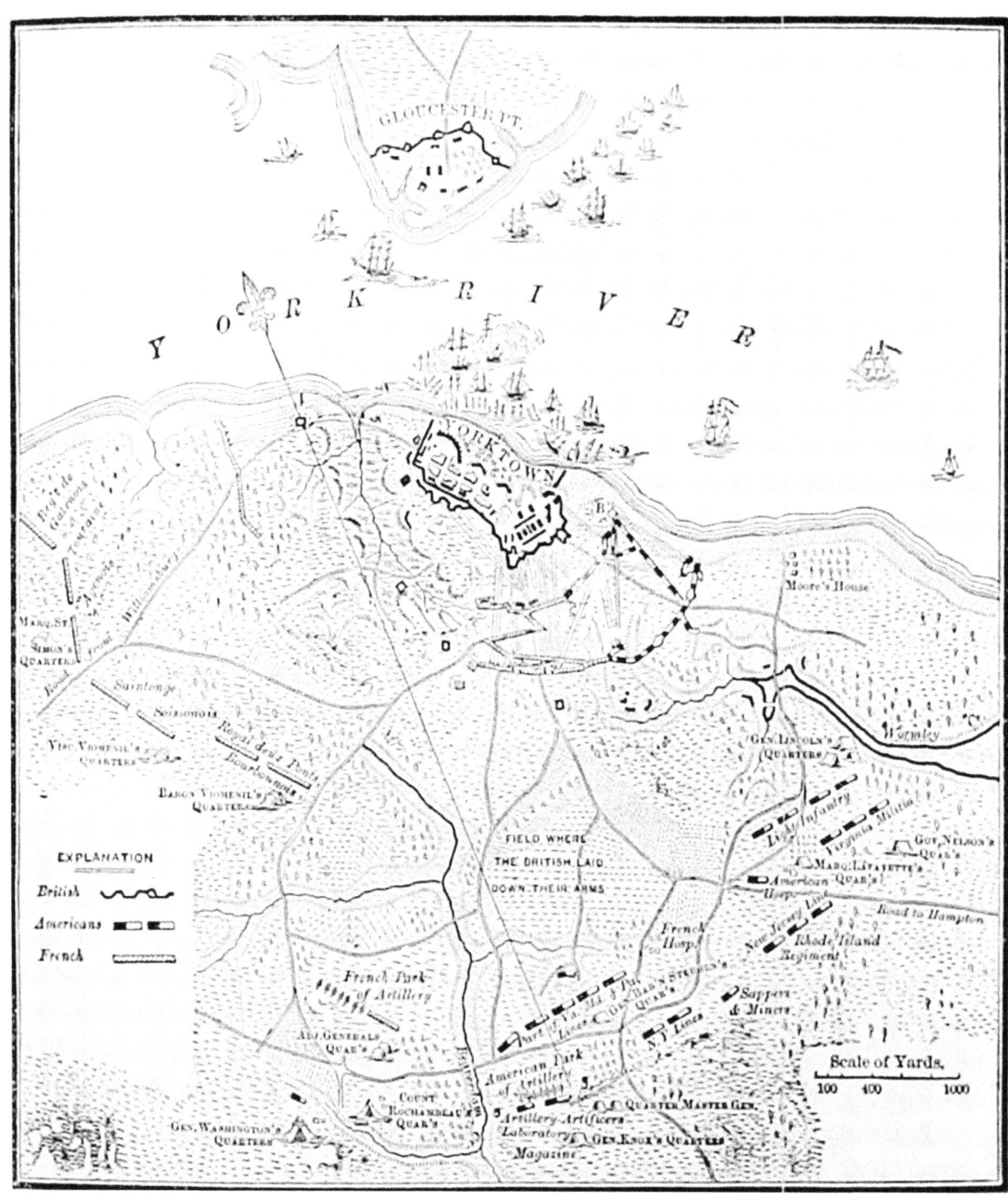

Map of Yorktown, Virginia, showing the military layout, etc., related to the American Revolutionary War siege there. From the book Edward J. Lowell, *The Hessians,* 1884, facing p. 278. {PD-US}

    It was decided that a series of parallels (trenches), that would run parallel to the British defenses, would be built. American and French cannons would be placed in the parallel to bombard British lines. The first parallel was 600 yards from the British line and was completed on October 7th. Colonel Tarleton reported on the parallel being built,

On the night of the 6th, a large detachment of American and French troops made considerable progress in the first parallel, which extended from the high ground above the river, along the left of the British lines, as far as the ravine that approached the hornwork, occupied by the light infantry. The length of the parallel was about one thousand yards, and its distance from the place, in general, six hundred. The Americans guarded the trenches, and conducted the attack upon the right of the combined forces; the French upon the left: The emulation of the officers communicated zeal to the soldiery.[17]

The following narrative is from Charles Cist's Cincinnati Miscellany, 1846: Cist's Advertiser a Weekly Sheet Vol. III Cincinnati, January 28, 1846. Fourteen year old John Hudson, an American soldier, recorded in his own words about digging the parallel,

The ground was of sand, which being thoroughly wet by the rain, was very easy digging. We shoveled until we filled these gabions, and finished by throwing up a bank in front, when the work was completed. The gabions being side and side the earth formed a solid line of breast works, through which a cannon ball could not pass. From what I afterwards saw of the efficacy of this description of defense in repelling cannon balls, there is no doubt that it is a better protection than a stone wall six feet thick, and has this advantage, that it can be made in a few hours. Not a single cannon ball penetrated this defense during the whole siege.

With the allied artillery in place, the French battery's guns began firing at 3:00 p.m. and the American guns followed at 5:00 p.m. The British defenses were torn apart, and they suffered many causalities which began to dampen their spirits. With the bombardment lasting day and night for several days, the British were not able to make necessary repairs. The British had no place safe to hide, and they began to desert in increasing numbers. In addition, the troops were weaken by sickness and lack of food. John Saunders reported in his pension application, "…the firing was so constant that they could not see the sun and could not tell whether it was clear or cloudy."[18]

Siege cannons in 1st parallel facing toward British positions at Yorktown. Photo by author.

On the night of October 11, Washington ordered the digging of the second parallel about 300 to 400 yards from the British lines. At this distance the gunners would be firing at point blank range. Without this parallel the siege would go on longer, and Washington, fearful that the French fleet might leave, needed to end this siege soon. General Von Steuben was ordered to have the second parallel completed quickly.

On October 12 back in New York City, the relief ships of Cornwallis had been loaded with supplies and troops. Prince William Henry traveled to Staten Island to see the troops off. A good show was given for the Prince, as the men marched around and flew their banners. This writer is sure that the British soldiers back at Yorktown, hugging the ground and trying not to get blown apart, would have been very happy that the troops in New York took the time to parade around for the Prince.

Washington knew that to complete the second siege line he would need to capture British redoubts No. 9 and 10. Once these forts were taken, British defenses would be severely weakened. As long as the British controlled both redoubts, the siege line could not be completed, and Cornwallis could hold out longer and perhaps even until help arrived. Washington met with Rochambeau to discuss strategy on taking them. On the evening of October 14, French and American troops captured the two redoubts, and Washington was able to bombard the British on three sides.

British redoubt at Yorktown with the York River in the background. Photo by author

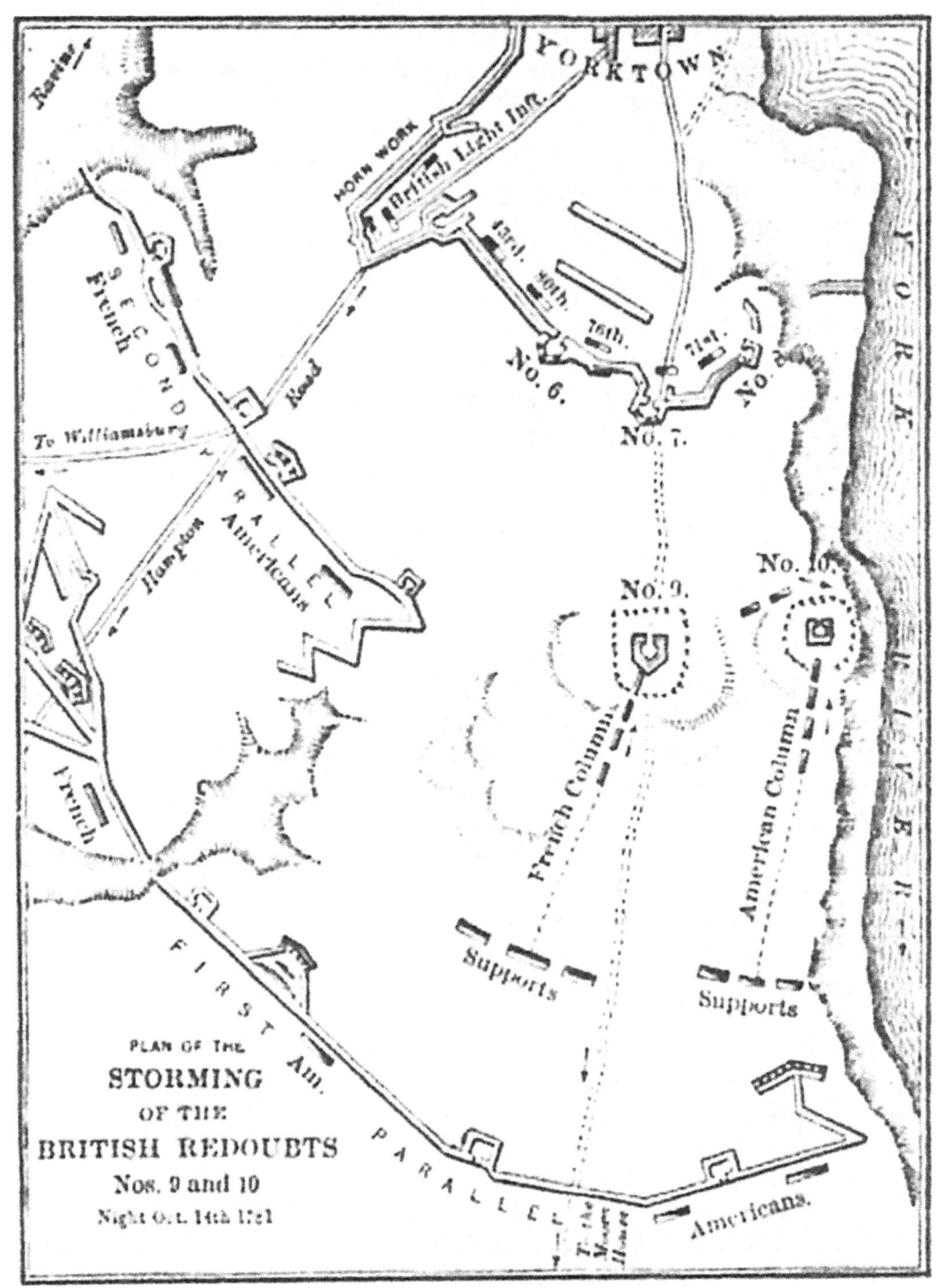

Storming of the Redoubts. Map from *The Yorktown Campaign and The Surrender of Cornwallis* by Henry P. Johnston, 1881, page 144.

Cornwallis wrote to Clinton in New York to give him the news that his situation in Yorktown had gone from bad to worse,

> Last evening the Enemy carried my two advanced Redoubts on the left by Storm, and during the Night have included them in their Second Parallel, which they are at present busy in perfecting. My Situation now

becomes very critical. We dare not shew a Gun to their old Batteries, and I expect their new ones will be open to-Morrow Morning. Experiences has shewn that our fresh earthen Works do not resist their powerful Artillery, so that we shall soon be exposed to an Assault in ruined Works, in bad position and with weakened Numbers.

The Safety of the Place is therefore so precarious that I cannot recommend that the Fleet and Army should run great Risque, in endeavouring to save us.[19]

Cornwallis knew that his defense would not be able to hold against this new bombardment, so he began to plan for an escape. He decided that crossing over to Gloucester with the majority of his troops, while leaving a small group behind to surrender, was his best option. If he could attack and defeat the allied troops at Gloucester, he could capture their horses and then move rapidly away from the allied forces. With a little luck he might be able to join forces with Clinton in New York. The plan was very risky and had little chance for success, but Cornwallis had run out of options.

Just before midnight of the 16th, the British were able to salvage sixteen boats that were seaworthy. They determined that it would require at least three roundtrips to carry the men across the York River and to Gloucester.

During the night, as the first group of men rowed across the York River, the winds began to pick up and a thunderstorm blew in. The boats began to bounce around in the high waves, and heavy rain fell as the winds grew in intensity. Two of the boats were blown off course and landed back on the Yorktown side shore where the frightened men were taken prisoner by the Americans. Fourteen boats made it across the river, and the water soaked men went ashore safely. It was impossible to bring any more men across until the storm blew itself out.

The weather did not break until around two in the morning. Cornwallis knew this would not be enough time to gather the scattered boats, so the escape was called off. Around noon the next day, he had the men that crossed earlier to Gloucester brought back. It was now clear to the British that their choice was annihilation or surrender.

At ten in the morning of October 17, a white flag was displayed by the British and talks of surrender began between the two sides. By the 19th terms of surrender were agreed upon and later that morning the British filed out of Yorktown to surrender.

At first glance as the British marched to surrender, it looked like they were marching out on a holiday. Drums were beating, and the men were in bright fresh uniforms. But then it was notice that the army's colors were cased and not flying. At an even closer look, some of the men were crying as they marched, while others were biting their lips to hold back the sorrow. There were some of the men who even appeared drunk. The British numbers also looked small, because they left over 2,000 sick and wounded men back at Yorktown.

The *New Jersey Gazette* reported a few weeks later, "The British officers behaved like boys who had been whipped at school, some bit their lips, some pouted, others cried; their round, broad-brimmed hats were well adapted to the occasion, hiding those faces they were ashamed to show."[20]

By October 24 the Americans had taken control of the British fortifications, and preparations were being made to move the British prisoners out. That same day, General Clinton finally arrived at Chesapeake Bay with reinforcements to save Cornwallis. He soon received the shocking news that days before Cornwallis had surrendered.

French Admiral de Grasse made no attempt to come out of the Chesapeake Bay to face the British. His job had been completed, and he was anxious to sail to the West Indies. Clinton found that the French fleet outnumbered his own, so after lingering for a few days off the Capes, he returned to New York on the 29th. The British quickly sent a ship to London with the sad news of the surrender.

Toward the end of November, the King received the news of the defeat, and his reply was returned with "calmness, dignity and self-command." Lord George did note, however, that the King "has omitted to mark the hour and the minute with his usual precision."[21]

On November 3 before Cornwallis was allowed to leave Yorktown, he was in the presence of General Washington and was standing with his head uncovered. Washington remarked to Cornwallis politely, "My lord, you had better be covered from the cold;" his lordship, applying his hand to his head, replied, "It matters not, sir, what becomes of this head now."[22]

Results of the British decisions at Yorktown:

The decision to fortify Yorktown left Cornwallis no place to run, when he was confronted with allied troops on land and the French fleet in the bay. Cornwallis had backed himself into a corner which was almost impossible to escape from. By not taking any action in August to try and escape, he sealed his eventual fate.

In August at Yorktown, Cornwallis had several chances to escape. Early in the month, he could have marched his men to Charleston which the British controlled, and the smaller force of Lafayette would not have been able to stop him. Once in Charleston, if he had joined with the army commanded by Francis Rawdon, their two armies could have remain or been withdrawn by the British navy to New York. Washington and Rochambeau would have been forced to remain in New York to keep General Clinton in check. When the French fleet reached Yorktown, there would have been no British army to face them, so the fleet most likely would have returned back to the West Indies.

Had this taken place, two possible scenarios might have played out. First, the escape of Cornwallis from Yorktown could have forced a stalemate in the south. The French, who had been growing weary of the war, might have pulled their support from the American cause. Congress was out of money to finance the war, and respect for them was fading with each day. Many in the colonies were sick of the war, and troops that had not been paid in months were deserting in increasing numbers, or in a few cases even mutinied. Now, with the war in the north and south at a standstill, the revolution might have been settled at the negotiation table. The total independence the colonists sought could have been postponed to a later date.

Or a second scenario could have taken place. Cornwallis would have defeated the smaller army of Lafayette, and then he could have turned his army south to join with Rawdon. The two British armies could have easily defeated the smaller southern army of Nathanael Greene. Next, the British could have traveled to the north, which would have placed the army of George Washington between Cornwallis and Clinton. With a little luck the British could have finally crushed the Revolution.

Of course there are many "what ifs" in each of these two scenarios. It would have meant that Cornwallis and Clinton would have to coordinate their efforts to a level that they had never reached in the past. Also, for these scenarios to work, the American armies would have found it necessary to engage the British in an all-out fight. This is something that Greene and Lafayette had been avoiding for the better part of a year.

Cornwallis also lost the chance to defeat some of his enemies before they had a chance to join forces. When 3,100 French troops landed just twelve miles from Yorktown, Cornwallis could have spared four or five thousand men to engage them. The French soldiers, who were travel weary and some sick from the voyage, would not have offered a stiff resistance. In fact, it is unlikely that Lafayette's troops would have joined the fight. They had been avoiding direct confrontation with the British and probably would have remained near Yorktown to keep the remaining British troops pinned down. By the beginning of September, the window of opportunity for the British army to escape was almost permanently shut.

Cornwallis failed to make any of these moves, for several reasons. First, he claimed that he felt safe to stay at Yorktown because he believed that Clinton would come with the navy and save him. He knew that Clinton was hesitant about leaving New York, since on several occasions he wanted Cornwallis to send him reinforcements. Yet even until the end, he held hope of being relieved by Clinton.

Secondly, Cornwallis claimed he stayed at Yorktown, because he was not authorized to escape to Charleston. Years later he wrote,

> The enemy were in a strong position and considerably superior in number, but I should have attacked them without hesitation if I had thought myself at liberty, after a victory, to escape into the Carolinas with the troops that were able to march. No other object appeared sufficient to justify this measure. But a defeat would probably have been followed with the immediate loss of our post, which until the end of September was in a

most defenceless state: and as I could never have proved that I should not have been relieved, I should have been exposed to public execration, as a man who, having reason to expect the early arrival of the Commander-in-Chief to supersede him in his command, had, in hopes of personal reputation from a victory, sacrificed the essential interest of his country.[23]

For months Cornwallis had been marching around in the south without paying much attention to any orders issued by Clinton, and at times he even kept his commander in the dark as to where he was and what he was doing. Yet, after his decisions led to his defeat at Yorktown, he later felt compelled to blame the defeat on being forced to follow orders and not be allowed any discretionary power.

Before he surrendered, Cornwallis complained that a successful defense of Yorktown was impossible, and he was forced by Clinton to stay there. He essentially blamed his defeat on Clinton for not letting him escape from the trap he managed to get himself into.

When all was lost, it was strange that Cornwallis decided to try to escape by sending his army across the York River to Gloucester in the middle of the night on October 16. He had the crazy idea that in doing so, he could move his tired and sick army several hundred miles northward, across many large rivers and through territory that could have easily raised a Patriot militia against him. Meanwhile, he would have been chased by a much larger combined American and French Army. This escape would have led either to his surrender, or complete destruction of his army.

Clinton denied all the charges leveled at him by Cornwallis. When the two men later met in New York, Cornwallis admitted that he had said too much, and that much of what he said was due to a, "great agitation of mind and might contain some mistakes."[24]

The poor decisions that Cornwallis made at Yorktown led to the surrender of a fourth of the British soldiers in the colonies. When he surrendered, he accepted terms that denied his Tory troops any protection as prisoners of war. They later received harsh punishment, and some were executed. This shocked and demoralized Tories throughout the colonies.

The American victory resulted in putting an end of any further major operations between England and the United States. However, the surrender of Cornwallis did not end the war. England continued fighting the French and Spanish elsewhere around the world. The British war effort was critically wounded but not defeated. King George wanted to continue the war in America, and he felt that the surrender of Cornwallis was just a setback. However, there was no support for the war in the House of Commons, so negotiations for peace were started at once. The House of Commons went on record to say that any Englishman who advised continuing the war would be considered an enemy to his country.

While peace talks were going on, the British military in America continued to fight. It would be another two years before American Independence was completed. At the end of 1781, there were still 30,000 British soldiers in America who continued to fight, but there were no large battles. The British occupied New York City, Savannah, Charleston, Canada, and parts of Florida. There were also pockets of Tory resistance particularly in New York, and the Indians would continue to be a problem as the Americans moved westward. General Washington now struggled to keep his army intact to face the remaining British in New York. Many of the French troops had returned home, and the American militiamen began to return to their farms and shops.

Conclusion

"Having now finished the work assigned me, I retire from the great theatre of action."

George Washington to Congress, December 23, 1783

Instead of continuing the war in America, the British chose to put its dwindling resources toward fighting the French and Spanish for control of Europe, and to keep the remainder of the British Empire intact. The final peace treaty was signed in Paris in September 1783, and the last of the British army left New York City in November. What most people thought was impossible eight years earlier had now become a reality. Washington was finally able to return to Mount Vernon and be relieved of his burden, or so he thought.

The war with the colonies was a war that England should have won. They had a professional army, the largest navy at that time, ample supplies, and a strong economy. The defeat came down to poor leadership and arrogance toward the handling of the American colonies. King George, Henry Clinton, Lord Cornwallis, Lord Germain, and the others in leadership lost America, and the Americans outlasted them.

There were bad military decisions on both sides during the war years. It seemed, however, that the Americans were able to overcome their mistakes and poor decisions much better than the British. That being said, you still can't place blame for the British loss entirely on bad decisions. At the time England was engaged in a war with several other countries around the world. The American Revolution was somewhat of a small conflict in British world events.

Because of this and the fact they were trying to conduct a war on the other side of the world, the British leadership, both at home and in the colonies, didn't appear to take too seriously what was happening in the American colonies. They displayed little respect for the colonial military and its leaders. For various reasons they chose, at crucial times, not to be aggressive enough during battle when victory was in their grasp.

The British leadership could have made better use of the Tories and Native Americans that supported them. Particularly in the south, their policy toward slaves could have been such, that it would have been an effective weapon against colonists. Instead, the British allow their prejudice and arrogance toward those that were not British affect their judgement and treatment of those groups that offered support.

The American military, even though they lacked the training of the average British soldier, must be praised, and this starts at the top. One cannot over emphasize the role of George Washington in the war. He was a leader so loved and respected by his men that they stayed and fought for him even without pay, while achieving only a few victories the first few years of the war. Years after the Revolution, Benjamin Franklin summed up Washington's importance at a dinner with some diplomats. Attending were the French and English Ambassadors along with Benjamin Franklin of the United States.

The English Ambassador rose and gave a toast to his homeland, "To England, the sun whose bright beams enlighten and fructify the remotest corners of the earth." Not to be outdone, the French Ambassador rose and politely said, "To France, the moon whose mild steady, and cheering rays are the delight of all nations, consoling them in darkness and making their dreariness beautiful."

Ben Franklin slowly rose and in a very dignified way he said, "To George Washington, the Joshua who commanded the sun and the moon to stand still, and they obeyed him."[1]

There was also the common soldier who showed a fighting spirit that could not be duplicated among the British troops. Men such as Samuel Whittemore nearly eighty years old and crippled, who on April 19, 1775, as the British were marching back from Lexington and Concord, was waiting for them near his home. With his musket, sword, and a pair of dueling pistols, he killed three of the British before they shot and bayonetted him and left him for dead. He survived for another eighteen years.

There was Richard Knight who served in a Pennsylvania regiment for four years and fought in four major battles. He left the army as a veteran at the age of thirteen. And there was Bishop Tyler who went off to war with a warning from his mother, which was to never let her hear that he died of a wound in his back.

There were women like Margaret Cochran Corbin who helped her husband and his cannon crew, when the British attacked Fort Washington in 1776. When her husband was killed, she took over the firing of the cannon. During the fight she was hit by three grape shots, which nearly severed her left arm, wounded her in the jaw, and left breast. She recovered, and when she died in 1800 and she was buried at West Point.

Oliver Cromwell was the son of a slave, who served in a New Jersey Regiment from 1777 until 1783. He fought in seven major battles including Yorktown. General Washington had such great affection for him, that after the war he personally wrote and signed Cromwell's discharge papers.

There was Nicholas Cusick, also known as Kaghnatsho, a Tuscarora Indian Chief. He formed a band of Indian Rangers that fought with Washington and was credited with saving the life of General Lafayette.

These are just a few of the thousands of Americans that believed in a dream and were willing to face countless personal hardships in the name of freedom. Most of their names will never be known, but what they accomplished will live on.

End Notes

1 Appointment of George Washington as Commander of the American Army

1. Moses Coit Tyler, *The American Statesman Patrick Henry*. (Boston, MA: Houghton, Mifflin, and Co., 1887), 99.
2. L.H. Butterfield, et al, editors, *Diary and Autobiography of John Adams Vol. 3*. (Cambridge, MA: Belknap Press, 1961), 322-23.
3. Wayne Whipple, *The Story of George Washington*. (Philadelphia, PA: Altemus Co., 1915), 209-210.
4. George Washington Parke Custis, *Recollections and Private Memoirs of Washington by his Adopted Son George Washington Parke Custis*. (New York, NY: Derby & Jackson, 1860), 519.
5. Whipple, 197-198.
6. Charles E. Claghorn, *Women Patriots of the American Revolution: a Biographical Dictionary*. (Metuchen, New Jersey: The Scarecrow Press, 1991), 129.
7. Whipple, 207.
8. Lawrence B. Evans, editor, *Writings of George Washington*. (New York and London: The Knickerbocker Press, 1908), 33-35.
9. Jack Darrell Crowder, *Strange, Amazing, and Funny Events that Happen during the Revolutionary War*. (Baltimore, MD: Clearfield), 2019), 25.
10. Letter from John Adams to Elbridge Gerry, June 19, 1775, Founders Online, National Archives.
11. Edmund C. Burnett, editor, *Letters of Members of the Continental Congress Vol. 1, August 29, 1774 to July 4, 1776*. (Washington D.C., Published by the Carnegie Institution of Washington, 1921).
12. Letter from John Adams to James Warren, Founders Online, National Archives.
13. Evens, 35-36.
14. George Washington letter of John Parke Custis June 19, 1775, Founders Online, National Archives.
15. George W. Corner, editor, *The Autobiography of Benjamin Rush, His Travels Through Life Together with his Commonplace Book for 1789-1813*. (American Philosophical Society, 1948), 113.
16. Paul Smith et al., editors, *Letters of Delegates to Congress, 1774-1789*. (Washington D.C.: Library of Congress, Vol. 1), 516
17. *Ibid.* 529.
18. Commission from the Continental Congress to George Washington, Founders Online, National Archives.
19. Smith, 500-501.
20. George Washington to Martha, June 23, 1775, Founders Online, National Archives.
21. Whipple, 212.
22. *Ibid.* 213.
23. Address from the Massachusetts Provincial Congress to General Washington, July 3, 1775, Founders Online, National Archives.
24. Letter from George Washington to his brother John on July 27, 1775, Founders Online, National Archives.
25. Letter from George Washington to John Hancock, July 21, 1775, Founders Online, National Archives.
26. Peter Force, *American Archives Fourth Series, Vol. II*. (Washington, April, 1843), 1438.
27. Daniel E. Harmon, *John Burgoyne British General*. (Philadelphia, PA: Chelsea House, 2002), 18.
28. Sidney Lee, editor, *Dictionary of National Biography Vol. XXXII*. (New York, NY: MacMillan and Co. 1892), 345.

2 The British Frontal Assault of Bunker [Breed's] Hill

1. Richard Frothingham, *History of the Siege of Boston and of the Battles of Lexington, Concord and Bunker Hill.* (Boston, MA: Charles C. Little and James Brown, 1849), 137.
2. Dorothy Dudley, *The Diary of Dorothy Dudley, In Theatrum Majorum.* (Cambridge, MA: Ladies Centennial Commission, 1876), 23.
3. Charles Coffin, *History of the Battle of Breed's Hill.* (William J. Cordon, 1831), 3-4.
4. _____, *The Detail and Conduct of the American War. Given Before a Committee of the House of Commons, Third Edition* (London, 1780), *13.*
5. John Clark Ridpath, *The New Complete History of the United States of America Vol. III.* (Washington, D.C.: Ridpath History Company, 1905), 2460.
6. Letter from Abigail Adams to John Adams, June 18, 1775, Founders Online, National Archives.
7. William W. Wheildon, *New History of the Battle of Bunker Hill, Its Purpose, Conduct, and Result, 2nd. Edition* (Boston, MA: Lee and Shepard, 1875), *26.*
8. Frothingham, 137.
9. Coffin, 6.
10. George Edward Ellis, *History of the Battle of Bunker's (Breed's) Hill, on June 17, 1775: From Authentic Sources in Print and Manuscript* (Boston, MA: Lockwood Brooks, 1875), *70.*
11. _____, *The Detail and Conduct of the American War. Given Before a Committee of the House of Commons, Third Edition.* (London, 1780), 13.
12. *Ibid.* 13.
13. Dorothy Dudley, *The Diary of Dorothy Dudley, In Theatrum Majorum.* (Cambridge, MA: Ladies Centennial Commission, 1876), 24.
14. *Ibid.* 24.
15. William B. Willcox, editor, *The American Rebellion: Sir Henry Clinton's Narrative of His Campaigns, 1775-1782.* (New Haven, CT: 1954), 19.
16. Frothingham, 210.
17. Ellis, 93-94.
18. _____, *The Detail and Conduct of the American War. Given Before a Committee of the House of Commons, Third Edition.* (London, 1780), 14-15.
19. Robert W Coakley and Stetson Conn, *The War of the American Revolution.* (Washington D.C.: Center of Military History United States Army. 1975), 27.
20. _____, *The Detail and Conduct of the American War. Given Before a Committee of the House of Commons, Third Edition.* (London, 1780), 14.
21. *Ibid.* 14.

3 The Battle and Siege of Quebec by the Americans

1. Edmund C. Burnett, *Letters of Members of the Continental Congress Vol. 1. August 29, 1774, to July 4, 1776.* (Washington D.C.: Carnegie Institution of Washington, 1927), 113.
2. Isaac Senter, *The Journal of Isaac Senter,* (Philadelphia, PA: Historical Society of Pennsylvania, 1846), 10.

3. John Codman, *Arnold's Expedition to Quebec.* (New York, NY: MacMillan Company, London, 1902), 60.
4. Senter, 22.
5. Gilman Bigelow Howe, *Genealogy of the Bigelow Family of America.* (Worcester, MA: Charles Hamilton, 1890), 78.
6. John Codman, *Arnold's Expedition to Quebec.* (New York, NY: MacMillan Company, London, 1902), 132-133.
7. Senter, 12.
8. Caleb Haskell, *Caleb Haskell's Diary, May 5, 1775-May 30, 1776.* (Newburyport: William H. Huskell & Co., 1881), 14.
9. Fred C. Wurtele, editor, *Blockade of Quebec in 1775-1776 by the American Revolutionists.* (Quebec, Canada: The Daily telegraph Job Printing House, 1905), 38.
10. Senter, 48.
11. Letter from Sullivan to Washington, June 7, 1776, Founders Online, National Archives.
12. Charles Royster, *A Revolutionary People at War: The Continental Army and American Character.* (Chapel Hill, NC: University of North Carolina Press, 1979), 100.
13. Charles Francis Adams, *Letters of John Adams, Addressed to his wife Vol. 1.* (Boston, MA: Charles Little and James Brown, 1841), 122.
14. William Henry Egle, editor, *Journals and Diaries of the War of the Revolution, Journal of John Joseph Henry,* (Harrisburg, PA: K.K. Meyers, 1893), 124.

4 British General Howe's Hesitation in Attacking Washington in New York

1. Letter from General Philip Schuyler to George Washington, July 12, 1776, Founders Online, National Archives.
2. Letter from George Washington to Lund Washington August 19, 1776, Founders Online, National Archives.
3. Letter from George Washington to John Hancock, June 17, 1776, Founders Online, National Archives.
4. Letter from General John Sullivan to George Washington, August 23, 1776, Founders Online, National Archives.
5. Letter from George Washington to General Putnam, August 25, 1776, Founders Online, National Archives.
6. Nedda C. Albray, *Flatbush The Heart of Brooklyn.* (Charleston, SC: Arcadia, 2004), 48.
7. Henry Whittemore, *The Heroes of the American Revolution and their Descendants, Battle of Long Island.* (The Heroes of the American Revolution Publishing Co., 1897), xiv. The Red Lion was kept as a public house for nearly a hundred years, and was the principal place of resort for the farmers of Gowanus and the surrounding country. Their hatred of the British was very strong, and for some time after the close of the war they refused to patronize it until the sign of the "Red Lion" was taken down. A bull's head was painted on the sign, and it retained the name of Bull's Head Tavern until its final destruction in the late 1800's.
8. *Ibid* 24.
9. *Ibid.* 22.
10. *Ibid.* 22.
11. Edward J. Lowell, *The Hessians and the Other German Auxiliaries of Great Britain in the Revolutionary War.* (New York, NY: Harper & Brothers, 1884), 64-66.

12. Joseph Plumb Martin, *Memoir of a Revolutionary Soldier.* (Mineola, NY: Dover, 2006).
13. Letter from George Washington to John Hancock, August 29, 1776, Founders Online, National Archives. Lord Stirling found himself surrounded and refused to surrender to the British. He broke through their lines and gave himself up to a Hessian regiment. Sullivan, seeing that all was lost, rode straight toward the enemy determined to sell his life as dearly as possible. He was surrounded by British soldiers and forced from his horse.
14. Letter from George Washington to John Hancock, August 31, 1776, Founders Online, National Archives.
15. Letter from George Washington to John Hancock, August 29, 1776, Founders Online, National Archives.
16. Whittemore, 30.
17. Henry P. Johnston, *The Battle of Harlem Heights.* (New York, NY: McMillan Company, 1897), 25.
18. Letter from George Washington to John Hancock, August 31, Founders Online, National Archives.
19. Letter from George Washington to John Hancock, September 2, Founders Online, National Archives.
20. ____, *Memoirs of the Long Island Historical Society Vol. III, The Campaign of 1776 Around New York and Brooklyn.* Brooklyn, (NY: Published by the Society, 1878), 228.
21. *Ibid.* 200-201.
22. Letter from George Washington to John Handcock, September 2, 1776, Founders Online, National Archives.
23. Martin, 20.
24. William Abbatt, editor, *Memoirs of Major-General William Heath.* (New York, NY: William Abbatt, 1901).
25. Henry B. Dawson, *Diary of David How, A Private in Colonel Dudley Sargent's Regiment in the Army of the American Revolution.* (Morrisania, NY: 1865), 29.
26. Johnston, 19.
27. Captain John Montresor, *The Journals of John Montresor, Collections of the New York Historical Society for the Year 1881.* (New York, NY: 1882), 130.
28. Letter from George Washington to John Hancock, September 25, 1776, Founders Online, National Archives.

5 Washington Makes a Bold Decision and Attacks Trenton

1. Lillian B. Miller, editor, *The Selected Papers of Charles Willson Peale and His Family.* (New Haven, CN: Yale University Press, 1983), 50.
2. Letter from George Washington to Lund Washington, December 10-17, 1776, Founders Online, National Archives.
3. Blackaby, Anita D., *Washington and the American Revolution: A Guide to the Campaigns in Pennsylvania & New Jersey.* (United States: Council of American Revolutionary Sites, 1986), 40.
4. Letter from Colonel Cadwalader to George Washington, December 15, 1776, Founders Online, National Archives.
5. Letter from George Washington to Jonathan Trumbull, December 14, 1776, Founders Online, National Archives.
6. Letter from George Washington to John Hancock, December 20, 1776, Founders Online, National Archives.
7. Letter from George Washington to John Hancock, December 20, 1776, Founders Online, National Archives.

8. Letter to George Washington from Robert Morris, December 21, 1776, Founders Online, National Archives.
9. David Hackett Fischer, *Washington's Crossing.* (New York, NY: Oxford Press, 2006), 189.
10. James W. Rabb, *Spain, Britain, and the American Revolution 1763-1783.* (Jefferson, North Carolina, NC: McFarland, 2008), 92.
11. George Morgan, *The Life of James Monroe.* (Boston, MA: Small, Maynard & Co., 1921), 50. Wilkinson was made a general after he embellished his small role in the American victory at Saratoga. He was later thought to be involved with the plot to have George Washing removed as commander-in-chief and replaced with General Horatio Gates. He was forced to resign in March 1778. In July 1779 Congress appointed him Clothier General of the Army, which he resign from in March 1781, citing his lack of aptitude for the job.
12. John Greenwood, *The Revolutionary Services of John Greenwood of Boston and New York, 1775-1783.* (New York, NY: The De Vinne Press, 1922), 38-39.
13. Letter from Washington to John Hancock, December 27, 1776, Founders Online, National Archives.
14. Letter from Washington to John Hancock, December 27, Founders Online, National Archives.
15. Greenwood, 41.
16. William S. Stryker, *The Battles of Trenton and Princeton.* (Boston, MA: The Riverside Press, 1898), 192.
17. Greenwood, 40.
18. Stryker, 225.
19. Lee, Francis Bazley, *History of Trenton, New Jersey.* (New Jersey, 1895), 48.
20. Greenwood, 41.
21. Letter from George Washington to Robert Morris, December 31, 1776, Founders Online, National Archives.
22. Letter from Robert Morris to George Washington, January 1, 1777, Founders Online, National Archives.
23. General James Wilkinson, *Memoirs of My Own Times, Vol. 1.* (Philadelphia, PA: Abraham Small, 1816), 139.
24. Henry W. Elson and Cornelia E. MacMullan, *The Story of Our Country Book 1,* (New York, NY: World Book Company, 1917), 174.
25. ____ *The Pennsylvania Magazine of History and Biography Vol. XVI.* (Philadelphia: PA, The Historical Society of Pennsylvania, 1892), 466.

6 British Decisions and Lack of Communication Results in a Defeat at Saratoga

1. Troy O. Bicham, *Savages within the Empire.* (New York, NY: Clarendon Press, 2005), 265.
2. Frank Moore, *Diary of the American Revolution from Newspapers and Original Documents Vol. I.* (New York, NY: Charles Scribner, 1860), 122.
3. Sydney George Fischer, *The Struggle for American Independence Vol. II.* (Philadelphia, PA: J.B. Lippincott Company, 1908), 92.
4. Henry Dearborn, *Journals of Henry Dearborn, 1776-1783.* (Cambridge, MA: John Wilson and Son, 1887), 6.
5. ____, *Proceedings of the Worcester Society of Antiquity Vol. XXV.* (Worcester, MA: Published by the Society, 1912), 157.
6. Madame De Riedesel, *Letters and Memoirs Relating to the War of Independence and the Capture of the German Troops at Saratoga.* (New York, NY: G. & C. Carvill, 1827), 169.

7. F.A. Gardner, *The Massachusetts Magazine, January 1908, Vol. 1 No. 1, Department of the American Revolution.* (Ipswich, MA: 1908), 55.
8. _____, *Proceedings of the Worcester Society of Antiquity Vol. XXV.* (Worcester, MA: Published by the Society, 1912), 157.
9. Henry B. Dawson, *Diary of David How, A Private in Colonel Dudley Sargent's Regiment in the Army of the American Revolution.* (Morrisania, NY: 1865), 48.
10. Moore, 511.
11. Henry Cabot Lodge, *George Washington Vol. I.* (New York, NY: Houghton Mifflin, 1889), 206.
12. Letter from George Washington to General Gates, October 30, 1777, Founders Online, National Archives.
13. Dearborn, 7.
14. Fischer, 97.

7 Washington Organizes a Spy Ring

1. Letter from George Washington to Robert Morris, January 1, 1756, Founders Online, National Archives.
2. George Washington, *The Journal of Major George Washington sent by Robert Dinwiddies,* Williamsburg, Virginia: 1754), 31.
3. Alexander Rose, *Washington's Spies: The Story of America's First Spy Ring.* (New York, NY: Bantam Books, 2006), 16-17.
4. Henry P. Johnston, *Nathan Hale 1776 Biography and Memorials.* (New Haven, CN: Yale University Press, 1914), 115.
5. _____, *Intelligence in the War of Independence.* (Washing D.C.: Public Affairs C.I.A., 1988), 36.
6. Orders from Washington to Sackett, February 4, 1777, Founders Online, National Archives.
7. From George Washington to Colonel Elias Dayton, July 26, 1777, Founders Online, National Archives.
8. Morton Pennypacker, *General Washington's Spies on Long Island and In New York.* (Brooklyn, NY: Long Island Historical Society, 1939), 214.
9. Letter from George Washington to Benjamin Tallmadge, October 6, 1779, Founders Online, National Archives.
10. Pennypacker, 214.
11. John Van Dyke, *An Unwritten Account of a Spy of Washington.* (Cincinnati, OH: Armstrong & Fillmore, 1892), 14.
12. *Ibid*, 13.
13. _____, *The Magazine of America History with Notes and Queries, Vol. II Part II.* (New York, NY: A.S. Barnes & Company, 1878,) 414-418.
14. Thomas J. Scharf & Thompson Westcott, *History of Philadelphia, 1609-1884.* (Philadelphia, PA: L.H. Everts & Co., 1884), 381. Other version of this story are less eventful describing McLane as distracting the British by making a sortie against the British lines and the defenders opened up with cannon that could be heard in the city.

8 How Decisions about African Americans as Soldiers Affected the War

1. Jack Darrell Crowder, *African Americans and Indians in the Revolutionary War.* (Jefferson, NC: McFarland, 2019), 4.

2. *Ibid*, 4.
3. Education and Outreach Division, Library of Virginia.
4. John W. Pulis, editor, *Moving On, Black Loyalist in the Afro-Atlantic World.* New York, NY: (Garland Publishing Co.. 1999), 4.
5. Cassandra Pybus, *Jefferson's Faulty Math: The Question of Slave Defections in the American Revolution, Third Series, 62, no. 2.* (Williamsburg, VA: Omohundro Institute of Early American History and Culture, 2005), 243.
6. *Ibid*, 255.
7. John A. Logan, *The Great Conspiracy: Its Origin and History.* (New York, NY: A.R. Hart & Co., 1886), 511.

9 Important Decisions at Valley Forge Save the American Army

1. John C. Fitzpatrick, editor, *The Writings of George Washington from the Original Manuscript Sources 1745-1799, Vol. 10.* Washington D.C.: (United States Government Printing Office, 1931), 196.
2. Sydney George Fischer, *The Struggle for American Independence Vol. II.* (Philadelphia, PA: J.B. Lippincott Company, 1908), 125.
3. Albigence Waldo, *Valley Forge, 1777-1778. Diary of Surgeon Albigence Waldo, of the Connecticut Line Diary of a Surgeon at Valley Forge.* (The Pennsylvania Magazine of History and Biography, 1897), 306-307.
4. Letter to John Trumbull from George Washington, March 31, 1778, Founders Online, National Archives.
5. Charlemagne Tower, *The Marquis de La Fayette in the American Revolution.* (Philadelphia, PA: J.B. Lippincott Co., 1895), 323.
6. Benson Bobrick, *Fight for Freedom The American Revolutionary War.* (New York, NY: Scholastic Incorporated, 2004), 52.
7. Baron Von Steuben, *Regulations for the Order and Discipline of the Troops of the United States.* (New York, NY: Evert Duyckinck, 1807), 35-37.
8. Jack Darrell Crowder, *Strange, Amazing, and Funny Events that Happen during the Revolutionary War.* (Baltimore, MD: Clearfield, 2019), 56.
9. Research Product - U.S. Army Research Institute for the Behavioral and Social Sciences. United States, U.S. Army Research Institute for the Behavioral and Social Sciences, 2003, 4.
10. Sir George Otto Trevelyan Bart, *The American Revolution Part IV.* (New York, NY: Longmans, Green and Co., 1922), 334.

10 Battle of Kings Mountain: The Beginning of the End

1. Sydney George Fischer, *The Struggle for American Independence Vol. II.* (Philadelphia, PA: J.B. Lippincott Company, 1908), 337.
2. Jack Darrell Crowder, *Strange, Amazing, and Funny Events that Happen during the Revolutionary War.* (Baltimore, MD: Clearfield, 2019), 120.
3. James W. Rabb, *Spain, British, and the American Revolution in Florida, 1763-1783.* (Jefferson, NC: McFarland & Company, 2008), 84-85.
4. _____Colonial and State Records of North Carolina, Vol. 15, 100-104.

5. Lyman C. Draper, *King's Mountain and Its Heroes.* (Cincinnati, OH: Peter G. Thomson, 1881), 246-247.
6. S.G. Heiskell, *Andrew Jackson and Early Tennessee History.* (Nashville, TN: Ambrose Printing Co. 1918), 247.
7. Draper, 289.
8. John M. Roberts, *Autobiography of A Revolutionary Soldier.* (Clinton, NC: Feliciana Democrat, Print, 1859), 51-52.
9. Samuel G. Williams, *Diary of Captain Alexander Chesney from Kings Mountain Battle, as Seen by a British Officer.* (Tennessee Historical Magazine, April 1921).
10. Roberts, 52.
11. Draper, 511.
12. Robert Mills, *Statistics of South Carolina, Including a View of the Natural, Civil, and Military History.* (Charleston, SC: Hurlbut and Lloyd, 1826), 282.
13. Pension application of Hughes S31764, National Archives.
14. Draper, 511.
15. *Ibid*, 244.
16. *Ibid*, 376.
17. *Ibid*, 560.
18. Lieutenant-Colonel Tarleton, *A History of the Campaigns of 1780 and 1781 in the Southern Provinces of North America,* (Dublin: T. Cadell, 1787), 167.
19. Charles Ross, *Correspondence of Charles, First Marquis Cornwallis Vol. I.* (London: John Murray, 1859), 315-316.
20. Draper, 377.

11 Washington Appoints Nathanael Greene Commander of the Southern Army

1. George Washington Greene, *The Life of Nathanael Greene Vol. I.* (New York, NY: G.P. Putnam, 1867), 27.
2. George Washington Greene, 48-49.
3. Francis Vinton Greene, *General Greene.* (New York, NY: D. Appleton and Company, 1893), 97.
4. Greene, 48.
5. *Ibid,* 366. Following the battle Gates never held a field command again. He was not court martialed due to his political connections.
6. *Ibid,* 367.
7. James D. McCabe, *The Centennial Book of American Biography, Embracing the Lives of the Great Men Whose Deeds Illustrate the First 100 Years.* (Philadelphia, PA: P.W. Ziegler and Co., 1876), 185.
8. Francis Vinton Greene, 174.
9. McCabe, 337.
10. William Seymour, *A Journal of the Southern Expedition 1780-1783.* (Wilmington, DE: The Historical Society of Delaware, 1896), 17.
11. McCabe, 189.
12. Francis Vinton Greene, 203.
13. John C. Hamilton, editor, *The Works of Alexander Hamilton, Vol II.* (New York, NY: John F. Trow, 1850), 450.
14. Seymour, 19.
15. Francis Vinton Greene, 226.

16. Henry B. Carrington, *Battles of the American Revolution 1775-1781.* (A.S. Barnes & Co., 1876), 564.
17. McCabe, 179.
18. *Ibid,* 191.
19. *Ibid,* 192.

12 Yorktown: No Where to Run

1. Letter from George Washington to John Laurens, 15 January 1781, *Founders Online,* National Archives.
2. ___, *The Letters of Horace Walpole Earl of Oxford, Vol. IV.* (Philadelphia, PA: Lea and Blanchard, 1842), 230 and 231.
3. Major Ebenezer Denny, *Military Journal of Major Ebenezer Denny, an Officer in the Revolutionary and Indian Wars.* (Philadelphia, PA: J.B. Lippincott, 1859), 35.
4. Colonel H.L. Landers., *The Virginia Campaign and the Blockade and Siege of Yorktown 1781.* (Washington D.C.: Government Printing Office, 1931), 115.
5. *Ibid,* 120.
6. Joseph Anderson, editor, *The Town and City of Waterbury Connecticut, From the Aboriginal Period to the Year Eighteen Hundred and Ninety-five, Vol. I, a Journal of Josiah Atkins.* (New Haven, CN: The Price and Lee company, 1896), 475.
7. Charles Ross, editor, *Correspondence of Correspondence of Charles, First Marquis Cornwallis Vol 1.* (London: John Murray, 1859), 105-106.
8. Edwin Martin Stone, *Our French Allies Rochambeau and His Army, Lafayette and His Devotion, D'Estaing, DeTernay, Barras, DeGrasse and Their Fleets in the Great War of the American Revolution from 1778-1782.* (Providence, RI: Providence Press Co., 1884), 405.
9. Colonel Tarleton, *A History of the Campaigns of 1780 and 1781, in the Southern Provinces of North America,* (London: T. Cadell, 1787), 363.
10. Anderson, 476.
11. Charles J. Stille, *Major-General Anthony Wayne and The Pennsylvania Line in the Continental Army.* (Philadelphia: PA: J.B. Lippincott, 1893), 271.
12. Stephan Popp, *Popp's Journal, 1777-1783.* (Philadelphia, PA, 1902), 17.
13. Craig L Symonds, *Battlefield Atlas of the American Revolution.* (Mount Pleasant, SC: Nautical & Aviation Publishing Company), 1986.
14. Burke Davis, *The Campaign that Won America.* (New York, NY: Harper Collins, 2007), 166.
15. Sir Henry Clinton, *Narrative of the Campaign in 1781 in North America,* (Philadelphia, PA: John Campbell, 1865), 22.
16. Joseph Plumb Martin, *Narrative of Some of the Adventures, Dangers and Sufferings of a Revolutionary Soldier.* (Hallowell, ME: Glazier, Masters & Co., 1830), 172.
17. Tarleton, 389.
18. Pension application [S7454] of John Saunders, National Archives.
19. Ross, 125.
20. Frank Moore, *Diary of the American Revolution, from Newspapers and Original Documents, Vol II.* (New York, NY: Charles Scribner, 1860), 508.
21. Henry P. Johnston, *The Yorktown Campaign and the Surrender of Cornwallis 1781.* (New York, NY: Harper & Brothers, 1881), 180.
22. James Thacher, *A Military Journal during the American Revolutionary War, from 1775 to 1783.* (Boston, MA: Cottons & Barnard, 1827), 302.

23. ____, *The Westminster Review, January and April 1868, Vol. XXXIII.* (London: Trubner & Co. 1868), 150.
24. Sydney George Fischer, *The Struggle for American Independence Vol. II.* (Philadelphia, PA: J.B. Lippincott Company, 1908), 501.

Conclusion

1. Sophie Lee Foster, *Revolutionary Reader, Reminiscences and Indian Legends.* (Atlanta, Georgia: Byrd Printing Company, 1913), 139.

Bibliography

Adams, Charles Francis, *Letters of John Adams, Addressed to his wife Vol. 1*. Boston, MA: Charles Little and James Brown, 1841.

Allbray, Nedda C., *Flatbush The Heart of Brooklyn*. Charleston, SC: Arcadia, 2004.

Anderson, Joseph, editor, *The Town and City of Waterbury Connecticut, From the Aboriginal Period to the Year Eighteen Hundred and Ninety-five, Vol. I, a Journal of Josiah Atkins*. New Haven, CN: The Price and Lee Company, 1896.

Bart, Sir George Otto Trevelyan, *The American Revolution Part III*. New York, NY: Longmans, Green and Co., 1907.

Bart, Sir George Otto Trevelyan, *The American Revolution Part IV*. New York, NY: Longmans, Green and Co., 1922.

Bickham, Troy O., *Savages Within the Empire*. New York, NY: Clarendon Press, 2005.

Blackaby, Anita D., *Washington and the American Revolution: A Guide to the Campaigns in Pennsylvania & New Jersey*. United States: Council of American Revolutionary Sites, 1986.

Bobrick, Benson, *Fight for Freedom The American Revolutionary War*. New York, NY: Scholastic Incorporated, 2004.

Bradford, Alden, *Complete and Authentic History of the Battle of Bunker Hill; Derived from the Best Authorities*. Boston, MA: J.N. Bradley and Co., 1825.

Bradford, Alden, *A Particular Account of the Battle of Bunker, or Breed's Hill on the 17th of June, 1775*. Boston, MA: Cummings, Hilliard & Company, 1825.

Burnett, Edmund C., *Ciphers of the Revolutionary Period. The American Historical Review 22, no. 2*, 1917.

Burnett, Edmund C., editor, *Letters of Members of the Continental Congress Vol. 1, August 29, 1774 to July 4, 1776*. Washington D.C., Published by the Carnegie Institution of Washington, 1921.

Butterfield, L.H., et al, editors, *Diary and Autobiography of John Adams Vol. 3*. Cambridge: MA: Belknap Press, 1961.

Carrington, Henry B., *Battles of the American Revolution 1775-1781*. New York, NY: A.S. Barnes & Co., 1876.

Carrington, Henry B., *Battle Maps and Charts of the American Revolution*. New York, NY: A.S. Barnes & Co., 1881.

Claghorn, Charles E., *Women Patriots of the American Revolution: a Biographical Dictionary*. Metuchen, New Jersey: The Scarecrow Press, 1991.

Clark, William Bell, editor, *Naval Documents of the American Revolution, Vol. II*. Washington D.C., 1966.

Clinton, Sir Henry, *Narrative of the Campaign in 1781 in North America,* Philadelphia, PA: John Campbell, 1865.

Coffin, Charles, *History of the Battle of Breed's Hill*. William J. Cordon, 1831.

Crowder, Jack Darrell, *African Americans and Indians in the Revolutionary War*. Jefferson, NC: McFarland, 2019.

Crowder, Jack Darrell, *Strange, Amazing, and Funny Events that Happen during the Revolutionary War*. Baltimore, MD: Clearfield, 2019.

Coakley, Robert W. and Stetson Conn, *The War of the American Revolution*. Washington D.C.: Center of Military History United States Army, 1975.

Codman, John, *Arnold's Expedition to Quebec*. New York, NY: MacMillan Company, 1902.

Cohen, Sheldon S., *Ainslie Journal entry, 23 December 1775, Canada Preserved: The Journal of Captain Thomas Ainslie*. New York, NY: New York University Press, 1968.

Corner, George W., editor, *The Autobiography of Benjamin Rush, His Travels Through Life Together with his Commonplace Book for 1789-1813*. American Philosophical Society, 1948.

Crowder, Jack Darrell, *Strange, Amazing, and Funny Events that Happen during the Revolutionary War*. Baltimore, MD: Clearfield, 2019.

Custis, George Washington Parke, *Recollections and Private Memoirs of Washington by His Adopted Son George Washington Parke Custis*. New York, NY: Derby & Jackson, 1860.

Davis, Burke, *The Campaign that Won America*. New York, NY: Harper Collins, 2007.

Dawson, Henry B., *Diary of David How, A Private in Colonel Dudley Sargent's Regiment in the Army of the American Revolution*. Morrisania, NY, 1865.

Dearborn, Henry, *Journals of Henry Dearborn, 1776-1783*. Cambridge, MA: John Wilson and Son, 1887.

_____, *The Detail and Conduct of the American War. Given Before a Committee of the House of Commons, Third Edition*. London, 1780.

Denny, Major Ebenezer, *Military Journal of Major Ebenezer Denny, an Officer in the Revolutionary and Indian Wars*. Philadelphia, PA: J.B. Lippincott, 1859.

De Riedesel, Madame, *Letters and Memoirs Relating to the War of Independence and the Capture of the German Troops at Saratoga*. New York, NY: G. & C. Carvill, 1827.

Doyle, Joseph B., *Frederick William Von Steuben and the American Revolution*. Steubenville, Ohio: The H.C. Cook Co., 1913.

Draper, Lyman C., *King's Mountain and Its Heroes*. Cincinnati, OH: Peter G. Thomson, 1881.

Duane, William, *Extracts from the Diary of Christopher Marshall*. Albany, NY: Joel Munsell, 1877.

Dudley, Dorothy, *The Diary of Dorothy, In Theatrum Majorum*. Cambridge, MA: Ladies Centennial Commission, 1876.

Dyke, John Van, *An Unwritten Account of a Spy of Washington*. Cincinnati, OH: Armstrong & Fillmore, 1892.

Egle, William Henry, editor, *Journals and Diaries of the War of the Revolution, Journal of John Joseph Henry*. Harrisburg, PA: K.K. Meyers, 1893.

Ellis, George Edward, *History of the Battle of Bunker's (Breed's) Hill, on June 17, 1775: From Authentic Sources in Print and Manuscript*. Boston, MA: Lockwood Brooks, 1875.

Elson, Henry W. and Cornelia E. MacMullan, *The Story of Our Country Book 1*, New York, NY: World Book Company, 1917.

Evans, Lawrence B., editor, *Writings of George Washington*. New York and London: The Knickerbocker Press, 1908.

Ferling, John, *A Leap in the Dark, The Struggle to Create the American Republic*. New York: Oxford Press, 2003.

Fischer, David Hackett, *Washington's Crossing.* New York, NY: Oxford Press, 2006.

Fischer, Sydney George, *The Struggle for American Independence Vol. II.* Philadelphia, PA: J.B. Lippincott Company, 1908.

Fisher, Sydney George, *The True History of the American Revolution.* Philadelphia, PA: J.B. Lippincott Co., 1902.

Fiske, John, *The American Revolution in Two Volumes Vol I.* Boston, MA: Houghton, Mifflin, and Company, 1891.

Fiske, John, *The American Revolution in Two Volumes Vol II.* Boston, MA: Houghton, Mifflin, and Company, 1891.

Fitzpatrick, John C. editor, *The Writings of George Washington from the Original Manuscript Sources 1745-1799, Vol. 10.* Washington D.C.: United States Government Printing Office, 1931.

Force, Peter, *American Archives Fourth Series, Vol. II.* Washington, April, 1843.

Foster, Sophie Lee, *Revolutionary Reader, Reminiscences and Indian Legends.* Atlanta, GA: Byrd Printing Company, 1913.

_____ *A Full and Correct Account of the Battle of Bunker Hill.* Boston, MA: 1825.

Frothingham, Richard, *History of the Siege of Boston and of the Battles of Lexington, Concord and Bunker Hill.* Boston, MA: Charles C. Little and James Brown, 1849.

Gardner, F.A., *The Massachusetts Magazine, January 1908, Vol. 1 No. 1, Department of the American Revolution.* Ipswich, MA: 1908.

Greene, Francis Vinton, *The Revolutionary War and the Military Policy of the United States.* New York, NY: Charles Scribner's Sons, 1911.

Greene, Francis Vinton, *General Greene.* New York, NY: D. Appleton and Company, 1893.

Greene, George Washington, *The Life of Nathanael Greene Vol. I.* New York, NY: G.P. Putnam, 1867.

Greene, George Washington, *The Life of Nathanael Greene Vol. II.* New York, NY: Hurd and Houghton, 1878.

Greenwood, John, *The Revolutionary Services of John Greenwood of Boston and New York, 1775-1783.* New York, NY: The De Vinne Press, 1922.

Hamilton, John C., editor, *The Works of Alexander Hamilton, Vol II.* New York, NY: John F. Trow, 1850.

Harmon, Daniel E., *John Burgoyne British General.* Philadelphia, PA: Chelsea House, 2002.

Haskell, Caleb, *Caleb Haskell's Diary, May 5, 1775-May 30, 1776.* Newburyport: William H. Huskell & Co., 1881.

Heiskell, S.G., *Andrew Jackson and Early Tennessee History.* Nashville, TN: Ambrose Printing Co. 1918.

Henry, John Joseph, *Account of Arnold's Campaign Against Quebec and of the Hardships and Suffering of that Band of Heroes,* Albany, NY: Joel Munsell, 1877.

Holloway, Charlotte Molyneux, *Nathan Hale the Martyr-Heron of the Revolution.* New York, NY: A.L. Burt Company, 1902.

Howe, Gilman Bigelow, *Genealogy of the Bigelow Family of America.* Worcester, MA: Charles Hamilton, 1890.

_____, *Intelligence in the War of Independence.* Washing D.C.: Public Affairs C.I.A., 1988.

Lamb, R., *An Original and Authentic Journal of Occurrences during the Late American War from Its Commencement to the Year 1783.* Dublin: Wilkinson & Courtney, 1809.

Irving, Washington, *Life of George Washington and the History of The American Revolution.* New York, NY: G.P. Putnam's Sons, 1883.

Irving, Washington, *Life of George Washington Vol. III.* New York, NY: G.P. Putnam and Sons, 1867.

Landers, Colonel H.L., *The Virginia Campaign and the Blockade and Siege of Yorktown 1781.* Washington D.C.: Government Printing Office, 1931.

____, *The Letters of Horace Walpole Earl of Oxford, Vol. IV.* Philadelphia, PA: Lea and Blanchard, 1842.

Logan, John A., *The Great Conspiracy: Its Origin and History.* New York, NY: A.R. Hart & Co., 1886.

Jameson, J. Franklin editor, *The American Historical Review, Vol. 29.* New York, NY: MacMillan, 1924.

Johnson, William, *Sketches of the Life and Correspondence of Nathanael Greene, Major General of the Armies of the United Stated, in the War of the Revolution, Volume 1.* Charleston, SC: A. E. Miller, 1822.

Johnston, Henry P., *The Battle of Harlem Heights.* New York, NY: Macmillan Company, 1897.

Johnston, Henry P., *Nathan Hale 1776 Biography and Memorials.* New Haven, CN: Yale University Press, 1914.

Johnston, Henry P., *The Yorktown Campaign and the Surrender of Cornwallis 1781.* New York, NY: Harper & Brothers, 1881.

Kapp, Friedrich, *The Life of Frederick William Von Steuben.* New York, NY: Mason Brothers, 1859.

Leffmann, Henry, *Notes on the secret Service of the Revolutionary Army Operating around Philadelphia.* Philadelphia, PA: The City History Society of Philadelphia, 1910.

Le Moine, J.M., *Quebec Past and Present A History of Quebec 1608-1876.* Quebec, Canada: Augustin Cote & Co., 1876.

Lee, Francis Bazley, *History of Trenton, New Jersey.* New Jersey, 1895.

Lee, Henry, *Memoirs of the War in the Southern Department of the United State Vol. I.* Philadelphia, PA: Bradford and Inskeep, 1812.

Lee, Sidney, editor, *Dictionary of National Biography Vol. XXXII.* New York, NY: MacMillan and Co. 1892.

Lodge, Henry Cabot, *George Washington Vol. I.* New York, NY: Houghton Mifflin, 1889.

Lossing, Benson J., *The Historical Field-Book of the Revolution, Vol. 2.* New York, NY: Harper & Brothers, 1860.

Lowell, Edward J., *The Hessians and the Other German Auxiliaries of Great Britain in the Revolutionary War.* New York, NY: Harper & Brothers, 1884.

____, *The Magazine of America History with Notes and Queries, Vol. II Part II.* New York, NY: A.S. Barnes & Company, 1878.

Martin, Joseph Plumb, *Memoir of a Revolutionary Soldier.* Mineola, NY: Dover, 2006.

Martin, Joseph Plumb, *Narrative of Some of the Adventures, Dangers and Sufferings of a Revolutionary Soldier.* Hallowell, ME: Glazier, Masters & Co., 1830.

Mayer, Brantz, *Journal of Charles Carroll of Carrollton during the Visit to Canada in 1776*. Baltimore, MD: John Murphy, 1876.

McCabe, James D., *The Centennial Book of American Biography, Embracing the Lives of the Great Men Whose Deeds Illustrate the First 100 Years*. Philadelphia, PA: P.W. Ziegler and Co., 1876.

McCullough, David, *1776*. New York, NY: Simon & Schuster, 2005.

Melvin, James, *A Journal of the Expedition to Quebec in the Year 1776*. Philadelphia, PA: The Franklin Club, 1864.

_____, *Memoirs of the Long Island Historical Society Vol. III, The Campaign of 1776 Around New York and Brooklyn*. Brooklyn, NY: Published by the Society, 1878.

Middlekauff, Robert, *Washington's Revolution, The Making of American's First Leaser*. New York: Alfred A. Knopf, 2015.

Miller, Lillian B., editor, *The Selected Papers of Charles Willson Peale and His Family*. New Haven, CN: Yale University Press, 1983.

Montresor, Captain John, *The Journals of John Montresor, Collections of the New York Historical Society for the Year 1881*. New York, NY: 1882.

Moore, Frank, *Diary of the American Revolution from Newspapers and Original Documents Vol. I*. New York, NY: Charles Scribner, 1860.

Moore, Frank, *Diary of the American Revolution from Newspapers and Original Documents Vol. II*. New York, NY: Charles T. Evans, 1863.

Morgan, George, *The Life of James Monroe*. Boston, MA: Small, Maynard, & Co., 1921.

O'Boyle, Rev. James, *From Washington to Roosevelt, Essays on the American Revolution*. New York, NY: Benziger Brothers, 1911.

Pennypacker, Morton, *General Washington's Spies on Long Island and In New York*. Brooklyn, NY: Long Island Historical Society, 1939.

_____, *Proceedings of the Worcester Society of Antiquity Vol. XXV*. Worcester, MA: Published by the Society, 1912.

_____*The Pennsylvania Magazine of History and Biography Vol. XVI*. Philadelphia: PA, The Historical Society of Pennsylvania, 1892.

Popp, Stephan, *Popp's Journal, 1777-1783*. Philadelphia, PA: 1902.

Pulis, John W., editor, *Moving On, Black Loyalist in the Afro-Atlantic World*. New York, NY: Garland Publishing Co., 1999.

Pybus, Cassandra, *Jefferson's Faulty Math: The Question of Slave Defections in the American Revolution, Third Series, 62, no. 2*. Williamsburg, VA: Omohundro Institute of Early American History and Culture, 2005.

Rabb, James W., *Spain, Britain, and the American Revolution 1763-1783*. Jefferson, North Carolina, NC: McFarland, 2008.

Randall, Willard Sterne, *George Washington, A Life*. New York: Henry Holt and Co., 1997.

Reed William B., *Life and Correspondence of Joseph Reed, Vol. 1*. Philadelphia, PA: Lindsay and Blakiston, 1847.

Reed William B., *Life and Correspondence of Joseph Reed, Vol. I1*. Philadelphia, PA: Lindsay and Blakiston, 1847.

Ridpath, John Clark, *The New Complete History of the United States of America Vol. III.* Washington, D.C.: Ridpath History Company, 1905.

Roberts, John M., *Autobiography of A Revolutionary Soldier.* Clinton, NC: Feliciana Democrat, Print, 1859.

Rose, Alexander, *Washington's Spies: The Story of America's First Spy Ring.* New York, NY: Bantam Books, 2006.

Ross, Charles, *Correspondence of Charles, First Marquis Cornwallis Vol. I.* London: John Murray, 1859.

Royster, Charles, *A Revolutionary People at War: The Continental Army and American Character.* Chapel Hill, NC: University of North Carolina Press, 1979.

Scharf, J. Thomas & Thompson Westcott, *History of Philadelphia, 1609-1884.* Philadelphia, PA: L.H. Everts & Co., 1884.

Senter, Isaac, *The Journal of Isaac Senter,* Philadelphia, PA: Historical Society of Pennsylvania, 1846.

Seymour, William, *A Journal of the Southern Expedition 1780-1783.* Wilmington, DE: The Historical Society of Delaware, 1896.

Smith, Justin H., *Arnold's March from Cambridge to Quebec.* New York, NY: G.P. Putnam's Sons, The Knickerbocker Press, 1903.

Smith, Justin H., *Our Struggle for the Fourteenth Colony, Vol. 2.* New York, NY: G.P. Putnam's Sons, The Knickerbocker Press, 1907.

Smith, Paul et al., editors, *Letters of Delegates to Congress, 1774-1789.* Washington D.C.: Library of Congress, Vol. 1.

Stille, Charles J., *Major-General Anthony Wayne and The Pennsylvania Line in the Continental Army.* Philadelphia: PA: J.B. Lippincott, 1893.

Stone, Edward Martin, *The Invasion of Canada in 1775: Including the Journal of Captain Simeon Thayer.* Providence, RI.: Knowles, Anthony & Co., 1867.

Stone, Edwin Martin, *Our French Allies Rochambeau and His Army, Lafayette and His Devotion, D'Estaing,*

DeTernay, Barras, DeGrasse and Their Fleets in the Great War of the American Revolution from 1778-1782. Providence, RI: Providence Press Co., 1884.

Stone, William L., *Memoirs and Letters and Journals of Major General Riedesel.* Albany, NY: J. Munsell, 1868.

Stryker, William S. editor, *Documents Relating to the Revolutionary History of the State of New Jersey, Vol 1,* Trenton, NJ: The John L. Murphy Publishing Co., 1901.

Stryker, William S., *The Battles of Trenton and Princeton.* Boston, MA: The Riverside Press, 1898.

Stuart, I.W., *Life of Captain Nathan Hale.* Hartford, CN: F.A. Brown, 1856.

Swett, S., *History of Bunker Hill Battle, 3rd Edition.* Boston, MA: Munroe and Francis, 1827.

Symonds, Craig L., *Battlefield Atlas of the American Revolution.* Mount Pleasant, SC: Nautical & Aviation Publishing Company, 1986.

Tallmadge, Col. Benjamin, *Memoir of Col. Benjamin Tallmadge.* New York, NY: Thomas Holman, 1858.

Tarleton, Lieutenant-Colonel, *A History of the Campaigns of 1780-1781.* Dublin, Ireland: Colles, Exshaw, White, H. Whitestone, Burton, Byrne, Moore, Jones, and Dornin, 1787.

Taylor, Alan, *American Revolution, A Continental History 1750-1804.* New York, NY: W.W. Norton & Co., 2016.

Thacher, James, *A Military Journal during the American Revolutionary War, from 1775 to 1783.* Boston, MA: Cottons & Barnard, 1827.

Tower, Charlemagne, *The Marquis de La Fayette in the American Revolution.* (Philadelphia, PA.: J.B. Lippincott Co., 1895), 323.

Tyler, Moses Coit, *The American Statesman Patrick Henry.* Boston, MA: Houghton, Mifflin, and Co., 1887.

Von Steuben, Baron, *Regulations for the Order and Discipline of the Troops of the United States.* (New York, NY: Evert Duyckinck, 1807).

Waldo, Albigence, Valley Forge, 1777-1778. *Diary of Surgeon Albigence Waldo, of the Connecticut Line Diary of a Surgeon at Valley Forge.* The Pennsylvania Magazine of History and Biography, 1897.

Washington, George, *The Journal of Major George Washington sent by Robert Dinwiddies.* Williamsburg, Virginia: 1754.

____, *The Westminster Review, January and April 1868, Vol. XXXIII.* London: Trubner & Co. 1868.

Wheildon, W., William, *New History of the Battle of Bunker Hill, Its Purpose, Conduct, and Result, 2nd. Edition.* Boston, MA: Lee & Shepard, 1875.

Whipple, Wayne, *The Story of George Washington.* Philadelphia, PA: Altemus Co., 1915.

Whittemore, Henry, *The Heroes of the American Revolution and their Descendants, Battle of Long Island.* The Heroes of the American Revolution Publishing Co., 1897.

Willcox, William B., editor, *The American Rebellion: Sir Henry Clinton's Narrative of His Campaigns, 1775-1782.* New Haven, CT: 1954.

Williams, Samuel G., *Diary of Captain Alexander Chesney from Kings Mountain Battle, as Seen by a British Officer.* Tennessee Historical Magazine, April 1921.

Wilkinson, General James, *Memoirs of My Own Times, Vol. 1.* Philadelphia, PA: Abraham Small, 1816.

Wilson, Joseph T., *The Black Phalanx; A History of the Negro Soldiers of the United States.* Hartford, CN: American Publishing Company, 1890.

Winsor, Justin, *Arnold's Expedition Against Canada 1775-1776, The Diary of Ebenezer Wild.* Cambridge, MA: John Wilson and Sons, 1886.

Wurtele, Fred C., editor, *Blockade of Quebec in 1775-1776 by the American Revolutionists.* Quebec, Canada: The Daily Telegraph Job Printing House, 1905.

Index

A

Adams, Abigail, 27
Adams, John, 10,11,14,16,27,44,58,139
Adams, Samuel, 9,11
Alexander, General William, (see Lord Stirling,)
Andre, Major John, 90
Armistead, James, 99,100
Arnold, Benedict, 95,97,131
    in Canada, 37-45
    battle of Saratoga, 78,80,81,83-85,88-90
Atkins, Josiah, 141

B

Balforr, Nisbet, 31
Basset, Burwell, 15
Battle of:
    Bemis Heights, 80,81,83
    Bennington, 78
    Brandywine, 89
    Bunker Hill, 17,19,23,25,31-36,50,55,60,62
    Camden, 117,131,158
    Cowpens, 121,133-135
    Freeman's Farm, 80-83,88
    Germantown, 89
    Green Spring, 141-144
    Guilford Courthouse, 135-137,140
    Kings Mountain, 107-128
    Lexington and Concord, 8,23,36,38,40,60,101,158
    Monmouth, 113,130
    Princeton, 73-75
    Stony Point, 98,99
    Trenton, 89,97,98
Bigelow, Timothy, 40,83,86
Bolton, John, (see Tallmadge)
Boston, 10,11,17,20,39,47,48,62
    Siege of, 22-36,44
Bowen, Charles, 125
Breed's Hill, 23,25,29,30
Brewster, Caleb, 94
Brooklyn Heights, 50,51,55
Bulford, Colonel Abraham, 121
Burgoyne, General John, 20,28,98
    Battle of Saratoga, 77-83
Butler, Jane, 11

C

Cabal, Conway, 78
Cadwalader, General John, 66,67,72
Callender, John, 19
Campbell, Colonel Arthur, 126

Campbell, Colonel William, 124-126
Carleton, General Guy, 40-42
Charleston, 103,117,131,132,137,154,155
Charlestown, 23,25,32
Charlestown Neck, 23,26-28
Chesney, Captain Alexander, 124
Church, Dr. Benjamin, 97
Cleveland, Colonel Benjamin, 125
Clinton, General Henry, 23,34,82,83,97-100,117,128,140,141,144,157
    at New York City, 145-147,151,153,155
    battle of New York, 49,51,52,62
Coburn, Corporal Samuel, 104
Coercive Acts, 7
Collins, James, 125
Congress,9,10,13,14,16,21,37,44,58,59,64,67,73,74
88,101,102105,154
Congress, First Continental, 8,10,37
Congress, Second Continental, 10,36,37
Conway, General Thomas, 20
Corbin, Margaret Cochran, 158
Cornwallis, General Charles, 117,121,126-128,132,134,135,140,145-147,150,151,154
    at Gilford Courthouse, 135-137
    at battle of New York, 49,50
    at Green Spring, 142-144,146
    at Trenton, 65,73-75
    at Yorktown, 99,100
    escape to Gloucester, 152
    marching to Yorktown, 139-144
    surrender, 152-153,155
    with slaves, 147
Cromwell, Oliver, 158
Culper, Spy Ring, 93-96-95,97
Cusik, Nicholas, 158

D

Danton, Colonel Elias, 93
D'Estaing, Admiral, 95
De Barras, Count, 145
De Grasse, Admiral, 145,146,153
DeLauzun, Duc, 147
Deerborn, Henry, 29,35,81,82,84,89
Denny, Lt. Ebenezer, 139
De Peyster, Captain, 125
Dinwiddle, Governor, 11
Dudley, Dorothy, 24,32,33
Dunmore, Lord, 104
Du Portail, General, 147
Dyer, Eliphalet, 14,16
dysentery, 40,47

E

Ewing, General James, 66,70,72

F

Ferguson, Major Patrick, 117-128
Franklin, Benjamin, 5,158
Fraser, General, 81-82,85,86
French and Indian War, 10,26,91
Forge, Valley, 21,44,105,107-116
    sanitation, 110-112
Fort Duquesne, 11
Fort Stanwix, 77
Fort Washington, 45

G

Gage, General Thomas, 9,23,25,26,35
    battle of Saratoga, 78
Gates, General Horatio, 10,20,35,131,132,138
    battle of Saratoga, 80,81,87-89
Germain, Lord George, 73,157
Gerry, Elbridge, 97
Gloucester, 144
Greene, Nathanael, 34,48,49,65,66,78,112,129-136,140
    at Gilford Courthouse,135-137
    description, 129
    appointed to Southern Army, 21,130,131
    wins the south, 137,138
Greenwood, John, 70-73
Grant, General James, 53,54,68

H

Hale, Nathan, 92
Hamilton, Alexander, 103,112,131,135
Hancock, John, 9,19,55-59,70,71
Harlem Heights, 58-62,92
Hart, Nancy Morgan, 95
Harris, Moses, 98
Haskell, Caleb, 42
Heath, General William, 25
Heister, General Leopold Philip von, 51
Henry, Joseph, 37,45
Henry, Patrick, 10,15
Henry, Prince William, 150
Hessians, 36,86,97,98,117
    at New York, 51,52,54,56,62
    at Trenton, 65,67-69,71-75
    at Yorktown, 144,147
Honeyman, John, 67,97,98
How, David, 60,87
Howe, Admiral Richard, 47
Howe, General William, 26-29,31,34,77,89,102,107-109
    attacking New York, 47-49,50,52,53,60-63
    at Trenton, 67,97,98
Hudson, John, 149
Hughes, Lt. Joseph, 126

Hunt, Abraham, 69

I

J

Jamaica Pass, 51-53
Jefferson, Thomas, 104

K

King George III, 8,9,15,73,146,153
Kip's Bay, 60
Knolton, Colonel Thomas, 60,92
Knox, General Henry, 65,132

L

Lafayette, General Marquis de, 98,103,137,139-141,145,154
Laurens, John, 103,105,113,139
Learned, General, 81,84
Lee, Charles, 10,17,20
Liberty, Sons of, 7
Lincoln, General Benjamin, 117,131
Livingston, Philip, 57
Long Island, 48,51,62
Loring, Elizabeth, 90
Lovell, James, 100
Loyalists (see Tories)

M

Manhattan, 56-61
Marion, Francis, 132
Martin, Joseph Plumb, 55,57,59
Maryland "400", 54
McDowell, Colonel Charles, 124
McLane, Captain Allan, 98-100
Mercer, Charles, 12
Mifflin, General Thomas, 17,57
Minutemen, 8,9
Montgomery, Richard, 10,37,40-43,45
Montresor, Captain John, 62
Morgan, General Daniel, 100,132-136
    battle of Saratoga, 78,79,81,82,85
Morris, Robert, 68,74,91
Murphy, Timothy, 95

N

New York City, 92,97,155,157
    attacked, 47-64
Nexsen, Elias, 97

O

"Overmountain Men", 119,120

P

Parliament, 7,49
Peale, Charles W., 12,65
Pendelton, Edmund, 10
Percy, General Hugh, 52
Phillips, Samuel, 119
Pompey, 98,99
Poor, General, 84
Popp, Stephen, 146
Porter, Elisha, 97,146
Prescott, William, 30
Proclamation of Bouquet River, 77
Putnam, General Israel, 10,49,50

Q

Quebec, 37-45 ,114

R

Rall, Colonel Johann, 65,68,69,72,73,97
Rawdon, Francis, 137,140
Read, James, 68
Reed, Colonel Joseph, 17,97
redoubts 9 & 10, 150,151
Riedesel, Baron, 94,95
Riedesel, Baroness, 77,85,86
Rivington, James, 94,95
Rochambeau, Comte de, 145-147,150,153
Rush, Benjamin, 15,58
Rutledge, Edward, 16

S

Sackett, Nathaniel, 93
Salisbury, Stephen, 86
Saunders, John, 149
Savannah, 132,155
Schammell, Major Alexander, 57
Schuyler, General Philip, 17,37,45,48,78,98
Scott, General John Morin, 57
Senior, Samuel Culper, (see Abraham Woodhull)
Senior, Samuel Culper, (see Robert Townsend)
Senter, Dr. Isaac, 39
Sevier, Colonel, 119,120,124,125
Seymore, William, 135,136
Shelby, Colonel, Isaac, 119,120,124,125,127
Shippen, Peggy, 90
Shippen, Dr. William, 109
Shoals, Sycamore, 119,120
slaves, 101
 after the war, 105
 during the revolution, 104
 Ethiopian Regiment, 101
 Importance to war, 108
 in British Army, 102
 in Georgia, 103
 in South Carolina, 103
 population, 102,105
 owners, 103,105
 recruitment quotas, 103
 why they fought, 104
Slocum, Giles, 118
smallpox, 21,42,48,109,110,113,114
Spelts, John, 126
spies,
 children, 82
 code breakers, 97
 codes, 95,96,98
 hidden letters, 95,96
 image, 91,92
 women, 92
St. Leger, Colonel Barry, 77
Staten Island, 49,93,97
Steele, Mrs. Elizabeth, 135
Steuben, General Baron von, 21,107,114-116
 description, 111
 improving sanitation, 110-112
 language, 112
 training, 112-113
 view of Americans, 112
Stirling, Lord, 50,53-55
Strong, Anna, 94
Sullivan, General John, 44,45,49,50,53-55,65,66,71

T

Tallmadge, Major Benjamin, 93-95
Tarleton, Colonel Banastre, 121,122,126-128,132,142,144
 at Cowpens, 133-135
 at Yorktown, 148
Tavern, Howard's, 52
Tavern, Red Lion, 53
Thomas, General John, 44
Thompson, Charles, 10
Tories, 8,59,68,69,90,94,105,157
 at Kings Mountain, 117-128
Townsend, Robert, 94
Trenton, 65-75
Trumbull, Joseph, 14,67,97,110
Tryon, William, 97
Tyler, Bishop, 158

U

V

Vernon, Mount, 11,49,157

W

Walker, Captain John, 112
Walpole, Horace, 139
Ward, General Artemas, 9
Warren, James, 37
Washington, General George, 7,12,27,40,44,78,88,90,130-132,135,137,157,158
    appointed commander, 16,18
    at siege of Boston, 35,44
    at Trenton, 65-75,97,98
    at Valley Forge, 21,107,116
    at Yorktown, 99,100,139-158
    black recruits, 101-105
    confidence in himself, 14,15
    defending New York, 47-64
    description of, 10
    expense account, 13,14
    his impact, 21
    impression of army, 20
    in French and Indian War, 11
    judge of men, 21
    spies, 91-100
    takes command of army, 18
Washington, John A., 16
Washington, Lund, 65
Washington, Martha, 13,15,16
Washington, William, 72
Wayne, General Anthony, 142-144
Weedon, Charles, 147
West, Rev. Samuel, 97
Whittemore, Samuel, 158
Wilkinson, Captain James, 70
Woodhull, Abraham, 94,95
Wooster, General, 40,42

Y

Yorktown, 139-156

www.ingramcontent.com/pod-product-compliance
Lightning Source LLC
Chambersburg PA
CBHW081420230426

43668CB00016B/2302